NATURAL SIGNS  OF GOD

Is there such a thing as natural knowledge of God? C. Stephen Evans presents the case for understanding theistic arguments as expressions of natural signs in order to gain a new perspective both on their strengths and weaknesses. Three classical, much-discussed theistic arguments—cosmological, teleological, and moral—are examined for the natural signs they embody.

At the heart of this book lie several relatively simple ideas. One is that if there is a God of the kind accepted by Christians, Jews, and Muslims, then it is likely that a 'natural' knowledge of God is possible. Another is that this knowledge will have two characteristics: it will be both widely available to humans and yet easy to resist. If these principles are right, a new perspective on many of the classical arguments for God's existence becomes possible. We understand why these arguments have for many people a continued appeal but also why they do not constitute conclusive 'proofs' that settle the debate once and for all.

Touching on the interplay between these ideas and contemporary scientific theories about the origins of religious belief, particularly the role of natural selection in predisposing humans to form beliefs in God or gods, Evans concludes that these scientific accounts of religious belief are fully consistent, even supportive, of the truth of religious convictions.

Natural Signs and Knowledge of God

A New Look at Theistic Arguments

C. STEPHEN EVANS

OXFORD
UNIVERSITY PRESS

Great Clarendon Street, Oxford OX2 6DP
United Kingdom

Oxford University Press is a department of the University of Oxford.
It furthers the University's objective of excellence in research, scholarship,
and education by publishing worldwide. Oxford is a registered trade mark of
Oxford University Press in the UK and in certain other countries

First published 2010
First published in paperback 2012

British Library Cataloguing in Publication Data
Data available

Library of Congress Cataloging in Publication Data
Library of Congress Control Number: 2009942581

ISBN 978-0-19-921716-8 (Hbk)
ISBN 978-0-19-966107-7 (Pbk)

Printed and bound by
CPI Group (UK) Ltd., Croydon, CR0 4YY

To Imogen Pearline Evans Bouwmeester
a sign of God's grace

Contents

Preface

At the heart of this book lie several relatively simple ideas. One is that, if there is a God of the kind accepted by Christians, Jews, and Muslims, then it is likely that a "natural" knowledge of God is possible. Another is that this knowledge will have two characteristics: it will be both widely available to humans and yet easy to resist. In the book I express these claims as the "Wide Accessibility Principle" and the "Easy Resistibility Principle." If these principles are right, and I have for many years been convinced that they are, then I believe that this makes possible a new perspective on many of the classical arguments for God's existence. These arguments can be seen as attempts to articulate and develop "natural signs" that lie at their core. I believe this helps explain both why these arguments have for many people a continued appeal but also why they do not constitute conclusive "proofs" that settle the debate once and for all.

I first expressed these ideas, in a somewhat popular form, in my book *The Quest for Faith: Reason and Mystery as Pointers to God*, a book that I later rewrote as *Why Believe?* Because of the popular character of these books, I have long felt that the power of the ideas they contain has not been fully appreciated. So I am glad to have the opportunity to express them here in a more developed and intellectually rigorous form. I believe that seeing the theistic arguments as expressions of natural signs gives a new perspective on both their strengths and weaknesses. Hence the greater part of this work consists in a study of various forms of the cosmological, teleological, and moral arguments, looking for the natural signs that they embody.

As I have worked through these ideas I have come to see the ways in which they connect with some contemporary scientific theories about the origins of religious belief, particularly the ways in which we have been "hard-wired" by natural selection to be predisposed to form beliefs in God or gods. Contrary to what some think, I am convinced that this kind of scientific account of religious belief is fully consistent, even supportive, of the truth of religious convictions.

Since I have lived with these ideas for a long time, I fear that I cannot properly thank all those who have helped nourish them. I am sure that epistemological conversations with Jay Wood over the years, many of them while running on the Illinois Prairie Path, were valuable. Perhaps my largest debt is to my students in philosophy of religion over the years, who have helped me come to see the theistic arguments as I do. More immediately, however, I must thank Baylor University for a research leave in the fall of 2008, which allowed me to write drafts of the majority of the chapters. Chapter 4 benefited from a thorough discussion by the colloquium of the Baylor Philosophy Department. Among my Baylor colleagues, Todd Buras was a tremendous help in understanding Thomas Reid's complex account of perception. Alexander Pruss read several chapters and gave me some very valuable suggestions. I also received some valuable help from Jonathan Kvanvig and Trent Dougherty. My good friend and department chair, Michael Beaty, has been a constant source of encouragement for all my work.

I must also thank Calvin College for welcoming me as a visiting scholar and providing an office during my 2008 leave. I am particularly grateful to the Calvin Philosophy Department for discussing two of the chapters in their weekly colloquium. The Calvin philosophy colloquium is surely one of the most rigorous and satisfying ongoing philosophical conversations anywhere; it is at least the best one I have ever had the privilege to be part of. I would be remiss if I did not mention Calvin philosophers Lee Hardy and Kelly Clark by name, since they provided particularly important help to me: Hardy in dealing with Hume and Kant, and Clark in dealing with contemporary evolutionary explanations of belief in God. What I have learned from them will be evident in the text. I must also thank Karl Ameriks, who generously read Chapter 4 and gave me some acute advice on my reading of Immanuel Kant. Finally, I am grateful to Nicholas Wolterstorff for generous help with some problems in Chapter 2. It hardly needs to be said that infelicities that remain in this book are solely my responsibility.

Kraig Martin, my research assistant for 2009–10, carefully read through large sections of the book and pointed out several errors to me. Julien Smith took time away from his own dissertation to work as my research assistant in the summer of 2009, when I was in Spain and away from my library. Julien tracked down a large number of quotations and bibliographical references for me, carrying out this difficult and important work with intellectual energy and aplomb. He also prepared the bibliography of works cited. I am grateful for his help and his friendship. Finally, I am grateful to Kelley Evans, who prepared the index with her usual care and excellence.

C. Stephen Evans

June 22, 2009

1

The Problem of Natural Theology

Since the time of the ancient Greeks, philosophers have given arguments for and against the existence of God, and such arguments continue to be presented. The attempt to show that there is a "natural" knowledge of God's existence—that is, knowledge of God that does not presuppose any special religious authority or revelation—is an important part of what is usually termed "natural theology." Natural theology includes more than just arguments for God's existence, of course. Traditionally, it has also included such things as the attempt to determine and define the attributes of God. However, the project of giving arguments for God's existence has long been a central component of natural theology, to such an extent that some simply identify natural theology with such arguments. In this book I shall examine whether there is such a thing as natural knowledge of God, and I shall begin by focusing on arguments for God's existence, even though my ultimate goal is to show that natural knowledge of God does not have to be derived from such arguments.[1] For convenience I shall henceforth refer to the project of gaining knowledge of God's existence as "natural theology," with an understanding that I am in reality only discussing a part of this subject.

Natural theology understood as the attempt to develop arguments for the existence of God poses a puzzle: arguments for God's existence are frequently criticized and declared to be conclusively refuted, yet the arguments continue to be presented. Some people, including well-trained, well-educated individuals—philosophers, scientists,

---

[1] Likewise, the project of developing arguments against the existence of God could be central to what could be called "natural theology," but my primary focus in this work will be on arguments for God's reality.

and other intellectuals—find the arguments convincing. Many others, equally well trained and well educated, find them to be without merit. The arguments never seem to convince the critics. However, the refutations never seem to silence the proponents, who continue to refine and develop the arguments.

There are, of course, many possible ways to explain this impasse. In this book I shall defend the claim that one important reason the debate continues stems from the nature of the arguments themselves. Many of the classical arguments for God's existence, such as the cosmological, teleological, and moral arguments, are grounded in what I shall call "natural signs" that point to God's reality. These theistic arguments derive their force and enjoy whatever plausibility they possess from the signs that lie at their core. The nature of a sign, as I shall develop the notion, is to be a "pointer," something that directs our attention to some reality or fact and makes knowledge of that reality or fact possible, and this feature is what explains the continuing appeal of the arguments.

However, these signs, like signs in general, do not point in a conclusive or compelling fashion. Signs have to be perceived, and once perceived must be "read." Some signs are harder to read than others, or, one might say, easier to interpret in alternative ways, even if not all of the possible interpretations are equally plausible. The natural signs that point to God's reality are signs that can be interpreted in more than one way and thus are sometimes misread and sometimes not even perceived as signs. They point to God but do not do so in a coercive manner. To function properly as pointers, they must be interpreted properly. It is for this reason that the theistic arguments, which are attempts to articulate these signs and develop them into inferential arguments, fail to be conclusive when they are considered as "proofs." As I have already noted, the evaluations of the arguments given by various individuals differ greatly. My main task is neither to attack nor to defend the arguments as arguments. In my own view, some of the arguments have considerable force in some of their forms. However, my main thesis will not require agreement about this.

Rather, I want to argue that, whether an individual thinks the arguments are strong or weak, that individual can recognize the natural signs that lie at the core of the arguments, and see these signs as having genuine force. If someone sees the arguments as weak, this will not necessarily undermine the value of the signs that are embodied in the arguments. Even if an argument developed from a sign fails as a coercive argument, the sign may still point to God and make knowledge of God possible for those who have the ability and will to read the sign properly. An important piece of evidence for this claim will be the way in which well-known critics of the arguments, philosophers who are recognized as having developed devastating refutations of them, continue to acknowledge the appeal and force of the very arguments they have criticized. I shall argue that this ambivalence reflects an awareness of the power of the sign, even when the argument developed from the sign is seen as less than compelling.

Seeing the theistic arguments as articulations of natural signs therefore helps us understand both the appeal of the arguments as well as their lack of conclusiveness. It also helps us resolve a lively current dispute in the philosophy of religion: the argument between evidentialists and so-called Reformed epistemologists.

Evidentialists, as the name implies, maintain that any knowledge we have about God must be based on evidence, a view that until recently was taken for granted by most defenders and critics of religious belief. Reformed epistemologists, such as Alvin Plantinga and Nicholas Wolterstorff, maintain that belief in God may be "properly basic," justified or rational without the support of any kind of inference.[2] Seeing the theistic arguments as articulations of natural signs helps to show how both camps may be correct in some of their main contentions.

The Reformed epistemologists are right to argue that the knowledge of God does not have to be based on formal arguments, since a natural sign is something that can direct an individual to the reality of which it is a sign without any process of inference. However, the evidentialists are right to insist that natural knowledge of God, at least in standard cases, is based on what may be called evidence. There are two senses in which this may be so. First, it is possible to become aware of the mediating role of the sign, and to use the sign as the basis

---

[2] Alvin Plantinga and Nicholas Wolterstorff (eds.), *Faith and Rationality: Reason and Belief in God* (Notre Dame, IN: University of Notre Dame Press, 1983)

for an inferential argument. On the view I shall defend, the main theistic arguments are arguments of just this kind. Second, however, even when the sign is *not* functioning as the basis for an inferential argument, it may still be regarded as evidence in the sense that it is something that makes a certain truth more evident to someone. This claim is not as contrary to Reformed epistemology as it might seem, since the Reformed epistemologists, while denying that belief in God is based on *evidence*, do claim that there is a *ground* for the belief. I hope to adjudicate the dispute between evidentialists and Reformed epistemologists by paying careful attention to the notion of evidence. This will help us understand in what senses a "ground" may be regarded as evidence, and that such "grounds" may legitimately be understood as natural signs.

WHAT IS NATURAL THEOLOGY AND WHY IS IT VALUABLE?

Before plunging into the case I wish to make for this way of looking at the theistic arguments, I must first discuss in more detail the nature of natural theology and consider whether it would be good to have such knowledge, and, if so, why it would be valuable. I have stipulatively described "natural theology" as the attempt to show that there is knowledge of God's reality without presupposing any special revelation, such as the Bible or the Koran, or perhaps the events described in the Bible or the Koran (acknowledging that in reality natural theology includes much more than this). However, this description is ambiguous in an important way. One might understand it as specifying that the attempt to gain knowledge of God must be undertaken without any prior commitment to the authority or truth of a special revelation. Such a description of natural theology would rule out any appeal to Scripture as "infallible" or "inerrant" or to church teaching as having any special authority. However, it would not necessarily preclude an appeal to those revelations or the events that they bear witness to, so long as they are simply considered as ordinary historical evidence. If, for example, there is good historical evidence for some particular miracle, it might be possible to cite this miracle itself as evidence for the existence of God, and such an argument would come under the category of natural theology. So in one sense natural theology can treat particular historical events, alleged miracles, and such things as part of its subject matter.

However, one can also define natural theology in a narrower sense, as the attempt to show that knowledge of God is possible independent of any specific historical revelation claim. Natural theology in this sense draws only on generally available features of the natural world or common human experiences. The potential value of natural theology in the narrow sense is that it can serve as the first component of what I have called "two-stage apologetics."[3] In such an apologetic, the first stage is an argument for the existence of a God with at least some of the properties of the God of the Abrahamic faiths. The second stage is an argument that this God has in fact revealed himself through particular historical events and/or a particular book that is a revelation from God. This kind of apologetic strategy has been exemplified within the Christian tradition time and time again, from the Middle Ages up until the present day, from Thomas Aquinas to Richard Swinburne, and is also seen in the more popular writings of a thinker such as C. S. Lewis.[4] Anyone who thinks that such an apologetic is an important component of a rational case for belief will accordingly regard arguments for God's existence that take as their starting point widely known features of the natural world or human experience as valuable. They will also regard knowledge gained from such features or experiences as valuable, even if that knowledge does not come through inferential arguments. I shall take natural theology in this narrower sense as my focus, looking at the traditional theistic arguments, such as cosmological arguments, teleological arguments, and moral arguments, as well as at the natural signs that I believe lie at the foundation of these arguments.

One might well ask: why not go with the broader, more-inclusive understanding of natural theology, which does not limit the grounds of knowledge of God to such general features or experiences? I do

---

[3] C. Stephen Evans, *The Historical Christ and the Jesus of Faith: The Incarnational Narrative as History* (Oxford: Oxford University Press, 1996), 233–7.

[4] Thomas Aquinas, *Summa contra Gentiles*, trans. Anton C. Pegis (Notre Dame, IN: University of Notre Dame Press, 1975), 1.6.1, 4 (71–3); Richard Swinburne, *Revelation: From Metaphor to Analogy* (Oxford: Oxford University Press, 2007), 94–5; C. S. Lewis, *Mere Christianity* (London: Collins, 1952), 51–3.

not say that in principle this would be impossible, but I think there are good reasons why many defenders of religious faith have followed the "two-stage" strategy. It might be difficult to start with a direct argument for some event or events as revelations from God if one does not already have some knowledge of God. Suppose someone wished to begin with an argument that some particular event is a miracle that has revelatory value. It might be hard to produce a good argument that the particular event is a miracle unless we already know that there is a God and perhaps even know something about God's character and intentions.

Since a miracle is a special act of God, to recognize an event as a miracle one must have grounds for attributing it to God as agent. To be sure, it does seem at least possible that one might be able to do this without prior knowledge of God's reality. One traditional basis for such an attribution would be a recognition of the event as being the kind of event that cannot be naturally explained, one that "surpasses the powers of nature."[5] For example, the event might be, in Hume's words, a "violation of a law of nature," or, perhaps, expressed more guardedly, an exception to a natural regularity.[6] There are, however, much-discussed problems as to how to ascertain that this condition, or some other that warrants ascription of the event to God, could be satisfied. Hume famously argued that the probability that an alleged miracle occurred would always be less than the probability that the testimony in favor of the alleged miracle was false, because of the sheer improbability of miracles as a type of event.[7]

Other thinkers raise problems distinct from Hume's worry about the relative probability of the alleged miracle as compared with the probability of the testimony being false. It always seems possible, for example, for someone who is skeptical about a miracle claim to hypothesize that the event can be explained by some unknown law of nature, or else that some unknown natural agent is responsible

[5] See Thomas Aquinas, *Summa Theologica*, trans. Fathers of the English Dominican Province (New York: Benziger Bros., 1947–8; repr. Allen, TX: Thomas More, 1981), I, q. 103, a. 5 and a. 7; q. 105, a. 4 and a. 5; *Summa contra Gentiles* 3.64, 72, 74, 89, 90.
[6] David Hume, "Of Miracles," in *An Enquiry Concerning Human Understanding*, ed. Eric Steinberg (Indianapolis: Hackett, 1977), 76.
[7] Hume, "Of Miracles," 76–7.

for what appears to be a contravention of natural law.[8] There are, of course, numerous ways that an advocate of miracles might respond to these types of objections, but it is likely that it will be much easier to do so if there is knowledge of God's reality that is independent of the miracle itself.

To see this, think of an analogous problem. Suppose that you are walking with a friend in a park and notice what appears to be evidence of cultivation; perhaps there are holes of various sizes that appear to be in some kind of pattern and/or the dirt is piled up into what could be taken to be rows and furrows, although they are not very straight or regular.[9] The evidence is somewhat ambiguous, and the observed soil formations might conceivably just be the result of the wind or animals. Your friend takes the apparent pattern to be the work of a gardener, but you are skeptical, and inclined to think that no human agent is required to explain the holes and rows in the dirt. Clearly, it will make a large difference to this dispute if it is antecedently known that there is in fact a gardener for the park. The case for interpreting the patterns as the work of a gardener will be much easier to make than would be the case if the only evidence you have for the gardener are the patterns in the ground. If something is known about the gardener's intentions and actions—that he is known to like small, natural-looking gardens within parks—the case will be easier still to make.

Knowledge of God that is independent of some alleged miracle would make the case for a miracle easier in a similar way. Hume's argument against belief in miracles hinges around the probability of a miracle's occurrence, but knowledge that there is a God and knowledge that God might be expected to act in particular ways at certain circumstances could significantly change our estimate of the probability of a miracle happening. In a similar way, the relative probability that an event has been caused by some unknown agent or can be explained by some unknown law instead of being the result of God's activity might be altered by prior knowledge of the existence of God. Even if it is possible that an event can be explained by some

[8] See, e.g., Hume, "Of Miracles," 77 n. 43.
[9] This example is, of course, inspired by the well-known parable by John Wisdom, *Philosophy and Psycho-Analysis* (New York: Philosophical Library, 1953), 154–6.

unknown natural law or unknown agent, this does not mean that it will always be reasonable to prefer that account to a supernatural explanation. If we know or have good grounds to believe God exists and is the kind of being who might perform the action in question, that could give a reason to prefer that explanation to the bare possibility of a natural explanation.

Similar remarks could be made if we shift from talking about miracles to talking about a special revelation. It may be possible for God's existence to be known by way of a special revelation of himself, but it will be much easier to argue that the Bible or Koran (or some other book) is such a revelation if we already know that there is a God who is likely to reveal himself to humans in some way. We can, therefore, see that there are good reasons for religious apologists to follow the "two-stage" strategy, and begin with showing that we have a natural knowledge of God that is grounded in general features of the world or of human experience. Such a strategy will clearly require natural theology in the narrower sense. Hence I shall consider theistic arguments that take such features as their starting points, along with the natural signs that I believe lie at the core of those arguments.

IS NATURAL THEOLOGY RELIGIOUSLY VALUABLE?

Despite the apparent value natural theology would appear to offer if it were viable, many theologians have been less than enthusiastic about such arguments. Not all of these thinkers have been as antagonistic as Kierkegaard, who seems to believe that such arguments are completely wrong-headed.[10] Nevertheless, it is not hard to find theologians and religious philosophers who, as Alvin Plantinga has quipped, think about arguments for God's existence the way some mainstream religious people look at faith healing: "It can't be done, but even if

---

[10] Kierkegaard is, of course, notoriously unsympathetic to apologetic arguments in general, going so far as to say that the person who first tried to defend Christianity with arguments was "Judas Iscariot No. 2." See *The Sickness unto Death: A Christian Psychological Exposition for Upbuilding and Awakening*, ed. and trans. Howard V. Hong and Edna H. Hong (Kierkegaard's Writings 19; Princeton: Princeton University Press, 1980), 87.

it could it shouldn't be."[11] Why is there this suspicion of natural theology? Doubtless there are several different kinds of reasons.

One is that natural theology in this sense leads only to what Pascal called the "God of the philosophers," rather than the "God of Abraham, Isaac, and Jacob."[12] The conclusion of the typical theistic argument is that some being exists with at least some of the classical "attributes" or properties of God, such as omnipotence, omniscience, and omnipresence. At best such arguments give us knowledge of God that is abstract and far removed from the conception of God that is part of a living faith, in which God is seen as a personal reality who acts concretely in history and relates to individuals. The philosophical arguments lead only to what one Christian philosopher has called "thin theism," and such a conception of God may be far from adequate religiously.[13] Thin theism does not give me knowledge of a God with whom I can have a personal relationship or tell me how to achieve such a relationship.

However, it is not just that the conception of God arrived at is religiously inadequate; it may also be epistemologically inadequate. The theistic arguments focus on an abstract conception of God that is supposed to be the common denominator for the great theistic religions: Christianity, Judaism, and Islam. Critics wonder whether such a thinned-out conception of God is in fact easier to defend than a richer, more concrete conception of God that is found in a full-fledged version of one of these faiths.

Some Christian critics of natural theology go even further, interpreting human attempts to develop such a natural knowledge of God as prideful self-assertion. If human beings are sinful beings, as Christianity claims, and if our sinfulness mars and distorts our cognitive capacity to know God rightly, then theistic arguments must fail, because of the vast gap between God and humans, what Karl Barth

---

[11] Alvin Plantinga, "Reason and Belief in God," in Alvin Plantinga and Nicholas Wolterstorff (eds.), *Faith and Rationality: Reason and Belief in God* (Notre Dame, IN: University of Notre Dame Press, 1983), 63.

[12] See Pascal's "Memorial," in *Pensées*, rev. edn., trans. A. J. Krailsheimer (London: Penguin, 1995), 285.

[13] See Paul K. Moser, "Cognitive Idolatry and Divine Hiding," in *Divine Hiddenness: New Essays*, ed. Daniel Howard-Snyder and Paul K. Moser (Cambridge: Cambridge University Press, 2002), 125–9.

called (following Kierkegaard) the "infinite qualitative difference" between God and humans.[14] Some worry that the arguments are not only epistemic failures, but actually forms of idolatry, by which humans create conceptions of God in their own image, echoing Feuerbach's claim about theology.[15] Rather than try to develop a natural knowledge of God, humans should simply recognize their dependence on God's own self-revelation.

These critics of natural theology have important points to make, at least from the perspective of a living faith such as Christianity. It is true that, in comparison with the conception of God found in the Bible or the Koran, the concept of God that is found in the theistic arguments is thin and abstract. Such a conception of God may have little religious value in and of itself. Imagine an individual who believes in God only on the basis of the theistic arguments discovering the kind of rich, concrete revelation to be found in the Bible as a result of a conversion to Christianity. We can understand why such a person might view his previous "knowledge" of God as having little or no value, perhaps even saying, "I really did not know God at all until I found him in Christ." However, these points, significant as they are, do not imply that natural theology, if it is possible, has no value.

Whether something has value or is to be judged a failure without value depends on the purposes to which it is being put. If one wanted to cross an ocean, a canoe would be of no use, but no one would say that this means that canoes are failures as modes of water transportation. They work quite well on rivers and small lakes. Similarly, an estimate of the value of theistic arguments, or natural theology in general, depends on what one is trying to accomplish via natural theology. If one is seeking what Christians call "salvific" knowledge of God, the kind of knowledge that is religiously adequate because it makes it possible to relate to God properly, then the theistic arguments, by themselves, will not do the job. However, few proponents of natural theology, if any, have ever thought of it as accomplishing such a task.

---

[14] Karl Barth, *The Epistle to the Romans*, trans. Edwyn C. Hoskyns (Oxford: Oxford University Press, 1933), 99; Søren Kierkegaard, *Philosophical Fragments; Johannes Climacus*, ed. and trans. Howard V. Hong and Edna H. Hong (Kierkegaard's Writings 7; Princeton: Princeton University Press, 1985), 44–6.

[15] This suggestion that theistic arguments lead to idolatry is made in Kierkegaard's *Philosophical Fragments*, ch. 3, pp. 37–48.

The goals of natural theology are more modest. The main goal may be simply to make belief in God a "live option," to use William James's term, by removing intellectual barriers to faith.

In the contemporary Western intellectual world, a naturalistic world view is often taken for granted, or expressly affirmed as the only respectable "scientific" view of reality (even though there is no logical connection between a commitment to natural science and naturalism as a world view; many natural scientists are also religious believers). As social beings, humans are inevitably influenced by what other humans think. On the whole this is not a bad thing; we probably would know little or nothing if we did not simply accept a great deal of what we are taught by our parents and teachers, and indeed what is generally accepted in our culture. It is obvious, however, that this leaves open the possibility that people's beliefs about God, positive or negative, are not wholly based on evidence, but are influenced by the social zeitgeist. Some grow up in fundamentalist homes where religious beliefs are never doubted; others grow up in atheistic homes where religious beliefs are never taken seriously. Regardless of upbringing, people may be influenced by intellectuals, such as Daniel Dennett or Richard Dawkins or Sam Harris, who argue—or at least loudly assert—that belief in God no longer makes sense or is not rational any more.[16] In such an intellectual climate, some people simply fail to take religious beliefs in any form seriously, whether those beliefs be thin and abstract or rich and concrete.

In such a world, natural theology may have real value. For, if it is successful, and there are rational grounds for belief in God, atheism as a kind of "default position" can no longer be taken for granted.[17] Natural theology does not bring us to what Christians call a "saving knowledge of God," but it may undermine the claim that naturalism is the only viable intellectual option and thus that religious beliefs should not even be seriously considered. The limits of natural theology must always be kept in mind, but within those

---

[16] Daniel Clement Dennett, *Breaking the Spell: Religion as a Natural Phenomenon* (New York: Viking, 2006); Richard Dawkins, *The God Delusion* (Boston: Houghton Mifflin, 2006); Sam Harris, *The End of Faith: Religion, Terror, and the Future of Reason* (New York: Norton, 2004).

[17] Antony Flew, *The Presumption of Atheism and Other Philosophical Essays on God, Freedom, and Immortality* (London: Elek/Pemberton, 1976).

limits it could have significant value, both for the honest atheist who wishes to give atheistic beliefs critical examination as well as for the religious believer who wonders whether his or her own beliefs are just the product of non-rational social influences.

What about the charge that natural theology leads to idolatry, in that it fails to recognize the "otherness" of God and the damage done to human reason by sinfulness? It may well be true that humans can use natural theology to create a God in their own image, for their own purposes. But it is equally true that sinful humans can use or misuse revealed religion in similar ways. A natural theology that is aware of its own limits is to some degree protected against such a danger, just because it must recognize that its understanding of God is impoverished. The natural theologian may argue that naturalism is false, and that it is plausible to believe that the natural world is the product of a personal being, one who is all-powerful, all-knowing, and all-good. However, even if we had good reasons to believe in such a being there would be a vast amount we would not know about God: Does he really care about humans? Does he act in special ways within the natural order? Has he revealed himself in history? Furthermore, the qualifications that God's power and knowledge are infinite implies strict limits on our ability to understand what God is like, for it is obvious that such a being must be vastly different from ourselves. The very thinness of the conception of God that is the conclusion of the theistic arguments should make us realize how little we know about God and make us wary of any attempt to be dogmatic in our claims about what we know about God through natural theology.

WHY WOULD GOD EMPLOY NATURAL SIGNS TO MAKE HIS REALITY KNOWN?

Obviously, if one wishes to show that there is a natural knowledge of God, one must not begin by presupposing that God exists. Rather, the question of God's reality must be an honest question. However, it does seem legitimate to think about God's existence as a possibility, in much the way scientists propose some hypothesis that is not yet known. When a hypothesis is posed, one must begin by thinking about what one would expect to find if that hypothesis were true. In order to determine what kind of evidence to look for, one must begin by imagining that the hypothesis is true and asking what we would expect things to be like if this were the case. Something similar is surely reasonable in the case of God. Hence I begin, not by assuming that God exists, but asking what would follow from God's existence. Even if we do not know precisely what kind of evidence God would provide, we might have some sense of what form such evidence might take.

Let us take as our hypothesis that the kind of God that many of the world's great religions accept is real. Suppose that God exists, and that God is the kind of being that Christians, Jews, and Muslims have traditionally believed in. Roughly, we can take this as meaning that there is an all-powerful, all-knowing, and completely good personal being who is responsible for the existence of every being other than himself in the universe.[18] Furthermore, let us assume, as do these great religions, that God created humans for a purpose involving a relationship to himself, and that God cares about humans and wants them to fulfill this purpose, a fulfillment that would involve eternal happiness for humans.

If all this were the case, what kind of knowledge of God would we expect God to make possible for humans? Of course our a priori expectations about such matters are fallible, and God might well have reasons for doing otherwise than we might expect. Still, it seems reasonable, if we seek knowledge of God, to think about what form we should expect such knowledge to take and how it might be gained.

One thing we might expect, given God's intentions for humans, is that the knowledge of God would be widely available, not difficult to gain. If we assume that God cares about all humans, and that all of them are intended by God to enjoy a relationship with God, then it seems reasonable to believe that God would make it possible at least for very many humans to come to know his existence, since one can hardly enjoy a special relationship with a being that one does

---

[18] We can take "beings" here as referring to all entities in the natural universe as well as any living immaterial beings there might be, such as angels or demons. I shall not here discuss the status of abstract entities such as numbers and propositions, since theists disagree among themselves as to whether they are properly thought of as entities and also about their relationship to God.

not know exists. I shall call this the "Wide Accessibility Principle." One might think that a stronger claim than this one is reasonable. Would not God make it possible for all humans to come to know his reality? Perhaps this is so, though I settle here for the weaker claim, because there may be constraints on how widely available God can make knowledge of himself because of other purposes God has. (I will explain what such constraints might be in due course.)

In positing the Wide Accessibility Principle, am I stacking the deck in favor of the theist? I do not think so. As evidence I cite the fact that such a principle is accepted by many non-believers in God, such as John Schellenberg, who in fact accepts a much stronger claim. Schellenberg argues that the knowledge of God, if God is real, would not just be possible but actual for anyone who wishes to know God.[19] Schellenberg's claim is much stronger than the one I am here making, in that he believes that, if there were a God, what he calls "reasonable nonbelief" would not exist.[20] On this view the knowledge of God would be not only widely available, in the sense that it ought to be possible for humans to gain it (perhaps given the fulfillment of certain conditions), but so evident that any genuine seeker would actually know God. Since Schellenberg believes that it is obvious that there are cases of non-resistant unbelief, he concludes that God's "hiddenness" or failure to disclose himself is in fact strong evidence that God does not exist. I shall deal with this argument of Schellenberg's later, by criticizing his stronger version of the Wide Accessibility Principle, but it clearly entails the weaker claim that the knowledge of God, if God exists, would be widely available.

Schellenberg is hardly alone among non-believers in endorsing a principle such as the Wide Accessibility Principle. The principle is tacitly presupposed in a famous anecdote about Bertrand Russell. According to the story, Russell was asked what he would say if, after death, he discovered that his atheism was mistaken and he found himself in the presence of God. What would he say to God in that situation? Russell thinks the answer is easy: "Not enough evidence, God." The answer clearly implies that Russell believes that, if there

[19] J. L. Schellenberg, *Divine Hiddenness and Human Reason* (Ithaca, NY: Cornell University Press, 1993), 1–57.
[20] Schellenberg, *Divine Hiddenness and Human Reason*, 58–9.

were a God, he would offer plenty of evidence, evidence that it would not be difficult to find.

The Wide Accessibility Principle can plausibly be combined with a certain egalitarian picture of how God relates to human beings. If there is a God who loves all humans and desires a relationship with them, we would not expect, for example, God to restrict the knowledge of God to philosophers capable of understanding extremely abstract and complicated arguments, just as we would not expect God to limit the knowledge of himself to one sex, or one race, or one nation. Similarly, if there is knowledge of God at all, we would not expect that knowledge to be limited to highly intelligent or highly educated people.

If God exists, what else, besides the Wide Accessibility Principle, would we expect to be true of any knowledge of God there is? I believe that the knowledge of God would not only be widely available but also easily resistible. I shall call this the "Easy Resistibility Principle." According to this principle, though the knowledge of God is widely available, it is not forced on humans. Those who would not wish to love and serve God if they were aware of God's reality find it relatively easy to reject the idea that there is a God. To allow such people this option, it is necessary for God to make the evidence he provides for himself to be less than fully compelling. It might, for instance, be the kind of evidence that requires interpretation, and include enough ambiguity that it can be interpreted in more than one way.

The plausibility of this principle stems from the assumption that God wants the relationship humans are to enjoy with him to be one in which they love and serve him freely and joyfully. Since God is all-powerful and all-knowing, one can easily imagine that people who do not love God would nevertheless, if his reality were too obvious, come to the conclusion that it would be foolish and irrational to oppose God and God's purposes, however grudgingly the conclusion might be held.

It might seem that the Easy Resistibility Principle stacks the deck in favor of the theist, making things too easy. However, once again Schellenberg can be called as a witness to the plausibility of the Easy Resistibility Principle, since even his strong version of the Wide Accessibility Principle admits that God would make it possible for those who did not want to love and serve God to remain ignorant of God's existence. It is true that Schellenberg thinks that God could make his reality much more evident than he has, and this is a claim I will address in Chapter 6. However, Schellenberg does concede that God would do what is necessary to allow those who would not wish to serve God to remain in a state of unbelief. Thus, a non-believer can nevertheless recognize the plausibility of the view that a God who wishes humans to relate to him would nonetheless allow some epistemic "distance" between himself and humans. The question should not be whether the Easy Resistibility Principle makes things easy or hard for the theist, but whether we have good reasons for thinking that God, if he existed, would follow such a policy.

One might think that the Wide Accessibility Principle and the Easy Resistibility Principle cannot be simultaneously implemented, but this is not necessarily the case. They do embody different divine purposes, and there might be tension between them in some cases, such that God cannot fully realize one purpose without compromising the other. However, we have no a priori reason to think that it would be impossible for God to make it possible for many (or even all) humans to know about him, and yet simultaneously make it possible for those who would not wish to serve him lovingly and freely to be ignorant of his reality.

The two principles I have here explained are memorably described by Pascal:

If he had wished to overcome the obstinacy of the most hardened, he could have done so by revealing himself to them so plainly that they could not doubt the truth of his essence . . . It was therefore not right that he should appear in a manner manifestly divine and absolutely capable of convincing all men, but neither was it right that his coming should be so hidden that he could not be recognized by those who sincerely sought him. He wished to make himself perfectly recognizable to them. Thus wishing to appear openly to those who seek him with all their heart and hidden from those who shun him with all their heart, he has qualified our knowledge of him by giving signs which can be seen by those who seek him and not by those who do not. "There is enough light for those who desire only to see and enough darkness for those of a contrary disposition."[21]

21 Blaise Pascal, *Pensées* (New York: E. P. Dutton, 1958), 118.

Pascal is probably thinking here about the Christian doctrine of the incarnation rather than any natural knowledge of God, but it is surely in the spirit of his thought to extend the claims he has made to natural theology. If Pascal is right in his views about the form we should expect the knowledge of God to assume, then we would expect both the Wide Accessibility Principle and the Easy Resistibility Principle to hold. God would make knowledge of himself widely available for those who wish to have it, but God would not force such knowledge on those who do not wish to know God. Those who wish not to know God should be able to explain away or "discount" any evidence God presents for his reality. I believe that the notion of a "natural sign" will meet these Pascalian constraints on the knowledge of God. Such signs are widely available "pointers" or clues to God's reality, but they point to God in a way that allows those who do not wish to believe in God to reinterpret or dismiss the sign.

THE MAJOR THEISTIC ARGUMENTS

In this work I shall focus on three main types of theistic arguments: cosmological arguments, teleological arguments, and moral arguments. I shall understand cosmological arguments as ones that take as their starting point the sheer existence of the universe or its parts, such as arguments that claim that God must exist as the "first cause" or ultimate cause of the universe, or that maintain that the contingency of the universe requires that it be grounded in God as a necessary being. I shall classify as teleological arguments for God those that take as their starting points certain special characteristics of the universe, such as its intricate order or apparent purposiveness, and try to show that these characteristics imply that God, understood as an intelligent designer, exists. Moral arguments I will understand as those that begin with some feature of human morality or human moral experience, such as the sense that there are binding moral duties or obligations, and try to show that God is the best explanation of this feature.

I shall focus on these types of arguments for several reasons. To begin, they are the forms of theistic arguments most often considered and discussed in the philosophy of religion. The only other type of argument that might be claimed to be as frequently discussed are ontological arguments, those arguments that try to show that God's existence is implied by the very concept of God. However, ontological arguments, even though much discussed by philosophers because of the fascinating array of philosophical issues they raise, are rarely viewed as convincing by non-philosophers; they are not, for example, typically used by popular apologists. Cosmological, teleological, and moral arguments, however, are commonly used by such apologists, because they make contact with the experience and thinking of ordinary people. In any case, ontological arguments, just because of their a priori character, are not plausibly viewed as grounded in an experience of some aspect of nature or human experience that is a natural sign.

I shall also try to show that cosmological, teleological, and moral arguments are widely recognized as having some degree of force even by some non-theists, as well as those who may be theists but who ultimately do not find the arguments convincing. Perhaps the clearest examples of this are seen in the responses of David Hume and Immanuel Kant to the teleological argument. I shall here briefly look at those responses to illustrate my point that a critic of a theistic argument can still find himself moved by the force of that argument, postponing a more detailed look at Hume's and Kant's views of the teleological argument until Chapter 4.

HUME AND THE DESIGN ARGUMENT

David Hume's most influential discussion of the teleological argument is found in his posthumously published *Dialogues Concerning Natural Religion*.[22] As the title would imply, the book is written in the form of a dialogue between three characters: Demea, Cleanthes, and Philo. Demea, who seems to be intellectually weaker than the other two characters, defends the view that belief in God is founded on a priori proofs, but also that the nature of God is essentially mysterious.

[22] David Hume, *Dialogues Concerning Natural Religion*, ed. Richard H. Popkin (Indianapolis: Hackett, 1980).

Cleanthes, however, defends an a posteriori argument for God's existence that is teleological in character:

Look round the world: Contemplate the whole and every part of it: You will find it to be nothing but one great machine, subdivided into an infinite number of lesser machines, which again admit of subdivisions to a degree beyond what human senses and faculties can trace and explain. All these various machines, and even their most minute parts, are adjusted to each other with an accuracy which ravishes into admiration all men who have ever contemplated them.[23]

Cleanthes concludes, using a principle of analogy, that the resemblance between the natural world and human contrivances implies that "the Author of Nature is somewhat similar to the mind of man, though possessed of much larger faculties, proportioned to the grandeur of the work which he has executed."[24]

Throughout much of the book, Philo criticizes this argument of Cleanthes, and, to many commentators, appears to get the best of the exchange, to such a degree that many have argued (or assumed) that Philo's views are close to those of Hume himself.[25] I shall consider Philo's criticisms of the teleological argument in some detail in Chapter 4; here I will merely sketch some of the main points.

In general Philo relies on the view of causation that Hume defends elsewhere—namely, that our knowledge of causes and effects depends on experience. Since we have no experience of universe-making, our knowledge of the causes of the order of the universe will necessarily be uncertain. In response to the claim that we can infer that the cause of the universe will resemble the causes of human-made machines because there is an analogy between the universe and machines, and if effects are analogous the causes will be as well, Philo raises a host of objections. First, he argues that it is difficult to know how strong the analogy really is. The universe resembles many things other than machines, and thus there are many rival explanations to the design hypothesis. In any case, it is risky to make claims about the character

---

[23] Hume, *Dialogues Concerning Natural Religion*, 15.
[24] Hume, *Dialogues Concerning Natural Religion*, 15.
[25] In what follows I do not assume that Philo necessarily represents Hume at every point. I am inclined myself to agree with those who think that in different parts of the *Dialogues* Hume allows all three of the characters to embody his views at various points.

of the universe as a whole from our limited experience of a small portion of it. He also argues that, if the argument from design were successful, it would have undesirable consequences from the point of view of orthodox theism, since it would imply that the designer may be less than perfect, may be morally neutral rather than good, and might not even be a single being.

Philo's arguments here may or may not fully represent Hume's own views, though they seem to many to embody views that Hume would endorse. Regardless of the extent to which this may be so, two points are, I believe, non-controversial. (1) Philo's arguments have been historically very influential; and (2) Hume's own reputation as a powerful critic of theistic arguments in general and the teleological argument in particular rests to a substantial degree on Philo's reasoning. It thus seems highly significant that Philo himself, near the end of the work, seems to accept a weak version of the claim that the character of the universe points towards an intelligent designer: *"That the cause or causes of order in the universe probably bear some remote analogy to human intelligence."*[26] Philo posits this proposition as something maintained by "some people" to be "the whole of natural theology." To be sure, he regards the proposition as "ambiguous, or at least undefined." Nevertheless, he gives it at least this qualified endorsement, in the form of an apparent rhetorical question. Suppose we assume that the proposition in question cannot really be explained in detail, and that it has no real implications for human life: "If this really be the case, what can the most inquisitive, contemplative, and religious man do more than give a plain, philosophical assent to the proposition, as often as it occurs, and believe that the arguments on which it is established exceed the objections which lie against it?"[27]

Whether this is Hume's own view or not, it is undeniably the view of a character that Hume has invented who has himself developed strong and powerful objections to the argument from design. It therefore represents testimony that a philosophical critic who, perhaps for good reasons, regards the argument from design as far from compelling, nevertheless acknowledges the force of what we might call a natural inference. One might think that this admission of Philo is too weak

[26] Hume, *Dialogues Concerning Natural Religion*, 88 (emphasis in original).
[27] Hume, *Dialogues Concerning Natural Religion*, 88.

to be significant, and that Philo does not really acknowledge that the inference from the apparent order in the universe to a designer is one that has force. However, in another passage earlier in the book, Philo makes the point that the inference to a designer is in some sense natural and hard to resist. After discussion of the difficulties that stand in the way of inferring the goodness of a creator if we begin with our experience of nature, Philo makes a sharp contrast between his skeptical claims about the moral qualities of an inferred creator, where he feels he has a very strong case, and his previous skeptical claims about the status of the inference to an intelligent designer:

> Here Cleanthes, I find myself at ease in the argument. Here I triumph. Formerly, when we argued concerning the natural attributes of intelligence and design, I needed all my skeptical and metaphysical subtilty to elude your grasp. In many views of the universe and of its parts, particularly the latter, the beauty and fitness of final causes strike us with such irresistible force that objections appear (what I believe they really are) mere cavils and sophisms; nor can we then imagine how it was ever possible for us to repose any weight on them.[28]

Here is clear testimony on Philo's part that the apparent design experienced in nature has a natural force; one of the severest critics of the *argument* from design nevertheless finds these characteristics of nature that suggest a designer to be obvious and irresistible, at least at certain moments. This is precisely the characteristic to be expected in a natural sign of God's reality. Such a sign points toward God; we might say, to change the metaphor, that it "pulls" us toward God. Even one who ultimately resists the pointing may feel and acknowledge the force of the pull.

KANT ON THE TELEOLOGICAL ARGUMENT

Immanuel Kant is, along with Hume, justly regarded as one of the great critics of the teleological argument, which he terms the "physico-theological proof" of God's existence, an argument that

---

[28] Hume, *Dialogues Concerning Natural Religion*, 66.

begins with our "determinate experience" of the world as orderly and purposive. Kant, like Hume, gives a number of different criticisms of the argument, and Kant's criticisms of the argument, like Hume's, depend heavily on his general philosophical outlook. For Kant the concept of God is what he terms an "Idea of pure reason," an a priori conception of a "necessary and all-sufficient original being."[29] Kant argues that it is impossible to gain knowledge of such an a priori Idea by empirical means: "To advance to absolute totality by the empirical road is utterly impossible. None the less this is what is attempted in the physico-theological proof."[30]

Kant claims, echoing one of Philo's arguments from Hume's *Dialogues*, that empirically the design we observe in nature could never prove the existence of an all-perfect being who created the universe from nothing, but at best could demonstrate the existence of a divine architect who fashioned the universe from pre-existing material, and is perhaps limited by the nature of the material he is forced to employ.[31] Besides this problem, as a proof of God's reality, such an empirical argument is subject to a fatal flaw: the concept of causality can be legitimately applied only to objects of possible experience, and this leads the proponent of the teleological argument into a dilemma. If God is understood to be a cause that is a link in a causal chain, then it would be legitimate to inquire about the cause of God. If, however, the ultimate cause of the universe is conceived as separate from the causal chain, then "by what bridge can reason contrive to pass over to it?"[32]

Kant argues that these defects in the argument from design imply that as a proof of God's existence the argument must depend on the cosmological argument, which attempts to infer the existence of a necessary being from the contingency of the natural universe.[33] The teleological argument appears to be an empirical argument that gains its power from "convincing evidence derived from experience," but Kant argues that in the end the argument from design rests on a

[29] Immanuel Kant, *Critique of Pure Reason*, trans. Norman Kemp Smith (New York: St Martin's, 1965), A621, B649.
[30] Kant, *Critique of Pure Reason*, A628, B656.
[31] Kant, *Critique of Pure Reason*, A627, B655.
[32] Kant, *Critique of Pure Reason*, A621, B649.
[33] Kant, *Critique of Pure Reason*, A629, B657.

"transcendental argument" that rests entirely on "pure reason."[34] Unfortunately, for the proponent of the argument, this cosmological argument that attempts to establish the existence of a necessary being in turn is only a "disguised ontological proof," since it depends on the claim that God is a necessary being—that is, that the very concept of God implies that God must exist.[35] Kant, however, believes that he has already established that the ontological argument must fail, since it depends on the illegitimate claim that "being" or "existence" is a real predicate, designating a property that an entity may or may not possess.[36]

For my purposes it is not necessary to determine whether or not Kant's criticisms of the argument from design are decisive. What is important is that Kant himself clearly believed that they are. What is remarkable is that in Kant's eyes the failure of the argument as a proof of God's existence by no means undermines the power and force of the design we observe in nature as legitimately leading us to belief in God. In reality, Kant says that when we consider the purposiveness we observe in nature, our belief in "a supreme Author [of nature] . . . acquires the force of an irresistible conviction."[37] The argument in fact has great value:

It would therefore not only be uncomforting but utterly vain to attempt to diminish in any way the authority of this argument. Reason, constantly upheld by this ever-increasing evidence, which, though empirical, is yet so powerful, cannot be so depressed through doubts suggested by subtle and abstruse speculation, that it is not at once aroused from the indecision of all melancholy reflection, as from a dream, by one glance at the wonders of nature and the majesty of the universe—ascending from height to height up to the all-highest, from the conditioned to its conditions, up to the supreme and unconditioned Author [of all conditioned being].[38]

Kant objects to the argument only as one that provides "apodeictic certainty" that would demand "unconditional submission."[39] If,

---

34 Kant, *Critique of Pure Reason*, A629–30, B657–8.
35 Kant, *Critique of Pure Reason*, A629, B657.
36 See chapter III, section 4, of Kant, *Critique of Pure Reason*, A592–602, B620–30.
37 Kant, *Critique of Pure Reason*, A624, B652.
38 Kant, *Critique of Pure Reason*, A624, B652.
39 Kant, *Critique of Pure Reason*, A624–5, B652–3.

however, we look to the argument as a basis for a "belief adequate to quieten our doubts," it is more than adequate for the task.[40]

There is little doubt that Kant's criticisms of the argument have attracted more attention than his commendation. However, there is no reason to think that a philosopher of Kant's rigor and honesty would be insincere in such a claim. Given the proximity of the criticisms to the commendation, it certainly seems reasonable to conclude that Kant himself saw the two as consistent with each other. I believe that Kant's claims here, like those of Philo in Hume's *Dialogues*, should be viewed as testimony that the design and order in nature that provide the basis for the teleological argument are natural signs that point to God's reality, signs that can be recognized and acknowledged even by someone who ultimately rejects the argument itself as conclusive.

In the chapters that follow, I will try to support the claim that the cosmological, teleological, and moral arguments are plausibly viewed as rooted in natural signs. The arguments themselves are best understood as attempts to articulate those signs and make their evidential force more apparent. Such attempts are legitimate and may in fact be helpful. However, I shall try to show that the force of the signs is not exhausted by such arguments, and that the signs may have power even for those who do not see the arguments as conclusive, or even powerful. My strategy will require close attention to each of the three types of arguments, which will occupy the greater part of Chapters 3, 4, and 5. However, before looking in detail at the arguments, I need first to explain in more detail the concept of evidence and the notion of a natural sign, which will be the main focus of Chapter 2. Chapter 6 will conclude the work with some reflections on the human epistemic situation with respect to the knowledge of God.

The concept of evidence is ambiguous in an important way. When we say that some experience or object constitutes evidence, we may mean that it is putative evidence, something that purports to be good evidence and should be considered as evidence. But we may also mean that it is good evidence, something that leads us to truth, or leads us closer to the truth, making the truth more evident. In Chapters 3–5,

---

[40] Kant, *Critique of Pure Reason*, A625, B653.

I shall argue that the natural signs for God are evidence in the former sense, possible evidence that we should consider. In Chapter 6 I shall consider the question as to whether they constitute good evidence, and discuss how we should decide such a question.

A crucial objection to the claim that there are natural signs for God's reality can be mounted from the fact that many people, including some who profess to want to believe in God, apparently do not believe in God. Can this be the case if the knowledge of God is grounded in natural signs? Consideration of this question will require discussion of the "hiddenness of God," looking at John Schellenberg's argument that the failure on the part of some "seekers" to believe in God casts doubt on God's reality.

2

The Concept of a Natural Sign

My thesis is that some natural signs point to God's reality, and that these signs lie at the core of many of the arguments that have traditionally been given for God's existence. To develop this thesis let me first try to explain in some detail what I mean by a natural sign.

I borrow the term from Thomas Reid; my concept is in several respects inspired by Reid's work and overlaps with his concept significantly.[1] However, there are also significant differences between my project and Reid's philosophy. First of all, Reid's concept of a natural sign is primarily used by him in his account of perceptual knowledge. As far as I can tell, Reid does not use the concept in philosophy of religion or as part of his philosophical theology, where he defends traditional theistic arguments. There is an aspect of Reid's philosophical theology that seems close to the view I wish to defend, in that he argues that there is a natural knowledge of God possessed by ordinary people that does not depend on philosophical argument.[2]

---

[1] Reid himself probably took the term "sign" from George Berkeley, who employed it in his *New Theory of Vision* (Everyman Edition; New York: E. P. Dutton, 1910) to explain the perception of distance by sight. There Berkeley develops a distinction between types of signs that seems close to Reid's distinction between natural and artificial signs. See, for example, section CXLIV, pp. 79–80. Although I believe Berkeley was probably the most direct influence for Reid, the term "natural sign" has a long history, with use in both ancient and medieval philosophy, and Reid very probably knew of this history. For an informative discussion of evidence and natural signs in the ancient world, see J. Allen, *Inference from Signs: Ancient Debates about the Nature of Evidence* (Oxford: Oxford University Press, 2001).

[2] See Dale Tuggy, "Reid's Philosophy of Religion," in Terence Cuneo and René van Woudenberg (eds.), *The Cambridge Companion to Thomas Reid* (Cambridge: Cambridge University Press, 2004), 289–312. In this article Tuggy explains Reid's account of the teleological argument as a rigorous philosophical argument, but argues

However, in developing this view, he does not employ his own concept of a natural sign.

Moreover, I am not merely putting the concept of natural signs to use in an area where Reid did not employ it, but modifying the concept in significant ways. I do not claim, therefore, that my concept of a natural sign is the same as Reid's, even if his work provides the inspiration for my concept.

As we shall see, Reid sees natural signs as causally linked in two directions: "upstream" to the objects that the signs point to or represent, and "downstream" to characteristic mental acts that culminate in beliefs about the objects pointed to.[3] In Reid's own language, natural signs "suggest" the things they are signs of, though the power of the "suggestions" can vary considerably. In both directions the links are not grounded purely on conventions, but in some way reflect dispositions grounded in our nature, or, as Reid would say, "our constitution." The major outlines of this story will apply to theistic natural signs as well. Hence, I shall begin with a detailed examination of Reid's concept, which is developed as part of his account of perception.

Although Reid is best known as the originator of "common-sense philosophy," I agree with Nicholas Wolterstorff and other commentators that this designation is apt to be less than helpful.[4] To begin, Reid's notion of "common sense" is a technical one and apt to be misunderstood, since all of us think we know what common sense is. More importantly, Wolterstorff argues, the notion of common sense does not capture what is deepest in Reid's philosophy, which is his epistemological account of how it is that we are able to gain awareness of non-mental realities and form beliefs about them. Only when we understand Reid's views on these issues can we properly grasp what he means by "common sense." To understand Reid's notion of natural signs, we must therefore begin with Reid's account

that Reid's account of the argument is also intended to be a description of "a process that occurs in most people, whether they ever get into the game of offering philosophical arguments" (p. 297).

[3] As I shall shortly make clear, I am here employing not Reid's own concept of causality, but what he would call causality in a loose and popular sense.

[4] See Nicholas Wolterstorff, *Thomas Reid and the Story of Epistemology* (Cambridge: Cambridge University Press, 2001), 1–2.

of perception, and pay particular attention to the role sensations play in perceiving the world around us.[5]

REID'S ACCOUNT OF SENSATIONS AS NATURAL SIGNS

Reid's account of perception is a spirited defense of a direct realist view of perception, one that tries to refute and replace the representational theories of perception employed by many of the early modern philosophers who were his predecessors. These representational accounts of perception hold that humans are not directly aware of mind-independent physical objects but only of mental entities, most commonly called "ideas" in the eighteenth century, that (for some of these philosophers) represent physical objects or allow us to infer their existence. On such an account when I look out of my window and gaze at a tree, what I directly see is not the tree itself, but a mental image of the tree, something occurring within my own consciousness. This type of representational account of perception, which Reid characteristically calls "the Way of Ideas" or "the Ideal philosophy," inevitably leads, on Reid's view, either to idealism or to skepticism, as Berkeley and Hume make clear, since there is simply no way to show that humans can gain knowledge of extra-mental realities if we are only directly aware of mental realities. Neither reason nor experience will allow us to bridge the chasm between our minds and the external world that looms if representationalism is true.

Much of the dispute between Reid and defenders of the "Way of Ideas" turns on the nature and function of sensations.[6] It is difficult to define what is meant by "sensation;" early modern philosophers typically explain the concept by giving examples, such as the feeling of warmth one gets from a fire, the smell of a fragrant rose, or the

[5] For a good account of Reid's account of perception, see James van Cleve, "Reid's Theory of Perception," in Cuneo and Woudenberg (eds.), *The Cambridge Companion to Thomas Reid*, 101–33.

[6] The best account of Reid's view of sensations I know is by Todd Buras, "The Function of Sensations in Reid," *Journal of the History of Philosophy*, forthcoming. Much of what I have to say about Reid on sensations and their role in perception is taken from Buras's work.

blueness of an image of the sky on a fine clear day. Philosophers such as Locke, who think of perception as rooted in sensations, typically see those special sensory "ideas" as immediate objects of awareness that give us an indirect connection to extra-mental entities. In the case of ideas of primary qualities, Locke sees these ideas as resembling or "mirroring" external entities. Such a relation between ideas and physical things allows the ideas to represent physical objects to us or else serves as the basis for an inference to such extra-mental entities.

Reid's account of sensations is entirely different. Reid learned from Berkeley that sensations (and mental ideas in general) do not resemble the physical objects they are supposed to represent. For Reid, sensations are not the primary objects of perceptual awareness but are "natural signs" that make perceptual awareness possible. Sensations are not (usually) the objects of perception, but the means whereby we perceive real objects.

The external senses have a double province; to make us feel and to make us perceive. They furnish us with a variety of sensations, some pleasant, others painful, and others indifferent; at the same time they give us a conception, and an invincible belief of the existence of external objects . . . This conception and belief which Nature produces by means of the senses, we call *perception*. The feeling which goes along with the perception we call *sensation*.[7]

By "conception" Reid does not mean exactly what someone schooled in modern philosophy might think, especially someone familiar with Kant's philosophy. For a Kantian to have a "conception" of something naturally suggests that one simply has a concept that can be applied to that thing. However, for Reid, conception of an object is not the application of a concept to an object; it is rather awareness of the object. To say that we have a "conception" of an object is to say that in some way it engages or is present to our consciousness. Our thought is directed to some object as an object of a certain sort, but "conception" in his sense does not imply belief in the reality of an object. If I merely imagine an object such as an apple I have a conception of it, but when I perceive an object, such as the Fuji

---

[7] Thomas Reid, *Essays on the Intellectual Powers of Man: A Critical Edition*, ed. Derek R. Brookes (University Park, PA: Pennsylvania State University Press, 2002), 210.

apple sitting on my desk, this conception is combined with a belief or judgment in the real existence of the apple.

Sensations are not linked to perceptions conceptually, and thus it is not a necessary truth that we perceive objects in the world by way of the particular sensations we in fact employ, or by means of any sensations at all. God could have created us as beings who perceived the world without sensations, or who could have perceived objects by way of very different sensations than the ones we actually rely upon. (Here we might think, as Thomas Nagel has done, about what it might be like to be a bat.[8]) Charmingly, Reid speculates that we "might have been made, so as to taste with our fingers, to smell with our ears, and to hear by the nose."[9] In fact, Reid considers and may even endorse the claim that for one special type of perception (that of visual figure) it is actually the case that we perceive without sensations.[10] If we could generally perceive the world without sensations or without the ones we actually employ, we would have to be physically different beings; in Reid's language there would have to be a difference in our "constitutions." Nevertheless, our actual constitutions are such that it is (with the one possible exception mentioned above) causally necessary (in a sense of "cause" explained below) for us to have sensations to perceive the world.

How are we able to perceive objects by way of sensations? Reid says it is not by way of inference; the transition from sensation to perception is "immediate" at least in a psychological sense. Nor is it by virtue of any relation of "resemblance" or "mirroring" between the sensation and the object perceived. Rather the sensation is a *sign*

[8] Thomas Nagel, "What Is It Like to Be a Bat?" *Philosophical Review*, 83 (1974), 435–50.

[9] Thomas Reid, *An Inquiry into the Human Mind on the Principles of Common Sense: A Critical Edition*, ed. Derek R. Brookes (University Park, PA: Pennsylvania State University Press, 1997), 176.

[10] Some commentators think that Reid actually endorses the claim that we perceive visual figures without sensations, but Todd Buras thinks that Reid may hold only that we perceive visual figures without any unique sensation rather than without any sensation at all, since Reid says, of sensation and perception, that "in our experience we never find them disjoined." See Buras, "The Function of Sensations in Reid." Buras draws on earlier work that supports this view, including Norman Daniels, *Thomas Reid's "Inquiry": The Geometry of Visibles and the Case for Realism* (Stanford, CA: Stanford University Press, 1989), 84–7; and Gideon Yaffe, "Reid on the Perception of Visible Figure," *Journal of Scottish Philosophy*, 1 (2003), 103–15.

of what is perceived. Signs in turn are either "natural signs" (which is the case for many sensations) or "artificial signs," signs that owe their status as signs to human conventions. The key idea is that sensations are not normally themselves the objects of perception, but are the means whereby we perceive other things.

We do not normally perceive sensations, but perceive by way of sensations. Of course it is possible to make sensations themselves the objects of conscious awareness, and for some special purposes we do this. For example, suppose some person is being examined by a physician who wants to determine whether that person's sense of smell is working properly. In such a case one might focus on the sensations themselves, rather than (as is normally the case) what one is smelling by way of the sensations.

Two things are required for the sensation to be a natural sign. First there must be a real causal connection between the thing and the sensation. There is one technical qualification that must be made at this point. Reid's own theory of causation is one that reserves the term "cause" for agent causation, since only agents possess "active power." Strictly speaking, there is no "event causation" in nature, but merely "constant conjunctions" that we recognize and call natural laws. Reid recognizes, however, that in ordinary life we typically call the physical conditions that are nomologically sufficient for some event the cause of that event. Thus, even if sensations are not caused by external objects (in Reid's strict, technical notion of "cause"), it is still true that, in the "loose and popular sense" of "cause," the one most of us employ in our daily lives, it is correct to say that sensations are caused by the objects that they help us to perceive.

The second condition that is required for a sensation to be a sign is that the sensation must play a key role in producing, again in the "loose and popular sense" of causality, the conception and belief that are the constituents of perception. Reid's characteristic way of putting this is to say that the sign "suggests" what is perceived by means of the sign. The term "suggest" is somewhat misleading, however, since the process by which we move from sensation to perception is immediate and spontaneous, and for one type of perception irresistible. The work of natural signs thus seems far stronger than what we would ordinarily call a suggestion.

There are two different ways in which sensations give rise to perceptions, corresponding to a distinction Reid draws between original and acquired perceptions. In original perception, we are "hard-wired" to take a particular type of sensation as a sign of a particular type of object that is being perceived. With respect to original perceptions, "nature hath established a real connection between the signs and the things signified; and nature hath also taught us the interpretation of the signs."[11] One of Reid's favorite examples is the way in which the sensation we get when we touch a solid object produces the perception of a body having the quality of "hardness."[12] Reid believes that without such original perceptions we would never gain perceptual knowledge of the external world. He also argues that the process by which we move from sensation as sign to the perception of an object in at least some original perceptions is one that is irresistible. Even philosophers such as Hume who profess to doubt the connections (as Reid interprets Hume as doing) confess that in daily life they are unable to do so.

In acquired perceptions, sensations also serve as natural signs of the objects perceived, but in this case the principles that govern the link between sensation and object perceived are more general in nature; there is no "hard-wired" link between a particular type of sensation and a particular type of perception.[13] Rather, the links are grounded in more general principles of our constitution, involving experience and reflection. For example, since lemons regularly are conjoined with a distinctive smell, the one we call "lemony," after experiencing lemons on a number of occasions I learn to recognize a lemony smell as the smell of a lemon. Once I learn this connection, however, the movement from sensation to perception is just as immediate as it is in the case of an original perception; no inference is necessary to perceive that a lemon is present by way of the smell of the lemon.

It is clear that acquired perceptions presuppose original perceptions, since I can learn by experience that a particular sensation is conjoined with a particular object only if I am able to know that the

---

[11] Reid, *Inquiry*, 190.   [12] Reid, *Inquiry*, 54–8.
[13] This paragraph and the one that follows are indebted to an email received from Todd Buras, which contained a particularly clear explanation of the distinction between original and acquired perception.

object is present.[14] Acquired perceptions are still natural in the sense
that they are the product of principles of our constitution. But their
involvement with experience and learning means they are subject to
improvement, correction, and variability in a way that our original
perceptions are not. For instance, when certain auditory sensations
suggest the location of an object, this is an acquired perception. Such
acquired perceptions, unlike original perceptions, are not irresistible.
As I gain more experience and reflect on that experience I may come
to believe that the perception of location by sound is unreliable in
certain circumstances (for example, an echo chamber). For Reid,
perception in general is not infallible; the justification provided to
our perceptions by the sensations that "suggest" them is always prima
facie. However, acquired perceptions are subject to defeat in ways
that is not the case for original perceptions.[15]

NATURAL SIGNS OTHER THAN SENSATIONS

Sensations are far from the only natural signs in Reid. Objects that are
perceived can themselves serve as natural signs for other perceptions,
and this is true for both original and acquired perceptions. Our ability
to recognize other persons as conscious beings and to communicate
with them depends on natural signs: perceptual recognition of the
"thoughts, purposes, and dispositions of the mind" are made possible
originally by way of perceptions of "the features of the face, the
modulation of the voice, and the motion and attitude of the body."[16]
These natural signs of human mental states constitute a "natural
language of mankind," without which communication in general,
including the use of artificial signs such as those employed in human
language, would be impossible. The signs in these cases are not the
perceptions, but the actual physical states perceived. This is important,
since it means that natural signs do not have to be mental realities

---

[14] Reid makes this explicit in *Inquiry*, 191.
[15] For Reid's discussion of the way experience and reflection give rise to acquired
perceptions, see *Essays on the Intellectual Powers*, essay 2, chapter 21 (pp. 234–41).
For Reid's explanation of how it is that we make mistakes in perception, see essay 2,
chapter 22 (pp. 241–52).
[16] Reid, *Inquiry*, 59.

such as sensations, but can themselves be perceived objects in the world.

These perceived facial and bodily characteristics are interesting, in that, although they give rise to perceptions that are original, they do not seem to be irresistible, since we do learn through experience that people can simulate these signs in an attempt to deceive others. Our disposition to rely on them is very strong, but that disposition, like our disposition to believe in the testimony of others, is one that can be strengthened, modified, and even blocked on some occasions by other experiences, background beliefs, and the influence of one's community.[17] So the tendency of a natural sign to produce belief is one that can vary in strength, and can be modified or overridden altogether by other factors.

To summarize, a natural sign for Reid is something, either mental (such as a sensation) or physical (such as a perceived facial gesture), that has a causal connection (in the "loose" sense of causality) "upstream" with what the sign signifies and also plays a causal role (again in the loose sense) "downstream" in generating a characteristic judgment. Reid says that some of the natural signs that produce original perceptions are irresistible, because we are hard-wired to move from the particular sign to a particular type of perceptual judgment. In other cases, the natural signs, both for original perceptions and especially for acquired perceptions, are not irresistible, because the dispositions to form judgments they occasion can be strengthened, modified, or overridden by experience. When a sign is functioning as a sign, one's conscious attention is not focused on the sign but on what the sign signifies, though it is possible to turn one's attention to the sign itself, something we do on some occasions for special purposes.

NATURAL SIGNS FOR GOD

So how is the concept of natural signs that I want to employ in looking at the theistic arguments similar to or different from Reid's

---

[17] For Reid's view of testimony, see *Inquiry*, 190–5; *Essays on the Intellectual Powers*, 487–8.

concept? I shall term natural signs that point to God as "theistic natural signs." There are many fundamental similarities between theistic natural signs and Reidian natural signs. The most important of these is simply the root idea of a sign as something that brings an object to our awareness and also produces a belief in the reality of that object. Natural signs of God would be a means whereby a person becomes aware of God. As is the case for Reidian natural signs, theistic natural signs should be linked upstream to what the sign signifies, and downstream to a conception of what is signified as well as a belief in the reality of what is signified. In other words, a natural sign for God ought to be something that is connected both to God and to a human disposition to conceive of God and believe in God's reality.

These two conditions merit some further consideration. Let us look first at the link between the sign and God. To look at the hypothesis that there are natural signs for God, it is legitimate to employ the content of the hypothesis, which in this case includes the existence of God. If God exists, then God is the creator and sustainer of every finite reality, so the idea of a causal link between God and the sign is unproblematic. However, just because God is the creator of everything finite, such a causal connection seems insufficient. Presumably, natural signs for God will be distinctive in some way. There may be some sense in which everything in the natural world can serve as a natural sign for God. However, if everything is a natural sign for God, then there will be no theistic natural signs in any distinctive sense. What is needed, I think, is the idea not only that God is the cause of the existence of the sign, but that God created the sign to be a sign. The function of the sign needs to be part of the reason why the sign exists, and this function must be anchored in God's creative intentions.

This is not really a significant difference from a Reidian perceptual sign, since the idea of a function seems to be a key part of the Reidian notion as well. Reid, who is of course a theist, thinks that God has designed the natural order in such a way that there is a regular link between the signs and what is signified by them. An atheist who wishes to be a Reidian would not, of course, see things this way. However, even an atheistic Reidian would presumably have to see the link between the sign and what is signified in perception as non-accidental, perhaps seeing the link as one that has some functional value that has provided an evolutionary edge.

What about the other link, the connection "downstream" to the belief or judgment about God? Theistic signs here, much like Reidian signs, must have the power to dispose us to form judgments that what the sign signifies, in this case God, is real. Again, this must be understood not merely as a causal relation, but as a functional one. For Reid, our tendency to form certain judgments because of signs is part of our "design plan," so to speak. If there are theistic natural signs, part of their intended function must be to give rise to beliefs about God.

However, this disposition to form beliefs about God is not the whole story about the "outputs" of a theistic natural sign. In Reidian natural signs, the sign does not lead merely to belief, but also to "conception," an awareness of the thing the beliefs are about. In a similar way I shall think of theistic natural signs as pointing us to God as a reality, not merely disposing us to form beliefs about God. We form beliefs about God as a result of an awareness of God that the sign makes possible. To go back to Reidian natural signs, it is possible to have a real awareness of an object while having all kinds of false beliefs about that object. I might, for example, see my sister walking up the driveway without realizing that it is my sister. Instead, I form the belief that my next-door neighbor is walking up my driveway. In some sense the sign has made my sister present to me, and I have some true beliefs about what I perceive. For example, I correctly believe that a woman is walking up my driveway. However, though the sign has given me a *de re* awareness of my sister, that is consistent with my developing some false beliefs about what I perceive through the sign.

Similarly, I shall maintain that theistic natural signs in some way point us toward and make possible a *de re* awareness of God. However, this is quite consistent with the fact that, for all kinds of reasons, the persons who have a *de re* awareness of God may have very different beliefs about the object of their awareness. And many of those beliefs may be false. This is one way in which a natural sign differs from a theistic argument, even one developed from reflection on a natural sign, since an argument has as its final goal acceptance of a conclusion—that is, a proposition. Theistic natural signs dispose individuals to form beliefs as well, but fundamentally serve to point to a reality. It will turn out to be the case that individuals can be in touch with that reality while having many false beliefs about it.

How strong must the connection be between a theistic natural sign and the beliefs that the sign gives rise to? We have seen that, for Reid, some natural signs are very powerful indeed, giving rise to perceptual judgments that are irresistible. However, other natural signs are variable in their effects; there must be some reasonably strong disposition for the sign to produce its characteristic outcome, but, in cases of acquired perceptions, and even for some original perceptions (such as those grounded in the signs provided by facial expressions), signs are not irresistible; they can be strengthened, weakened, or even blocked on particular occasions by such factors as other experiences, prior beliefs, and social influences.

Theistic natural signs are more like the second type of Reidian natural signs. On the one hand, to be a natural sign at all, there must be some in-built propensity, when the sign is encountered, to form some relevant judgment as a result of the encounter with the reality mediated by the sign. If there are such theistic natural signs, we would then expect belief in God to be widespread, found in reasonably young children and across many cultures, and we would expect that those beliefs would be typically occasioned by the same types of experiences. This expectation is consistent with the "Wide Accessibility Principle" explained in Chapter 1. In the next section, I shall discuss contemporary scientific theories on the origins of religious belief that support the idea that there is a natural propensity to form beliefs in God that is cross-cultural and found in young children.

However, this propensity to believe in God, though strong, is far from irresistible. First, there is every reason to think that the beliefs that theistic natural signs give rise to are subject to modification (strengthening, weakening, or even being blocked) in just the same ways as Reidian natural signs. In other words, the theistic natural signs are more like Reidian natural signs in acquired perceptions, where experience plays a role in their development, than like those sensation signs that irresistibly produce certain perceptions. Or at the very least theistic signs will be like the facial expression signs, which, though original, are certainly modifiable by experience and are far from irresistible. It is not uncommon to find ourselves suspicious that some person is attempting to deceive us by simulating natural signs that suggest mental states such as sincerity or compassionate concern.

Certainly among the factors that will determine how signs are modified, strengthened, and overridden will be social factors. How a sign is interpreted, whether it is taken seriously or discounted, what role the judgments arising from the sign will play in an overall system of beliefs—all these things will be influenced by the community of the individual who is perceiving the sign. All this will be true for both Reidian and theistic natural signs.

However, theistic natural signs may be even more subject to disturbance in their operations than Reidian natural signs. The reason this is so has to do with what I called in Chapter 1 the "Easy Resistibility Principle." Since God wishes humans to relate to him freely and in love, and since an irresistible awareness of God's reality would make this difficult, there is good reason to think that those who might be motivated to disbelieve in God would be able to inhibit the operation of the natural disposition to form a belief in God when one encounters a theistic natural sign. The fact that theistic natural signs are easier to resist than Reidian natural signs is the greatest difference between the two concepts.

Another similarity between theistic natural signs and Reidian natural signs is that in both cases the signs may be either mental or physical in character. We have seen that Reidian natural signs can be sensations, but also perceived physical states of affairs. I want to leave open the possibility that some theistic natural signs might consist of experiences of a certain sort, where "experience" is a term for a mental state. An example might be the feeling of guilt in a person who has just performed some tawdry action. However, other signs might consist of actual features of the natural world, such as the beauty or grandeur of a sunset over the ocean or a mountain vista.

COGNITIVE SCIENCE AND BELIEF IN GOD

As noted above, if there are natural signs that point to God's reality, then there should be natural mechanisms whereby human persons form beliefs about God in certain circumstances. According to the Wide Accessibility Principle explained in Chapter 1, these circumstances should be common, and thus belief in God should be very widespread, arising at an early age and appearing in all or nearly all cultures. It is significant that there is increasing agreement among scientists, including psychologists, cognitive scientists, sociologists, and anthropologists, that there are indeed natural mechanisms that predispose humans to belief in God.[18] Contrary to earlier social scientific theories about religious belief, which tended to explain such beliefs in terms of environmental stimuli related to social or psychological functioning, contemporary scientists are prone to think that humans are "hard-wired" to be religious; belief in God or gods is the result of the operation of a cognitive faculty. Pascal Boyer, for example, a cognitive scientist, affirms that "the content and organization of religious ideas depend, in important ways, on noncultural properties of the human mind-brain."[19] A large number of scientists agree with Boyer.[20]

The great majority of the scientists who are working in this area do not think of these natural mechanisms that produce religious beliefs as reliable sources of knowledge. On the contrary, many of them seem to think that explaining religious beliefs in this way undermines their rationality. Daniel Dennett, for example, claims that the cognitive faculty that produces religious faith is a "fiction generating contraption."[21] Rather than thinking of this natural faculty as operating in connection with natural signs to produce true beliefs, these scientists usually interpret the cognitive faculty that produces

---

[18] Here I must acknowledge the help of Kelly Clark and Justin Barrett. Their forthcoming article "Reidian Epistemology and the Cognitive Science of Religion" was most helpful to me in summarizing the scientific literature on cognitive explanations of religious belief.

[19] Pascal Boyer, *The Naturalness of Religious Ideas: A Cognitive Theory of Religion* (Berkeley and Los Angeles: University of California Press, 1994), 3.

[20] See, e.g., Scott Atran, *In Gods we Trust: The Evolutionary Landscape of Religion* (Evolution and Cognition; Oxford: Oxford University Press, 2002); Justin L. Barrett, *Why Would Anyone Believe in God?* (Cognitive Science of Religion Series; Walnut Creek, CA: AltaMira Press, 2004); Stewart Elliott Guthrie, *Faces in the Clouds: A New Theory of Religion* (New York: Oxford University Press, 1993); Dean Hamer, *The God Gene: How Faith is Hardwired into our Genes* (New York: Doubleday, 2004). This is just a fraction of the new books that have appeared in this area, and does not include the large number of articles that have appeared in scholarly journals.

[21] Daniel Clement Dennett, *Breaking the Spell: Religion as a Natural Phenomenon* (New York: Viking, 2006), 184.

belief in God as a "spandrel," an unintended by-product of a faculty that evolved for entirely different purposes.

A common version of such a view is that religious belief is a by-product of a human propensity to interpret events in nature as the result of intentional actions. The reasoning behind this is grounded in the assumption that humans would have paid a heavy evolutionary price for a failure to detect threats from enemies, whether other humans or animals. The need to detect other agents in the environment, whether promising or threatening, eventually led to what some cognitive scientists have called a "hypersensitive agency detection device" (HADD).[22] It is not surprising that such a cognitive device would produce many false positives, since there is little price to be paid if someone thinks an enemy is near when there is none, but survival may be on the line if a real, present enemy is not detected. On this interpretation, the human tendency to believe in God is the result of such a false positive. We have a natural, in-built tendency to attribute significant results, good and bad, to the work of an agent, as well as to explain such things as striking patterns as the work of an agent. If no natural agent can be found, an invisible, supernatural agent is invoked.

I shall not attempt to evaluate the strength or weakness of this evolutionary explanation of the existence of what we may call the human God-faculty. It is, like many evolutionary explanations of human behavior, in many ways a "Just-So" story that is speculative in character, and many such stories can doubtless be told. The point I wish to make is that, even if this explanation is correct, it does not have the reductive implications its proponents believe it has, nor does it imply that the God-faculty is unreliable in producing belief in God. We should remember at this point that, if humans are physical creatures who have evolved in a Darwinian way, then all our human cognitive capacities can in principle be explained as a result of the struggle for survival. If evolutionary explanations automatically discredit a cognitive faculty, then all of our cognitive faculties would be discredited, including those faculties that enable us to do science.

Nor are "spandrels" necessarily unreliable from a cognitive point of view. Since it is unlikely that a capacity for high-level mathematical

---

[22] See Barrett, *Why Would Anyone Believe in God?*, 32.

theory is a direct result of the evolutionary struggle to survive, it is likely that the capacity for mathematics is also a "spandrel." Yet few would want to challenge the outputs of our cognitive capacity to do mathematics. It is possible, of course, that people such as Dawkins are right, and that the human tendency to believe in God is a "delusion." If we know independently that God does not exist, then certainly some such explanation will be plausible. However, the plausibility of such an account, on the assumption that God does not exist, does not amount to powerful evidence that God does not exist. The fact that there is a natural tendency to believe in God and that an evolutionary story can be told about the causal origins of such a tendency does not establish that the outputs of the cognitive process are delusory.

The scientific evidence in favor of a God-faculty can in fact be seen as supporting an important part of traditional theology. Many theologians have maintained that God has created humans with an in-built tendency to believe in God. John Calvin, for example, famously posits that humans possess what he calls a *sensus divinitatis*: "There is within the human mind, and indeed by natural instinct, an awareness of divinity. This we take to be beyond controversy. To prevent anyone from taking refuge in the pretense of ignorance, God himself has implanted in all men a certain understanding of his divine majesty."[23] These claims of Calvin and other theologians show that the idea of a natural disposition to develop a belief in divinity, an inherent part of the idea that there are natural signs that point to God's reality, is not an ad hoc suggestion, but a standard part of the way religious believers have thought about these matters. One might say that Calvin here licenses a prediction: if there is a God of the sort religious people affirm, then there will be a natural tendency to believe in God. The theories of contemporary cognitive scientists affirm that Calvin's prediction has been fulfilled. I do not claim that this in itself is powerful evidence for the reality of God. But the fact that something that should be true if God is real seems in fact to be true is certainly not evidence *against* the reality of God.

---

[23] John Calvin, *The Institutes of the Christian Religion*, ed. John T. McNeill, trans. Ford Lewis Battles, in collaboration with the editor, and a committee of advisers; 2 vols. (Library of Christian Classics 20–1; Philadelphia: Westminster Press, 1960), bk. I, ch. 3.

Someone might object at this point that the evolutionary explanation of religious belief offered by skeptical cognitive scientists undermines the claim that this tendency to believe in God is a God-implanted faculty. Since we can give a perfectly natural explanation for this faculty that does not presuppose God, there is no need for a supernatural explanation. Such an objection assumes that natural and supernatural explanations are rivals, such that the success of the natural explanation undermines the supernatural. However, it is an essential part of a theistic world view that whatever happens in the natural world can ultimately be traced back to God's creative and conserving actions and intentions. The fact that an object falls off a shelf because of gravity does not preclude the possibility that this happens because it is God's will, since theists believe that the law of gravity—and all the laws of nature—hold because God wills the universe to be a certain way. In a similar way, the fact that a natural explanation can be given for the existence of the God-faculty does not show that this faculty is not the result of God's creative intentions, since whatever natural explanation is given may simply be an account of the natural process God has chosen to realize his creative intentions. If it is the case that humans have a natural tendency to postulate an agent who lies behind the apparent designedness and purposefulness of the natural world, this tendency is not delusory if there is in fact a God who is responsible for that designedness and purposefulness. HADD in that case will not be producing false positives when it produces beliefs in God.

In any case, I want to emphasize that the evolutionary explanation of the fact that humans have a natural tendency to form beliefs in God in certain circumstances presupposes that it is a fact that humans have such a tendency. The science under discussion thus supports belief in the reality of such a human cognitive tendency, regardless of how we interpret or explain such a tendency. Hence I claim that in one important dimension the idea that there are natural signs that point to God's reality is fully consistent with contemporary scientific theories about the origins of religious belief. This, of course, is far from establishing the truth of the natural theistic signs view. However, if there were no such natural dispositions, the theistic natural signs view would be a non-starter.

ARE THEISTIC NATURAL SIGNS EVIDENCE FOR GOD?

In the chapters that follow, I shall examine three types of theistic arguments and look for the theistic natural signs that, on my view, lie at their core. Before examining these signs in some detail, it is worth asking whether or not the signs I am looking for should be thought of as evidence for God's reality. There are several things that one might mean by asking this question. One is whether the signs constitute good evidence. Do they provide justification for belief in God? I shall present my answer to this question in Chapter 6, after looking at the signs in detail.

However, there is a prior question that should be answered before embarking on a detailed examination of the signs, and that is whether it is right to think of the signs as evidence at all. In looking for natural signs that point to God, are we looking for something that could properly be described as evidence? Here I am thinking of evidence, not as what actually makes some proposition true or probable, the question to be dealt with in my concluding chapter, but rather what purports or is alleged to do so. In looking at theistic natural signs, should we think of ourselves as looking at things that purport to be evidence, and should be assessed as potential evidence? The answer depends, as is so often the case in philosophy, on how we understand "evidence."

Reformed epistemology famously claims that belief in God can be "properly basic," that "it is entirely right, rational, reasonable, and proper to believe in God without any evidence or argument at all . . . "[24] It is clear, however, that in this context philosophers such as Plantinga are thinking of "evidence" as propositional evidence, the sort of thing that could serve as a premise in an argument. This is certainly a legitimate way to think about evidence, but it is not the only way to think about it. Many philosophers have thought that evidence should be understood as whatever a person apprehends

---

[24] Alvin Plantinga, "Reason and Belief in God," in Alvin Plantinga and Nicholas Wolterstorff (eds.), *Faith and Rationality: Reason and Belief in God* (Notre Dame, IN: University of Notre Dame Press, 1983), 17.

that makes it more likely for that person to achieve true beliefs. On such a view, evidence is simply whatever makes the truth "evident" to us, or that tends to do that. Clearly, propositional evidence can do this, but there may also be forms of non-propositional evidence. Paul Moser, for example, claims that the "subjective contents" of "non-conceptual, perceptual experiences" are basic forms of evidence; they are "evidential probability-makers" for propositions.[25] Obviously, the subjective contents of non-conceptual experiences are not propositional in character, and thus cannot serve as evidence in the sense of being premises in arguments. However, for philosophers such as Moser, such experiences are not only properly described as evidence; they are the foundational kind of evidence.

There are, of course, reasons why some philosophers reject the notion of non-propositional evidence. While we have some clarity about what it means to say that the truth of one proposition entails the truth of another proposition or makes it more likely or probable that some proposition is true, it seems more difficult to say how something that is non-propositional can make a proposition true or probable. Nevertheless, if these difficulties could be surmounted, it would seem possible to employ a concept of evidence that is broad enough to encompass non-propositional forms of evidence.

Hence, I shall reformulate my original question by distinguishing the two senses of evidence. Do natural signs constitute propositional evidence for God's reality? The correct answer, I believe, is "sometimes, but not necessarily." Recall that, for Reidian natural signs, the sign is not normally the object of awareness, but is rather the means whereby we become aware of something else. So, for example, sensations are not normally propositional evidence for the reality of the things we perceive by means of the sensations. Nevertheless, though we normally focus not on the sign, but on what the sign signifies, it is possible to direct attention to the sign itself. Furthermore, it is possible for the person who does this to treat the sign as the basis for an argument. Indeed, according to Reid, this is precisely what some of the early modern philosophers, such as Descartes and Locke, tried to do: construct arguments for the reality of external physical objects beginning with premises about sensations, or how the world appears to an individual.

According to Reid, however, those arguments are spectacularly unsuccessful. However, not all philosophers agree with Reid about the prospects for such arguments. In any case, if we think of propositional evidence as alleged or purported evidence, it seems clearly possible to take Reidian natural signs as evidence. However, if we follow Reid himself, we will recognize that it is not necessary to do so. Reid himself thinks that we will be much more likely to make epistemic progress if we do not do so. Instead of taking the natural signs as premises for arguments, we are better off allowing them to function purely as signs.

I shall leave it as an open question whether this is so for theistic natural signs as well. There are points to be made on both sides. On the one hand, the signs can and do function as signs without serving as premises for an argument. The individual is normally consciously aware of the signs as pointing beyond themselves to the reality signified, which is, of course, God in this case. On the other hand, it is possible to make the signs themselves the focus of attention, and use them as the basis for arguments. Even if Reid is right in thinking that the arguments developed from natural perceptual signs are bad ones, it does not follow that arguments developed from theistic natural signs will necessarily be bad ones. If it turns out to be the case that these arguments are strong, this is not a problem for my thesis. My aim is not to polemicize against theistic arguments. In some cases it may be that the signs that I claim lie at the core of theistic arguments may have enough force to make those arguments powerful. So it may be possible for theistic natural signs to function as propositional evidence.

However, just as was the case for Reidian signs, I shall argue that it is not necessary to develop arguments from the signs in order for the signs to make knowledge possible. The signs can point to God's reality with no argument or conscious inference being part of the process, and in such a case the signs will not be propositional evidence.

However, if someone employs the broader concept of evidence, which allows for non-propositional evidence, then I think that it is correct to say that theistic natural signs are evidence, even in cases where the knowledge the signs make possible is psychologically immediate and no inferential argument is involved. Here "evidence" comes close to what the Reformed epistemologist calls "grounds." Of course calling them evidence in the sense of alleged or purported evidence does not mean they constitute good evidence. That question remains on the table.

3

Cosmic Wonder and Cosmological Arguments for God

In this chapter and the next two I shall discuss some of the natural signs for God's existence, developing my claim that a particular sign lies at the core of each of three types of classical theistic arguments: cosmological, teleological, and moral arguments respectively. I shall discuss the signs and the corresponding arguments in what I regard as an ascending order, beginning with the least clear and least powerful sign, which is embedded in cosmological arguments for God, and moving to the teleological and then the moral arguments with the signs that each incorporate.

I have already noted in the previous chapter that theistic natural signs, like some Reidian natural signs, are not irresistible, but subject to modification in light of experience, social influences, and other beliefs: strengthening, alteration, and outright suppression. However, as will become clear in the discussion, theistic natural signs differ from each other with respect to their force and clarity, and thus differ with respect to how easy they are to modify. Some are easier to read and interpret than others. Some are easier to dismiss outright than others. They also differ with respect to what we might call their information content. While all the signs point to God, some provide more insight into God's character than others, and thus are inherently more enlightening. The natural sign that underlies the cosmological argument is one that provides only a vague and indistinct concept of God. It is thus not only easy to resist, but can be interpreted or "read" in vastly different ways.

It is worth pointing out that there may be other natural signs than those that are embedded in these three arguments. Other arguments for God's reality, with corresponding signs, could be considered. Moreover, there are, I believe other natural signs for God's reality that have not been developed into formal arguments at all, or at least not very commonly, and I shall at one point discuss some of these, particularly a certain kind of experience of gratitude.

I shall take cosmological arguments for God's existence as those that attempt to argue for God's reality from the sheer existence of the natural universe, or from very pervasive features of the universe, such as the fact that the world is constantly changing, or is in motion.[1] Such arguments were first developed by philosophers in ancient Greece, and have been put forward by Jewish, Islamic, and Christian philosophers. Notable defenders of the argument in the West include Thomas Aquinas, Maimonides, Leibniz, and Samuel Clarke.[2] Contemporary philosopher Richard Swinburne has developed the argument as an inductive argument that attempts not to prove the existence of God, but to raise the probability that God exists.[3] (I shall argue that the form of the argument given by Swinburne fits nicely with the claim that the argument rests on a perceived natural sign.)

TYPES OF COSMOLOGICAL ARGUMENTS

There are a number of ways of classifying different varieties of cosmological arguments. I shall begin this chapter by a sketch of some of these possible ways. No more than a sketch can be provided, since a full treatment of the various types of cosmological arguments would itself require a book-length treatment. However, for my purposes, a brief sketch will be adequate, since my main purpose is not to defend any particular argument or even such arguments in general, but to isolate and show the plausibility of the sign that lies at the core of the

[1] Here I follow J. L. Mackie's definition, in *The Miracle of Theism: Arguments for and Against the Existence of God* (Oxford: Oxford University Press, 1982), 81.

[2] For a good historical overview of the argument, see William Lane Craig, *The Cosmological Argument from Plato to Leibniz* (Library of Philosophy and Religion; London: Macmillan, 1980).

[3] For Swinburne's version, see his *The Existence of God* (2nd edn.; Oxford: Oxford University Press, 2004), particularly pp. 133–52, though his earlier discussions of the nature of inductive arguments and the intrinsic probability of theism are crucial for understanding his argument.

arguments. Nevertheless, I need to say enough about the arguments in their various forms for the common core to come into view.

"Part" Arguments and "Whole" Arguments

I begin with a distinction between versions of the argument that start from particular parts of the natural universe, and versions that start from the universe as a whole. The first type I call a "part" argument, while the latter I term a "whole" argument.[4] The former can be seen in several of the celebrated "Five Ways" of Thomas Aquinas. In these arguments Aquinas does not begin with the existence of the universe as a whole, but with such claims as the following: "It is certain, and evident to our senses, that in the world some things are in motion" and "We find in nature things that are possible to be and not to be."[5] Aquinas thus begins with particular objects in the world, albeit very common ones, that possess certain pervasive characteristics.

These arguments from Aquinas all seem to have several main elements. The first is what we have just seen: the claim that particular things exist that have certain features. In the second element Aquinas goes on to argue that these objects with these particular features require a cause or explanation. This cause may be some other object, or the explanation may posit some other object, but, if that object also has this feature that demands an explanation, then it will, in turn, have to be explained by something else. So, for example, in the First Way, Aquinas argues that anything that is in motion must be moved by something else; in the Second Way he argues that anything that is caused to exist must be caused to exist by something else. The third element is a claim that an infinite regress of such causes or explanations is impossible, but such a regress can be avoided only if there is something, such as an "unmoved mover," a "first cause," or a "necessary being," that lacks the features in the original objects that demand explanation, and that therefore itself requires no explanation. The final element in each argument is a claim by Aquinas that this

---

[4] I introduced this terminology in my *Philosophy of Religion: Thinking about Faith* (Contours of Christian Philosophy; Downers Grove, IL: InterVarsity Press, 1982), 51.

[5] Thomas Aquinas, *Summa Theologica*, trans. Fathers of the English Dominican Province (New York: Benziger Bros., 1947–8; repr. Allen, TX: Thomas More, 1981), I, q. 2, a. 3.

ultimate cause or explanation can be identified with what people understand to be God.

We can see then that the starting point of Aquinas's arguments is nothing so vast or grand as "the cosmos" or "the universe" but merely particular objects within the universe. Other cosmological arguments take as their starting point the whole of the natural universe, extended both spatially and temporally. Leibniz, for example, gives an argument from the contingency of the physical world that goes roughly like this.[6] The principle of sufficient reason (henceforth PSR), which Leibniz states in a variety of forms, and regards as necessarily true and self-evident, claims that there must be a sufficient reason for the existence of anything that exists.[7] Everything in nature that we are aware of is contingent, meaning that it exists but might not have existed or might have existed in some other form. This means that there must be some reason why these contingent things exist in the form that they do, an explanation for their reality. Perhaps a reason for the existence of every particular finite thing can be found in other finite things that are the cause of that first finite thing. Those finite things that explain the existence of the first finite object may in turn have finite causes that provide a reason for their existence. However, Leibniz says that, since each finite thing in the natural world that exists is contingent, that world as a whole is contingent.[8] This would be true, according to Leibniz, even if the universe were infinitely old and thus consisted of an infinite series of finite events; the existence of the series as a whole would still be unexplained. This means that, according to the principle of sufficient reason, there must be some explanation for the existence of the natural world as a whole, and this explanation must posit the existence of something that is not part of the collection of contingent things that make up the natural world. If the cause of the finite things in the natural world is itself contingent,

---

6 For Leibniz's own words, see "On the Ultimate Origination of Things," in G. W. Leibniz, *The Philosophical Writings*, selected and trans. Mary Morris (Everyman's Library; Theology and Philosophy 905; London: Dent, 1934), 32–41.

7 For a list of some of the versions of the principle that Leibniz gives, see Craig, *The Cosmological Argument from Plato to Leibniz*, 259–60.

8 By "natural world" I mean to refer to the totality of the finite objects in space and time here. There is an established sense of "world" in which God is also a part of a "possible world," but here I use the term "world" in a more restricted sense.

something that needs a cause to explain it, then it will in reality be part of that contingent world. Only a being that is not contingent, a being that exists necessarily, which means that it has its reason for existence within its own nature, can be the basis for an explanation for such a contingent universe. Leibniz's argument is thus a "whole" argument that takes as its starting point the entire natural universe.

Part and whole arguments, since they employ different premises, are vulnerable in different ways. I shall explain this in more detail below, but a short preview of the possible objections to the forms helps make their differences clear. Many critics object to the "part" arguments by questioning why an infinite regress in a series of causes or explanations is impossible. Why, says the critic, could there not be an infinite series of causes or explanations? If there were such a series, nothing would be unexplained, since every finite object or event could be explained by some previous object or event in the series.[9]

"Whole" arguments, however, are often criticized on the grounds that it is illegitimate to attribute a characteristic, such as contingency, to the whole of the universe, even if that property legitimately can be predicated of each part of the universe. Once one has explained why every particular object has the feature that is the beginning point of the argument, there is no need to explain why the universe as a whole has such a feature, for the universe as a whole does not have the property except in the sense that each part of the universe has it. For example, such a critic may argue that, if a cause for each event of the universe has been provided, then this also provides an explanation of the whole series of events.[10]

Causal Arguments and Explanation Arguments

A second way that one might try to classify cosmological arguments is to distinguish between "first-cause" arguments, which attempt to

---

[9] For an example of such an objection, see Mackie, *The Miracle of Theism*, 90–1.

[10] Alexander R. Pruss calls this objection the "Hume–Edwards Principle" (for David Hume and Paul Edwards) and argues against it in *The Principle of Sufficient Reason: A Reassessment* (Cambridge Studies in Philosophy; New York: Cambridge University Press, 2006), 41–4. Pruss also argues against a slightly weaker form of this principle, which he calls the "HEC Principle" (for Hume–Edwards–Campbell). The HEC Principle maintains only that, once a cause for all finite events has been given, possibly the whole series has been explained. My thanks to Pruss for clarifying this.

argue for God as the originating cause of the universe or objects within the universe, and "explanation" arguments, which argue for God as providing an ultimate explanation for the existence of contingent objects or the universe as a whole. One can immediately see from this wording that this distinction cuts across the first distinction, and thus there can be "part" and "whole" forms of both "first-cause" and "explanation" arguments. On the surface there is a significant difference between arguments such as the first two of Aquinas's Five Ways, which start, respectively, from objects in motion and the existence of chains of efficient causes in the world, and Aquinas's own Third Way, which begins with the fact that there are objects in the world that have the characteristic that it is both possible for them to exist and not to exist, and argues for a necessary being as providing an explanation of their existence. Perhaps an even better example of an "explanation" argument is Leibniz's, summarized in the previous section, which begins with the contingency of things in the world, and the world as a whole, and argues for the existence of God as a necessary or non-contingent being that satisfies the demand that there be a "sufficient reason" for whatever exists.

Certainly, the argument forms are different; the first seems to rest on some kind of causal principle, such as "anything that comes into existence requires a cause of its existence," while the second seems to rest on some form of the "principle of sufficient reason," such as "there must be an explanation for the truth of any positive fact." However, there may be less of a difference here than there appears. The reason this is so is that, as Alexander Pruss has argued, the notion of causation "is tightly bound up with the notion of explanation."[11] We believe that events have causes precisely because we believe they have explanations, and to give the cause of an event is to give a type of explanation, the type we regard as appropriate for events in the natural world. Thus, the causal principles that lie behind the first type of argument appear to presuppose some form of the PSR; perhaps such causal principles are simply particular applications of a PSR. One can see this if one asks why some contingent object could not simply pop into existence without any cause; anyone who rejects such a possibility is likely to say that this is impossible because there would simply be no reason in that case why the contingent being should have come into existence at just the time and place it did, or, for that matter, why it came into existence at all.

Temporal and Non-Temporal Arguments

Yet another way of categorizing cosmological arguments is to note that some forms of the argument rest on the claim that the universe had a beginning, while other forms are compatible with the claim that the universe might be infinitely old. William Lane Craig is well known for his defense of a temporal version of the argument, which he terms the "Kalam" argument because of its use by Arabic philosophers.[12] This argument begins with the claim that the universe had a beginning, and argues that it must have some cause outside itself on the basis of the principle that whatever has a beginning must have a cause, and nothing can be the cause of its own beginning, for that would require it to exist before it existed.

Temporal and non-temporal arguments have different strengths and weaknesses. On the one hand, a temporal argument requires only a weak form of a causal principle or PSR; it is not necessary to claim that everything that exists has a cause, or even every contingent thing, much less that there is a reason for every true fact, but only that whatever has a beginning must have a cause. On the other hand, such an argument will require defense of the claim that the universe actually did have a beginning.

Craig himself defends the claim that the universe had a beginning in two ways. First, he argues that an actual infinite series, as opposed to a potential infinite series, is impossible, but an infinitely old universe would require the existence of such an actual infinite series.[13] Second, he argues that there are empirical grounds, such as contemporary cosmology's postulation of a "Big Bang," for belief that the universe had a beginning.[14] Note that non-temporal arguments, such as those given by Aquinas, have the disadvantage that they require a stronger

---

[12] William Craig, *The Kalam Cosmological Argument* (London: Macmillan, 1979; repr. Eugene, OR: Wipf and Stock, 2000).
[13] Craig, *The Kalam Cosmological Argument*, 69–110.
[14] Craig, *The Kalam Cosmological Argument*, 110–40.

form of a PSR or causal principle, but the advantage that they would not be refuted if science were to develop evidence that the universe is infinitely old, since they rest on the claim that the universe (or parts of it) require an explanation regardless of how old it is, even if it has always existed.

Deductive and Inductive Arguments

The last of the possible ways of categorizing cosmological arguments I shall consider is the distinction between deductive and inductive forms of the argument. Valid deductive forms of the argument, as the name implies, put the argument in a form in which the premises entail the conclusion. If those premises are true, then the conclusion (such as "A necessary being must exist" or "A First Cause of the universe must exist") must be true as well. If the premises of the argument are known to be true with certainty, such an argument would constitute a proof of the conclusion. However, it would be a mistake to equate the notion of a deductive argument for God's existence with the notion of a proof. An argument that does not qualify as a proof might still have great epistemic value.

Suppose, for example, that one is considering a temporal argument that holds that God must exist as the cause of the universe. Such an argument might fail as a proof, because one or more of the premises, such as the claim that the universe had a beginning, might not be known with certainty. However, the premise in question might still be one that is more reasonable than its denial, and in that case the argument might show, if all else about the argument is in order, that belief that God exists is more reasonable than its denial. In that way an argument that is deductive in form but falls short of a proof might still lead to an important result: it might show that belief that God exists is justified, or plausible, or more reasonable than its denial.

Richard Swinburne develops an inductive form of the cosmological argument, using the term "inductive" in a broad sense, in which it applies to any argument in which some data are explained by some hypothesis in such a way that the probability of that hypothesis is raised.[15] On Swinburne's view, the evidence

---

15 See Swinburne, *The Existence of God*, 133–52.

in such a case will be something that confirms the hypothesis in the sense of raising the probability that the hypothesis is true. A case where the evidence raises the probability of the hypothesis to the point where it is more likely to be true than not is one Swinburne describes as a case of a "P-inductive argument," while a case where the evidence merely increases the probability of the truth of the hypothesis without necessarily making it more probable than not Swinburne describes as a "C-inductive argument."[16] In many cases, of course, whether evidence makes some hypothesis more probable than not depends, not merely on the strength of the evidence, but on the "prior probability" of the hypothesis, which in turn is shaped both by the intrinsic probability of the hypothesis as well as by our background knowledge.[17] These factors determine how probable the hypothesis is independently of the evidence.

With respect to the cosmological argument, Swinburne rejects a deductive argument, because "it seems coherent to suppose that there exists a complex physical universe but no God," and this seems to imply that there can be no valid deduction from the existence of such a universe to the existence of God.[18] Swinburne admits the logical possibility that the universe simply exists without a cause as a "brute fact." The existence of such a universe as ours, however, with its vast complexity, is, as Swinburne sees things, very improbable or unlikely as a brute, uncaused, and unexplained fact. The existence of God, on the other hand, seems intrinsically less unlikely or improbable, since "the supposition that there is a God is an extremely simple supposition."[19] If God exists, however, God would have very strong reasons to create a universe, especially one with free creatures capable of achieving moral goodness. Put simply, "It is very unlikely that a universe would exist uncaused, but rather more likely that God would exist uncaused."[20] Hence, a universe such as ours seems more likely to exist if there is a God to explain its existence.

[16] Swinburne, *The Existence of God*, 5–7.
[17] See Swinburne's discussion of these notions in *The Existence of God*, 52–72.
[18] Swinburne, *The Existence of God*, 148.
[19] Swinburne, *The Existence of God*, 150.
[20] Swinburne, *The Existence of God*, 152.

WHY THE ARGUMENTS ARE INCONCLUSIVE

Even this brief sketch of the various types of cosmological arguments can help us understand why the arguments are not universally compelling. Because the arguments are different, they are vulnerable in different places and in different ways, but each seems to include some element that some reasonable persons might reject. I do not wish to claim that all the arguments lack force or weight. It is possible, for example, that such arguments may be rationally convincing for some individuals, or at least show that belief in God is more reasonable than its competitors. However, the arguments fail as conclusive proofs; all have premises that seem less than absolutely certain.

Consider, for example, "part" arguments. The first premises of such arguments seem entirely above reproach. To use Aquinas's arguments as examples, it seems impossible to deny that there are some things that are in motion, or that there are series of efficient causes in the world, or objects that are contingent in the sense that it is possible for them both to exist but also not to exist.

However, in this case doubts about some other premise in the argument seem possible. For example, the claim that the feature identified in the first premise demands some kind of explanation may be doubted. Aquinas says that things that are in motion (or, in some translations, "things that are changing") require something outside themselves to be the cause of the motion. However, it has seemed possible to some philosophers that the fact that certain objects are in motion (or change in some other specified way) might just be a brute fact about objects of that type.[21] No explanation requiring some other cause is required.

If one admits that an explanation or cause of the initial feature is necessary, pressure may be put on the third element in the argument, the denial of the possibility of an infinite series of causes. Suppose that it is true that objects that are changing require a cause outside

---

[21] See, e.g., William L. Rowe, *The Cosmological Argument* (Princeton: Princeton University Press, 1975), 16–17, where Rowe says that Aquinas apparently does not consider the possibility that it may simply be a brute fact that certain things change in the way that they do.

themselves. It has seemed to many philosophers that the causes of every finite object or state of affairs might simply be another finite object or state of affairs. Each finite cause in turn may have some other finite cause. So long as the series of causes is infinite, there will be no element in the series that will lack a cause.

Defenders of the argument sometimes respond by claiming that, even if an infinite series of causes is sometimes possible, it is not possible in a case where the causes are operating simultaneously. On this (quite plausible) interpretation of Aquinas, when he says that there must be a "first cause," he is not using "first" in a temporal sense. Since Aquinas affirms the possibility that the world might be infinitely old, he is thinking of a chain of efficient causes not as a temporal series in which earlier events or objects bring about later events or objects, but as a series where all the causes are operating simultaneously, such as the example of a hand moving a stick that in turn is moving a stone. In this kind of causal series, it does seem plausible to say that, without the "first" cause of the series, the last element in the series would be unexplained.[22]

However, in this case the critic of the argument can again change focus. The worry in this case will be about how we can know that the features identified in the first premise do in fact require a cause or explanation *in this special sense* in which the explanation is a series of causes, all of which are acting simultaneously with what is being caused or explained. The critic may admit that particular objects in the world all have some causal explanation in terms of other particular objects. Thus, a person may be said to exist partly because of the parents who conceived that person. The defender of the argument may respond by insisting on something like the following: that every object whose existence is distinct from its essence requires a special kind of cause or explanation, a cause not of the objects' beginning, but of its continued existence. However, in this case the critic may simply wonder whether this is true and how we know it to be true.[23]

---

[22] There is a clear discussion of this kind of causal chain in William Rowe's interpretation of Aquinas's cosmological arguments in Rowe, *The Cosmological Argument*, 22–36.

[23] Something like this exchange seems to be present in the well-known BBC radio debate between Father Copleston and Bertrand Russell in 1948. Russell seems willing to concede that ordinary finite objects have causes, but does not admit Copleston's

A different set of concerns emerges if one turns from "part" arguments to "whole" arguments. One way to respond to objections to a "part" argument is to convert it to a "whole" argument. For example, suppose that one is uncertain about whether the "no-infinite-regress" premise is true, and wonders whether or not there might be an infinite series of finite causes that would leave no particular event or object unexplained. At this point the defender of the argument may claim, following Leibniz, that there is still something unexplained—namely, the existence of the whole infinite series. Every individual element in the series that constitutes the natural universe may be explained, but what is not explained is why there should be any such universe at all.

Such an argument has certainly seemed plausible to many, and will seem compelling to those who find the principle of sufficient reason in a suitably strong form to be true. However, many philosophers resist the claim that the existence of the universe as a whole cannot be a brute, unexplained fact. They may concede that for scientific and practical purposes we assume that there are explanations of the particular facts we encounter, while doubting that there is any explanation for the existence of the whole. In effect, such critics doubt whether the PSR is true in the strong form required by a "whole" argument.

Temporal arguments such as the one advanced by William Craig are a natural counter to such an objection, for such arguments require only a weaker form of the PSR. The defender of a temporal cosmological argument does not have to claim that there is an explanation for every positive fact, but only that there must be a cause that explains the existence of everything that has a beginning. The claim that everything that has a beginning has a cause ("nothing comes from nothing, nothing ever could," sings Julie Andrews in *The Sound of Music*) seems highly plausible to many, though even this principle has been doubted by philosophers such as Hume. However, if the critic concedes this point, the doubt may shift again to a

contention that everything whose existence is distinct from its essence requires a cause of its continuing existence that operates simultaneously with that existence. See Bertrand Russell, *Bertrand Russell on God and Religion*, ed. Al Seckel (Buffalo, NY: Prometheus Books, 1986), 123–46.

different point: whether we know with certainty that the universe had a beginning. The a priori arguments Craig presents for this claim are subtle and tricky, dependent on the concept of infinity, a concept that often produces uncertainty and puzzlement when used in logical arguments. The empirical arguments for the universe's having had a beginning may seem strong; however, like all empirical arguments, it seems that new scientific discoveries might shift the probabilities, in favor of an oscillating universe that is infinitely old.

Swinburne's argument is, of course, different in kind from all of the above, in that Swinburne does not even claim that the cosmological argument by itself is conclusive. He affirms only that the argument raises the probability that God exists, without specifying exactly how much it raises that probability, and with no claim that the argument by itself even makes God's existence more probable than not. If we think of the argument as resting on a natural sign, taking into account both the Wide Accessibility Principle and the Easy Resistibility Principle, then something like Swinburne's conclusion is exactly what we would expect. The sign that lies at the base of the argument, since it points to God's reality, would make it appear more likely, at least to many people, that God exists. However, given the fact that the sign is resistible, one would not expect that even the probability that God exists could be definitely fixed as high.

One difficulty with Swinburne's argument is justifying the "intrinsic probability" he assigns to the existence of God and the existence of the universe as a brute fact. Swinburne argues that the existence of the world as such a brute fact, while logically possible, is highly unlikely, while the existence of God, though perhaps also unlikely, is much less unlikely. After considering what we would expect God to do if God exists, he then argues that the creation of a universe like ours is likely if there is a God. The sheer existence of a complex universe is evidence that confirms God's existence.

Critics of course raise a number of difficulties with this series of claims. First, can we reliably estimate how probable or improbable the existence of a universe such as ours as a brute fact is, as well as how probable or improbable the existence of God is? Swinburne claims that the intrinsic probability of the universe as a brute fact is very low because of its complexity, with the probability of God's existence as the ultimate fact being higher, since the hypothesis that there is a God is a very simple hypothesis. He claims this is reasonable because it parallels the practice we follow in science, where simplicity is an important factor when rival theories are weighed. But, even if Swinburne is right in his claim that theism is a simpler hypothesis, can we trust our intuition that what is simpler is more likely to be true with respect to such a question, which is, after all, a question in metaphysics and not science? In the end it seems that Swinburne relies on what seems intuitively correct to him: the existence of the universe seems less puzzling if there is a God than if there is no God. I believe that the source of this intuition is Swinburne's experience of the world as mysterious and puzzling: a natural sign that points beyond itself.

COSMIC WONDER

I want to suggest that what lies at the bottom of all or at least most of the forms of the cosmological argument is a certain experience of the world or objects in the world, in which they are perceived as mysterious or puzzling, crying out for some explanation. I shall call this experience that of "cosmic wonder."[24] Even Swinburne's probabilistic argument, with its rigorous appeal to confirmation theory, rests in the end on such an experience: "A complex physical universe (existing over endless time or beginning to exist at some finite time) is indeed a rather complex thing. We need to look at our universe and meditate about it, and the complexity should be apparent."[25] Swinburne thinks that after this "meditating" it will be evident that "there is a complexity, particularity, and finitude about the universe that cries out for explanation."[26]

One might think that Swinburne is here providing a kind of implicit argument for the claim that the universe "cries out for an

---

[24] I first used this term in *Why Believe? Reason and Mystery as Pointers to God* (Grand Rapids, MI: Eerdmans, 1996), 32. This book is a revised edition of *The Quest for Faith: Reason and Mystery as Pointers to God* (Downers Grove, IL: InterVarsity Press, 1986). The term may actually refer to more than one type of experience. For example, my experience of my own contingency seems somewhat different from my wonder about the existence of the whole of the universe. However, for my purposes these experiences have enough in common to justify the common label.

[25] Swinburne, *The Existence of God*, 150.

[26] Swinburne, *The Existence of God*, 150.

explanation," an argument that goes something like this: "Things that are very complex require explanation. The universe is very complex. Therefore the universe requires an explanation." Perhaps this is what Swinburne intends, but the passage could be read in a different way. Perhaps the recognition that the universe is puzzling or mysterious is something that humans can immediately perceive, and the claim that it is such factors as complexity and particularity that are the basis of this puzzling, mysterious character is more the result of reflection that tries to explain or understand the perception than the premise of an argument. In support of this other interpretation is the fact that many ordinary people, who might be unable to cite the factors Swinburne cites, nonetheless agree with him that the sheer existence of a universe such as ours is surprising. We simply perceive the universe as surprising; on reflection we might cite various characteristics of that universe as the ground of the perception, but the perception itself is immediate and primary.

If something like this is right, then we can understand many of the forms of the cosmological argument as reflective attempts to pick out those characteristics of the universe that "cry out" for explanation. For Aquinas, one such characteristic is that objects in the universe are changing or "in motion" (the First Way), and another is that the objects in the universe are contingent ("things that can exist but also not exist," found in the Third Way). One might think that temporal versions of the cosmological argument would have a different ground, since the fact that the universe had a beginning (if it did) is not something that could be immediately perceived. That is certainly plausible, and there is no doubt that formulations such as Craig's, which rely on contemporary cosmology to ground the initial premise that the universe had a beginning, are different from other forms of the cosmological argument. However, it is worth noting how many ancient cultures have "origin myths" that tell a story about the beginning of the universe, which might suggest that there is something about the character of the universe itself that suggests that it had a beginning. At the very least it seems natural to see the universe in this way, and that may mean that at least the germ of the idea that lies behind temporal versions of the argument also rests on an experience of cosmic wonder. The fact that the universe seems puzzling or mysterious itself suggests it must have an explanation, which in turn leads to perceiving it as the kind of thing that must have had a beginning, inspiring various accounts of its origin.

Experiences of cosmic wonder are not, of course, common in the sense that they occur to everyone every day. However, they are common in the sense that almost everyone seems to have such experiences at times. It may begin with a disquieting thought like "Suppose I had never been born; suppose I had never existed." Zen masters sometimes unsettle their disciples by asking, "Where were you before your father was born?" One might say that this is a perception of oneself as possessing the property of "might-never-have-been-ness," or, in more standard philosophical language, contingency. In one sense everyone knows that he or she might never have existed, but nevertheless at certain times such a thought may strike a person with almost dizzying force. And the possibility is naturally extended to other things. Not only is it the case that I might never have existed; my parents and friends might never have existed. I may naturally think, "Suppose there had been no humans at all, or no living things of any kind." In the end it may strike one as odd that there should be a universe at all, a world with objects, all of which possess the property of "might-never-have-been-ness." At such times a person may experience something like intellectual vertigo; the ordinary familiar world seems almost to crumble away. It appears as something fragile, something remarkable.

The perception of the world as contingent, as something that might never have been, is closely linked to the contrasting notion of something that lacks this character, something whose existence is in some way impervious to non-existence. Descartes argued that our recognition of objects in the world as finite shows that we have at least an implicit conception of the infinite.[27] For how could we recognize something as finite if we had no idea of what it would mean for something to be infinite? In a similar way, the recognition of things in the universe as contingent shows we at least have a grasp of the idea that there might be something that lacks this characteristic, something that exists in some deeper, more secure manner. Whatever else may be said about God or the gods, such beings are always perceived in

---

[27] René Descartes, *The Philosophical Works of Descartes*, trans. Elizabeth S. Haldane and G. R. T. Ross (2 vols.; Cambridge: Cambridge University Press, 1967), ii. 165–6.

just this way. They are "immortals," different from us mortals. To put this in philosophical language, God is a necessary being, unlike the contingent beings we observe all the time.

There are a number of different ways philosophers have conceived of the idea of a necessary being. At one extreme some have said that God's existence is logically necessary, a claim that underlies the ontological argument. Others have held that God exists necessarily in some weaker sense, ranging from the claim that God's existence is "metaphysically necessary," to the claim that God's existence is factually necessary, meaning that nothing can in fact threaten his existence. It is not important at this point to decide which of these senses is best, or even carefully to distinguish between them. My point is simply that implicit in our experience of cosmic wonder, in which we perceive the world as contingent, is a grasp of the idea that there could be a different manner of existing, a reality that has a deeper and firmer grip on existence than the things we see around us.

A natural sign must do things: it must lead to the conception of the thing for which it is a sign and it must naturally lead to belief in the reality of that thing. The experience of cosmic wonder, in which we experience the universe as contingent, does both of these things. It puts the idea of a "necessary being" in our minds. However, it also suggests to us, perhaps somewhat vaguely and tentatively, that the universe must somehow rest on this different kind of reality.

If it is true that God created the universe, then it is literally true that the universe "might never have been," for the classical theistic claim is that God's creation was a free act on his part. The world is created out of nothing; nothing in God necessitated such an action. The suggestion I wish to make is that the experience of cosmic wonder, when we encounter objects in the universe or the universe as a whole and see this natural order as "contingent," might simply be a perception of the createdness of the natural world. Cosmic wonder would then be a natural sign that points to God, a "calling card," so to speak, that reflects God's own creative work. It would not only be the case that the sign naturally tends to produce belief in God; it would do this because God created a contingent universe and gave humans a natural sense of wonder when they encounter that universe. We do find it natural to see the universe as something whose existence is surprising, something that "cries out" for explanation and naturally suggests to us that behind the universe lies something—or someone—that exists in a deeper and less surprising way.

As a natural sign that points to God, cosmic wonder may seem both vague and not very powerful. We may not have a clear idea of the "something or someone" pointed to as having a more secure form of being than the universe itself does, and the sign may be one that is easily resisted. Skeptics may think we are making too much of a strange and infrequent experience. To be sure, when immersed in the daily grind—commuting to work, dropping off the kids at the daycare center, answering the email, earning the paycheck—we may find such a sign has little hold on us. Nevertheless, we must also consider the possibility that the concerns of "real life" may be ones that immerse us in the relative and the superficial, concerns that lessen our ability to perceive what is really deep and profound about our lives and our world. Compared with the other natural signs that will be discussed in Chapters 4 and 5, cosmic wonder is both vaguer and less powerful in its action. Nevertheless, it has genuine force.

In any case, it would seem unphilosophical to dismiss our experience of cosmic wonder as meaningless. Aristotle says that philosophy itself begins with wonder. Why should we not pay attention to the fact that we wonder about the sheer existence of the universe? Why should we not wonder about our own sense of wonder?

NATURAL SIGNS AND ARGUMENTS

If I am right in claiming that the experience of cosmic wonder is a natural sign, and also that it lies at the core of various forms of the cosmological argument, then this explains why the arguments continue to have appeal, despite the difficulties discussed in this chapter. Given the nature of a theistic natural sign, it is only to be expected that any attempt to convert the argument into a conclusive proof will fail. Given the constraint of the Easy Resistibility Principle on signs, it will always be possible for a critic to find some possible way that the argument might fail. It is the very nature of a sign that it points without necessitating. Furthermore, as we have noted, theistic natural signs are not irresistible, but subject to modification and even suppression in light of other experiences and other beliefs.

A critic may even find fault with a probabilistic argument such as Swinburne's, claiming, for example, that we cannot reliably estimate the relative antecedent or intrinsic probability of the existence of God and the universe as ultimate, brute facts.

The point is not that it is in principle a mistake to develop a natural sign into an argument, or even that such arguments are necessarily weak, as philosophical arguments go. Philosophical arguments for any significant claim are rarely conclusive. Given certain plausible assumptions, the various forms of the cosmological argument appear strong. If someone accepts a reasonably strong form of the principle of sufficient reason, such as that there must be an explanation for every contingent fact, then the Leibniz-type arguments, in their "whole" and non-temporal "explanation" versions, are very appealing.[28] If one accepts the claim that the physical universe had a beginning, and there are good empirical reasons for thinking this is so, then temporal arguments such as Craig's are similarly appealing. If Swinburne's claims about the intrinsic improbability of a brute, unexplained physical universe are plausible, then his claim that the cosmological argument at least provides confirming evidence for God's existence appears strong.

So the claim that the arguments are not conclusive or coercive does not imply that the arguments are weak. I wish to make two claims about such arguments. First, I want to maintain that whatever force the arguments have is significantly dependent on cosmic wonder, the natural sign that lies at the core of the argument. Second, I want to claim that the sign can function as a sign even for someone who does not develop the sign into an argument. For the person who has the inclination and ability to read the sign, cosmic wonder can point directly to God.

SHOULD WE WONDER ABOUT GOD'S EXISTENCE?

It is now time to pose and respond to an objection to the claim that cosmic wonder is a natural sign that points to God's reality. One

[28] Alexander Pruss gives a powerful, extended argument for the truth of the principle of sufficient reason in just this form in *The Principle of Sufficient Reason*.

might think that what I have been calling cosmic wonder is captured in the question, "Why is there something and not nothing?" Many philosophers have agreed that in some sense this question is the most profound and fundamental question that can be asked, and one might think that cosmic wonder is what inspires this question. In other words, cosmic wonder is at bottom sheer wonder that anything should exist at all. However, if this is right, then one might think that God's existence has no power to resolve this mystery. After all, God himself, on the kind of view I am considering, is a being. God's existence, rather than explaining why anything should exist at all, would appear to be one more thing to be explained. The critic of my view here maintains that cosmic wonder is grounded not in a perception of a characteristic possessed by objects in the natural world, but rather in the sheer fact that anything, including God, should exist at all.

The key to a response to this objection is to understand why God must be defined as or understood to be a necessary being. If God is a necessary being, then his existence is not surprising or mysterious in the same way that the existence of finite, natural objects is surprising or mysterious. This idea is implicit in many forms of the cosmological argument, where the conclusion of the argument is that there must be a being whose existence is necessary (in some sense of "necessary"), and it is simply stipulated that "God" is being used as a term to refer to such a being. As many critics have pointed out, such an argument does not by itself show that the "necessary being" thus inferred has all or even many of the characteristics of God, as God is understood by major religions. Further argument is needed to show that God, in the sense of a necessary being, is a personal being who has such properties as omnipotence and omniscience.

This limitation on cosmological arguments seems right, and by itself is not necessarily problematic. Many proponents of cosmological arguments, such as Aquinas, recognize the need for further arguments to settle questions about the nature of God's other properties. However, the point is that, if God is defined as a being that exists necessarily (whatever other properties such a being may have), then in an important sense his reality will be less surprising, less in need of explanation, than is the case for finite natural objects. If someone asks why God exists, the answer will be that God necessarily exists. As

Aquinas puts it, God's nature is such that he must exist.[29] His essence entails his existence. This simply does not seem to be true for any other being that we encounter, since an understanding of the nature of a thing, whether that thing be a person, an island, or whatever, seems entirely independent of the question as to whether something with that nature actually exists.

One might think that such a view would imply that the ontological argument must be sound. If God's essence includes his existence, we should be able to reason from the concept of God to the reality of God. Perhaps something like this thought underlies Kant's well-known attempt to argue that the cosmological argument really rests on the ontological argument. However, Aquinas helps us to see that this is not the case. If we look at what Aquinas says about the ontological argument, we find an interesting and complex view.[30] In discussing the question as to whether God's existence is "self-evident," Aquinas makes a distinction between truths that are "self-evident in themselves" and those that are "self-evident to us." God's existence, he claims, is one of those that is self-evident in itself, because "God is his own existence, as will hereafter be shown." However, God's existence is not self-evident to us, because "we do not know the essence of God."

The terminology Aquinas uses here is not the best from a contemporary point of view, since it is hard to see what it means to say that a proposition is self-evident but not self-evident to us. I suggest, however, that what Aquinas means is that God's existence is necessary; his nature or essence does indeed entail that he exists. However, since we do not know that essence, this is not a truth that is directly evident to us. One might say that, if we were God, and understood God's essence as God himself does, we would see that God necessarily exists. Since we are not God and do not have a direct grasp of God's essence, this is not something we can know simply by reflection on God's nature or essence. If we can come to know it at all, we must come to know it by some other means. For Aquinas this means we must start with the created objects we are directly aware of; any knowledge we have about God is grounded in the knowledge we have of finite things.

---

[29] Aquinas, *Summa Theologica*, I, q. 2, a. 3.
[30] Aquinas, *Summa Theologica*, I, q. 2, a. 1.

I believe that Aquinas is right here; we human beings do not have a clear grasp of God's essence or nature. This is hardly surprising, given that God is infinite and we are finite. The claim that we do not know God's essence does not imply that we have no direct experience of God. Even if such experiences are possible, it does not follow that the person having the experience would gain an understanding of God's essence, since it is quite possible to experience an object without having an understanding of the essence of that object.

If we have no experience of God that provides us with an understanding of God's nature as a necessary being, it follows that we are only acquainted with the natures of realities that are contingent. All of our experience of beings is an experience of beings that are contingent, for, even if we do experience God, who is in reality a necessary being, we do not experience his nature as a necessary being. This means that when a person asks "Why is there something and not nothing?" the "somethings" that give rise to the question are all contingent somethings.

If we were God or if we understood God's nature, we would see that the existence of God himself is not surprising. God exists necessarily. However, we have no such grasp of God's nature. All the beings whose nature we can understand are beings that exist contingently, that have "might-never-have-been-ness" and elicit from us cosmic wonder. It is thus natural for us to ask "Why is there something and not nothing?" The origin of the question lies in our experience of the contingency of the finite objects of whose nature we have some awareness. We may find the existence of God mysterious or puzzling also, but that does not show that it is. For we do not have any grasp of God's nature, no understanding of what it would be like to be God. And it follows from this that we do not know that God's existence is, like the existence of everything we see in nature, something that demands an explanation beyond itself.

What I am suggesting is that the experience of cosmic wonder is derived from our experience of created objects. We wonder about the existence of the things we see around us, because all of those things are experienced as contingent. Since contingent things are the only things whose natures we grasp, it is natural for us to express that wonder by asking why "anything" should exist at all. I suggest that we cannot infer from this that God's existence is mysterious or surprising in the same way, for the truth is that we have no direct understanding of God's nature.

Can we know something about God's nature indirectly? On my account, the experience of cosmic wonder is one in which we grasp the contingency of the objects around us, gain a sense of them as things that exist in a fragile way. But such an experience can also suggest to us a kind of reality that exists in a deeper and stronger way; such a concept is implicit in the awareness of contingent objects as things that lack this deeper, stronger mode of being. I conclude that the experience of cosmic wonder is not a generic wonder about any kind of being, but a wonder inspired by the particular kind of being we encounter in the natural order. I shall therefore interpret the questions, "Why is there something and not nothing?" and "Why is there anything at all?" as expressions of cosmic wonder.

COSMIC WONDER IN OPERATION

I shall conclude this chapter with a look at some of the ways cosmic wonder manifests itself. If it is a natural sign for God, then we should be able to find clear instances of it in operation. To begin, we should notice the fact that the cosmological argument itself continues to be persuasive for many. If I am right in claiming that the experience of cosmic wonder is what primarily motivates such arguments, this is itself evidence that our experience of the natural universe as contingent is one that points people in the direction of God.

An interesting example of an individual who finds the cosmological argument convincing is Paul Williams, a professor specializing in Buddhist philosophy who converted to Catholicism after twenty years as a practicing Buddhist. Williams claims that Buddhism, which does not posit a God of the sort Christians believe in, has "an explanatory gap."[31] The gap is found when we ask questions such as the following: "Why is there something rather than nothing? Why is there anything at all? And why is there a world in which, among other things, the processes (causation, etc.) detected by the Buddha are the

---

[31] Paul Williams, *The Unexpected Way: On Converting from Buddhism to Catholicism* (London: T. & T. Clark, 2002), 19.

case? Why is it that this way of things *is* the way of things? . . . Why are things just like that, and not otherwise?"[32]

Williams goes on to develop a form of the cosmological argument in which he claims that the only possible answer to such questions is the existence of a necessary being.[33] However, it is clear that it is his experience of cosmic wonder that motivates the argument: "For me the question 'Why is there something rather than nothing?' has become a bit like what Zen Buddhists call a *kōan*. It is a constant niggling question that has worried and goaded me (often, I think, against my will) into a different level of understanding, a different vision, of the world and our place in it."[34] Williams, being a philosopher and an adult convert from another religion, has a particularly clear and powerful sense of the power of cosmic wonder. However, we may take him as representing many people who may have not the ability to articulate their views in clear philosophical terms, but share a sense that the physical universe, including ourselves, is dependent upon something that lacks the contingency that characterizes everything in the world. Such a sense of dependency is clearly closely linked to the religious impulse. No less a theologian than Friedrich Schleiermacher argues that a sense of "absolute dependency" lies at the very heart of religious belief.[35]

However, as one would expect in a natural sign for God, the power of the experience is by no means one that is accessible only to orthodox theists, or those who accept some form of the cosmological argument. William James, for example, though he seems favorably disposed towards some vaguely religious belief that there is something "more" than the natural world, something disclosed in religious experiences, is far from an orthodox theist and certainly does not regard the cosmological argument as decisive. Nevertheless, James feels the force of the experience of cosmic wonder:

One need only shut oneself in a closet and begin to think of the fact of one's being there, of one's queer bodily shape in the darkness (a thing to make children scream at, as Stevenson says), of one's fantastic character and all,

[32] Williams, *The Unexpected Way*, 27–8.
[33] Williams, *The Unexpected Way*, 30.   [34] Williams, *The Unexpected Way*, 30.
[35] Friedrich Schleiermacher, *The Christian Faith*, trans. H. R. Mackintosh and J. S. Stewart (Edinburgh: T. & T. Clark, 1928), 16.

to have the wonder steal over the detail as much as over the general fact of being, and to see that it is only familiarity that blunts it. Not only that *anything* should be, but that *this* very thing should be, is mysterious.[36]

James pointedly says that some philosophies attempt to "banish" this question or paper over the mystery, but he insists that we must feel the force of the mystery.[37] The experience is not one that pushes James into full-fledged belief in God, but it does successfully unsettle any dogmatic confidence that the natural world is the whole of reality.

The final examples I shall give of those who exhibit an awareness of cosmic wonder are clearly non-believers. One might question whether a natural sign for God's reality can be seen at work in a person who does not believe in God. However, it must be remembered that theistic natural signs are resistible and defeasible. We saw that this is true even for Reidian natural signs, but it holds even more strongly in the case of theistic natural signs. Hence it is possible for an individual to recognize the sign and even to feel its force without forming any belief in God. Suppose, for example, that a person believes that there are powerful reasons to deny the existence of God. Of course, the possible reasons for believing that God does not exist are legion. The person might think that the existence of evil provides one with very powerful evidence that God does not exist.[38] Or, someone might simply believe that the idea of a God who is responsible for the existence of the universe is impossible, on the grounds that an immaterial being cannot causally interact with a physical creation.[39] Such individuals might well feel the force of a sign pointing to God while failing to believe in God.

Consider the case of J. J. C. Smart. In *Our Place in the Universe* Smart considers and rejects the cosmological argument in various versions, chiefly because he sees that the conclusion of the argument must be

---

[36] William James, *Some Problems of Philosophy: A Beginning of an Introduction to Philosophy* (New York: Longmans, Green, and Co., 1916), 39–40.

[37] James, *Some Problems of Philosophy*, 40.

[38] This may well be the situation of William Rowe, who gives a sympathetic treatment of the cosmological argument in *The Cosmological Argument*, but also a powerful argument from evil against the existence of God.

[39] This seems to be the view defended by Bede Rundle in *Why There is Something Rather than Nothing* (Oxford: Oxford University Press, 2004), in which he admits the profundity of the question as to why there is something but denies that God can be an answer to the question.

the existence of a "necessary being," a concept that he avers that "he can make no sense of."[40] Despite his rejection of the argument, however, Smart cannot quite let go of the experience that drives such arguments, and wonders if there is room in his naturalistic world view for "genuine mysticism." Such mysticism is one that Smart says he "feels" with "the question 'Why is there anything at all?' even though it seems impossible that the question should ever have an answer."[41] Given Smart's own claim that the concept of a "necessary being" makes no sense, it is clear why he thinks the question cannot have an answer. Nevertheless, he finds himself still uneasy, wondering whether the feeling is one that he ought to "cherish" or one "to be explained psychologically."[42]

Smart is a distinguished philosopher in what is usually termed the "analytic tradition." However, some of the most profound descriptions of cosmic mystery have come from those European philosophers termed "existentialists," Albert Camus pre-eminent among them. Camus, like Smart, is unable to believe in God or any final explanation for the existence of the world. He belongs to a group of European intellectuals whose background beliefs make it impossible or at least very difficult to form a belief in God. Nevertheless, he offers eloquent testimony that the world as we encounter it is a world that in some way demands an explanation; our failure to find any such explanation constitutes what he calls "the Absurd." In some way we sense that the world should make sense, that there should be a reason why things are the way they are, even a reason that gives us a sense of meaning and an understanding of our place in the universe, to use Smart's phrase. However, Camus, like Smart, cannot believe in God, and thus finds no answer to his questions: "This world in itself is not reasonable, that is all that can be said. But what is absurd is the confrontation of this irrational [world] and the wild longing for clarity whose call echoes in the human heart."[43]

[40] J. J. C. Smart, *Our Place in the Universe: A Metaphysical Discussion* (Oxford: Blackwell, 1989), 182.

[41] Smart, *Our Place in the Universe*, 183.

[42] Smart, *Our Place in the Universe*, 183.

[43] Albert Camus, *The Myth of Sisyphus and Other Essays*, trans. Justin O'Brien (New York: Vintage, 1955), 16.

For Camus, the world cries out for an explanation; we experience a "wild longing for clarity," and it is clear that scientific explanations do not provide the kind of explanation he is seeking: "I realize that if through science I can seize phenomena and enumerate them, I cannot, for all that, apprehend the world."[44] Camus experiences the world as one that posits a fundamental mystery, that poses a question it cannot itself answer. Like many European intellectuals, Camus does not regard belief in God as a "live option," and so he resolves courageously and honestly to face "the Absurd." The attempt to resolve the mystery and find an answer, which he sees in various ways in figures as diverse as Husserl and Kierkegaard, is rejected.[45] Nevertheless, the power of cosmic wonder is evident for Camus. *If* Camus had not seen belief in God as intellectually impossible, and thus dishonest, it is easy to see how such an experience could have pushed him toward religious faith. Thus, the power of cosmic wonder can be seen even in the life of a non-believer.

[44] Camus, *The Myth of Sisyphus*, 15.

[45] In Camus's view, these philosophers have allowed the human need to find an explanation to motivate them to take "the leap," a choice to believe in some final account. See *The Myth of Sisyphus*, 24–31.

4

Beneficial Order and Teleological Arguments for God

The experience of cosmic wonder discussed in the previous chapter suggests that the natural world depends on some kind of superior being, a reality that exists in some deeper and more secure way than the contingent beings of the natural world do. However, as I noted at the end of the chapter, the concept of a "necessary being" that the sign gives rise to is somewhat vague, and by itself leaves out a good deal of the concept of God that is found in a living religion.

This does not mean that the experience of cosmic wonder is not a genuine natural sign that points us to God. For, as I noted in Chapter 2, the function of a theistic natural sign is to point us to the reality of God. While this undoubtedly includes a disposition to form some beliefs about God, it is compatible with a great deal of incompleteness, variation, and even outright falsehood in those beliefs. If God is in fact a reality who exists necessarily and on whom the natural world depends, then someone who forms a belief about God on that basis of cosmic wonder, developing a conviction that there is some "necessary being" that underlies the natural world, has formed a belief about the real being (God) of whom the person is in some way aware. The person is aware of God as a real being, however ignorant the person may be about God's true nature. This is so, even if the person has many false beliefs about the being whose reality he has come to know.

What we might call the information content of the sign of cosmic wonder is, therefore, somewhat low, corresponding to the fact that the cosmological arguments that are developed from this sign similarly reach a somewhat meager conclusion, taken by themselves. In this chapter I shall discuss the natural sign that lies at the heart of a different type of argument for God, those arguments usually termed "teleological arguments" or "arguments from design." The information content delivered by this sign is greater than that provided by cosmic wonder, though also subject to limitations. The sign points to God as the designer responsible for the order found in the natural world, and the notion of design suggests a more personal conception of God. The sign points to God as an intelligent being with goals, a being who cares about some ends and has the knowledge and power to implement those ends. As in the previous chapter, before focusing on the sign, I shall first reflect on the arguments developed from the sign.

THE TELEOLOGICAL ARGUMENT OF AQUINAS

Thomas Aquinas provides a classical statement of a teleological argument in his Fifth Way:

The fifth way is taken from the governance of the world. We see things which lack knowledge, such as natural bodies, act for an end, and this is evident from their acting always, or nearly always, in the same way, so as to obtain the best result. Hence it is plain that they achieve their end, not fortuitously, but designedly. Now whatever lacks knowledge cannot move towards an end, unless it be directed by some being endowed with knowledge and intelligence; as the arrow is directed by the archer. Therefore some intelligent being exists by whom all natural things are directed to their end; and this being we call God.[1]

Several things about this argument are noteworthy. First, it is, to use the terminology of the last chapter, a "part" argument rather than a "whole" argument. That is, Aquinas does not begin with the natural universe as a whole, but with particular objects within the world. As we shall see, there are forms of the argument from design that do start with the whole of the world, considered as one complex system, but it is important to see that not all arguments from design have this feature.

---

[1] Thomas Aquinas, *Summa Theologica*, trans. Fathers of the English Dominican Province (New York: Benziger Bros., 1947–8; repr. Allen, TX: Thomas More, 1981), I, q. 2, a. 3.

Second, the objects that Aquinas singles out as the starting point of his argument have two features. There are things in nature that "act always or nearly always in the same way," and those things thereby obtain "the best result." In other words, the natural world often exhibits orderly patterns, and those patterns make possible outcomes that are good. I shall say that objects or systems in nature that have both of these properties, orderly structure that leads to valuable results, exhibit "beneficial order."

It is worth noting here that I believe Aquinas overstates things and claims more than is necessary when he says that the things in nature that form his starting point achieve "the *best* result." It is not clear that there is always a "best result" in the natural world. We may observe an outcome of a natural process as good, but it is unclear how to determine whether that outcome is "best" or even what that would mean. In any case, while I do think rational agents necessarily seek what they perceive as good, I do not think a rational being must be pictured as a kind of "rational maximizer," always seeking to obtain some "best" outcome. Hence I shall say that beneficial order requires only two things: orderly structure that seems to result in a good outcome.

Aquinas clearly thinks that beneficial order is not something to be taken for granted; it is a marker for intelligence. Intelligent beings themselves exhibit beneficial order; they typically order their actions so as to obtain desirable results. When we observe things that themselves lack intelligence that have this characteristic, Aquinas says that this is a sign that an intelligent being is shaping the process, since such things do not happen "fortuitously, but designedly."

Using my terminology, this argument could be boiled down to this simple syllogism:

1. There are many examples of beneficial order in nature.
2. Beneficial order is the result of an intelligent designer.
3. The natural world is (at least partly) the result of an intelligent designer.

The qualification "partly" in the conclusion seems necessary for several reasons. One is because the argument is a "part" argument, beginning with specific things in nature rather than the natural world as a whole. Another is that the argument by itself suggests only that the "designedness" of the objects is the product of the designer, but this seems compatible with a designer who works with pre-existent materials rather than a God who creates from nothing.

Most of the criticisms of such arguments focus, as we shall see, on premise 2. How do we know that beneficial order must be the work of an intelligent designer? One could protect premise 2 against such attacks by modifying the first premise in the following way:

1. There are many examples of design in nature.
2. Design is the result of purposive intelligence.
3. The natural world is (at least partly) the result of purposive intelligence.

The new premise 2 now seems secure, since design simply is an application of purposive intelligence. However, the critic will now shift the focus to the first premise. How do we know that the examples of beneficial order we observe in nature are genuine examples of design? Perhaps what we observe is merely apparent design, something that mimics the design we recognize in human artifacts. How do we know that the order we observe in nature is not, in Aquinas's words, merely "fortuitous?"

ANALOGY VERSIONS OF THE ARGUMENT FROM DESIGN

One way to bolster the second premise in the original argument above is to appeal to our experience of the origins of analogous entities that also display beneficial order, but that we know to be the work of intelligent designers. This transforms the argument into one that rests on analogies drawn between objects in nature and human artifacts. It is noteworthy that no such appeal to analogy is made in Aquinas's argument. Rather, Aquinas seems to think that it is simply evident that beneficial order is the result of intelligence.

Versions of the argument that do turn on analogies are common, however, and were popular in the eighteenth century and the early part of the nineteenth century. A particularly famous version is found in the writings of William Paley, who describes finding a watch while walking:

In crossing a heath, suppose I pitched my foot against a stone, and were asked how the stone came to be there; I might possibly answer, that, for anything I knew to the contrary, it had lain there forever: nor would it perhaps be very easy to show the absurdity of this answer. But suppose I had found a watch upon the ground, and it should be inquired how the watch happened to be in that place; I should hardly think of the answer I had before given, that for anything I knew, the watch might have always been there . . . . There must have existed, at some time, and at some place or other, an artificer or artificers, who formed [the watch] for the purpose which we find it actually to answer; who comprehended its construction, and designed its use . . . . Every indication of contrivance, every manifestation of design, which existed in the watch, exists in the works of nature; with the difference, on the side of nature, of being greater or more, and that in a degree which exceeds all computation.[2]

Paley's type of argument provides empirical support for the claim that orderliness seen in beneficial order is the work of intelligent design. We have observed countless human artifacts that we know to be the work of design. Many objects in nature are analogous to human artifacts in that they appear to be contrivances in which complex means work together to achieve desirable ends. Since like effects come from like causes, if human artifacts are the work of intelligent design, this suggests that the same is true for many objects or systems found in nature.

HUME'S ATTACK ON ANALOGICAL TELEOLOGICAL ARGUMENTS

Although Paley wrote some time after David Hume, many philosophers today consider Hume's *Dialogues Concerning Natural Religion*, briefly discussed in Chapter 1, to be a powerful critique of the teleological argument in the form defended by Paley. Hume's character

---

[2] William Paley, *Natural Theology: Or Evidences of the Existence and Attributes of the Deity, Collected from the Appearances of Nature* (Boston: Gould & Lincoln, 1853), 5–13.

Philo makes a number of criticisms of the argument, all of which seem directed against analogical forms such as Paley's. Since Hume is Philo's creator and Hume is commonly credited with having developed the classical critique of the argument on the strength of Philo's objections, I shall speak of these objections as Hume's, dividing them into two main categories.

The objections in the first category focus on what we might call the religious inadequacies of the concept of God that the argument leads to. Hume argues that, since the design we see in nature is not perfect or infinite, it is not necessary to infer a perfect or infinite designer as the cause of that design.[3] For all we know, he says, the designer might be a junior deity who was still improving his skill at universe-making, or a geriatric deity who has seen better days.[4] Or, the designer might not be a single being at all, but a committee.[5] Furthermore, and this is a point I have already conceded in my formulation of the argument, a designer is not necessarily a being who creates from nothing, but could be a being who works with pre-existent materials. Worst of all, from a religious perspective, the natural world, even if it shows evidence of design, also seems to contain a great deal of suffering and evil. Hence, if we relied solely on the natural order to form an idea of God, we would have no basis for concluding that God is completely good or morally perfect.[6] Hume admits that it is possible that a completely good and perfect God might have reasons for allowing evil and suffering; hence the design argument is compatible with an all-perfect God.[7] However, the argument by itself would not justify belief in such a God.

Proponents of the argument have responded to such criticisms in a number of ways. Swinburne, for example, argues that the hypothesis of a single designer is superior to multiple designers on grounds of simplicity.[8] He also argues that a God of unlimited power is more

[3] David Hume, *Dialogues Concerning Natural Religion*, ed. Richard H. Popkin (Indianapolis: Hackett, 1980), 35–6.

[4] Hume, *Dialogues Concerning Natural Religion*, 37.

[5] Hume, *Dialogues Concerning Natural Religion*, 36.

[6] Hume, *Dialogues Concerning Natural Religion*, 67–81.

[7] Hume, *Dialogues Concerning Natural Religion*, 83.

[8] Richard Swinburne, *The Existence of God* (2nd edn.; Oxford: Oxford University Press, 2004), 145–6.

likely than one of very great though limited power, again on grounds of simplicity, since, if God had limited power, we would need an explanation of why God has just the degree of power that he has. However, it seems to me that the proponent of the argument can simply concede the force of this type of criticism. All that such objections show is that the teleological argument by itself, at least in its analogical form, does not lead to a fully adequate conception of God.

However, it seems quite possible that the argument could be supplemented by other arguments. For example, if the teleological argument suggests only that God is a designer and not a creator, it may be combined with a cosmological argument that suggests that the natural world depends on a necessary being. One could imagine that the being responsible for the existence of the universe differs from the being responsible for its design, but it seems much more plausible (and simpler, as Swinburne reminds us) to suppose that the being responsible for the existence of the universe also accounts for its design. Similarly, one might argue that the moral qualities of God could be made known through the moral argument, and this argument could supplement the design argument. In any case, natural theologians do not typically claim that the arguments given in favor of the existence of God by themselves settle all or even many of the questions that arise about God's nature. Aquinas, for example, devotes a huge amount of his work in both the *Summa Theologica* and the *Summa contra Gentiles* to separate arguments designed to show the unity of God, goodness of God, and so on.

Alternatively, the proponent of the argument may admit that, even when supplemented by other arguments, the output of natural theology is meager and religiously inadequate. The point is that it is not the purpose of natural theology to give us an adequate and complete understanding of God. Rather, natural theology is designed to show us the inadequacy of a naturalistic world view, and open us to the possibility of a special revelation that will give us the knowledge of God that is needed. Those who employ natural theology in what I called "two stage apologetics" in Chapter 1 will not hesitate to admit the limits of natural theology, taken alone. No less a champion of natural theology than Aquinas makes this forthright statement about the limits of natural theology when compared with special revelation: "If the only way open to us for the knowledge of God were solely that of the reason, the human race would remain in the blackest shadows of ignorance."[9]

The other category of objections raised in Hume's *Dialogues* concern what we may properly call alleged epistemic deficiencies in the argument, rather than the limitations of the designer the argument infers. Some of these objections reflect Hume's doctrinaire empiricism, and may reveal more about the limits of that epistemology than problems with the design argument. For example, Hume claims that knowledge of cause and effect comes from repeated experiences in which we have observed one type of event, the cause, succeeded by another, the effect. Since we have no experience of universe-making, we have no observational basis for any reliable inferences about the causes of universes.[10] The universe is too singular a phenomenon to have any causal knowledge about it.

This objection seems weak, since scientists do not regard the singularity of a phenomenon as a barrier to forming and supporting hypotheses about the cause of that phenomenon. It seems possible, for example, that life (at least on earth) is a singular phenomenon that began at one point in time, but, if that is the case, it would not prevent theorizing about the causal process that gave rise to life. In any case, the whole point of reasoning from analogy is to give us information about some reality of which we do not have direct experience; if we had repeated direct experience of a phenomenon, we would have no need for analogical reasoning.

A second objection in this category that Hume raises is that the analogy that underlies the argument from design is weak. Here Hume assumes, not only that the argument must rest on an analogy, but that it is a "whole" argument, in which the universe as a whole is claimed to be similar to a human artifact such as a house or a watch. However, Hume argues that the analogy between the universe and something such as a house or a watch is faint, and therefore any inference that the cause of the universe will resemble the cause of things such as houses and watches will be highly uncertain: "But surely you will not

[9] Thomas Aquinas, *Summa contra Gentiles*, trans. Anton C. Pegis (Notre Dame, IN: University of Notre Dame Press, 1975), I, q. 4, a. 4 (p. 67).
[10] Hume, *Dialogues Concerning Natural Religion*, 148–50.

affirm that the universe bears such a resemblance to a house that we can with the same certainty infer a similar cause, or that the analogy here is entire and perfect. The dissimilitude is so striking that the utmost you can here pretend to is a guess, a conjecture, a presumption concerning a similar cause."[11]

This objection to the strength of the analogy between the universe and human artifacts is reiterated and deepened later in the *Dialogues*, when it is claimed that the universe actually bears a stronger analogy to things like seeds and plants than it does to things such as watches and houses.[12] Since we know by experience that things such as plants and seeds come from other plants and seeds, and like effects require like causes, the hypothesis that the universe germinated from a seed may be just as strong or even stronger than the hypothesis that it is the result of an intelligent designer.

This line of thought has real force, I think, but only when directed at "whole" versions of the teleological argument that are analogical in form. It is noteworthy that Aquinas's argument has neither of these features. It begins, not with the universe as a whole, but with particular parts of the universe that are observed to have beneficial order. Furthermore, the argument rests, not on any alleged analogy between the universe as a whole and human artifacts, but on the claim that the beneficial order observed in nature is itself immediate evidence of design.

This last claim is one that Hume clearly rejects, since it conflicts with his empiricist account of how we gain knowledge of causes and effect: "order, arrangement, or the adjustment of final causes, is not of itself any proof of design, but only so far as it has been experienced to proceed from that principle. For aught we can know *a priori*, matter may contain the source or spring of order originally within itself, as well as mind does."[13] Hume in fact uses this principle to argue that the design argument begs the question. If we take seriously the possibility that matter can somehow produce order, then mind itself

11   Hume, *Dialogues Concerning Natural Religion*, 16.
12   Hume, *Dialogues Concerning Natural Religion*, 44.
13   Hume, *Dialogues Concerning Natural Religion*, 18.

may be explained by matter, and the claim that the universe must be the work of a mind will not lead to the conclusion that mind is the ultimate cause of things, since mind itself may be the product of something more ultimate.[14]

This is an interesting claim, but it may be one that cuts two ways. Hume here suggests that, if we start with the assumption that matter can itself produce order, we can explain mind itself. In that case we will err if we assume that the cause of the universe must be a mind, basing the assumption on the view that it must resemble the minds that create artifacts, because the ultimate cause of the artifacts themselves will not be minds but the matter that produced minds. To assume that mind is an original cause would beg the question against the materialistic world view. However, it looks as though the defender of the design hypothesis can make a similar move. Hume argues that the universe is similar not only to a house, but to things like a plant. However, this claim threatens the design hypothesis only on the assumption that we know that plants are *not* the work of design. However, to recall Aquinas's argument again, a proponent of the design argument (in a different form) may claim that plants themselves are among the objects that clearly possess beneficial order and thus point to an intelligent cause.

Hume further develops this materialistic hypothesis in part VIII of the *Dialogues*, in which Philo tentatively spins out the possibility of what he calls the "Epicurean hypothesis," not as a view known to be true but as another possibility that experience cannot rule out. On such a view, the order that we observe in nature is regarded as simply the outcome of principles that are inherent in the operation of matter, perhaps operating randomly over a long period of time, until a state of the universe appears that is orderly and relatively stable.[15] Writing more than a half century before Darwin, Hume had no clear conception as to how such a materialistic story might go, but the possibility he here spins out seems prophetic in light of *The Origin of Species*.

[14] Hume, *Dialogues Concerning Natural Religion*, 47.
[15] Hume, *Dialogues Concerning Natural Religion*, 49.

DOES EVOLUTIONARY THEORY UNDERMINE
THE DESIGN ARGUMENT?

There is little doubt that Darwinian evolutionary theory has had a fundamental impact on the popularity of teleological arguments. Prior to Darwin, despite the efforts of philosophers such as Hume, atheists had no plausible means of explaining the apparent design in the natural world. Hence, it is not surprising that Richard Dawkins has famously said that "Darwin made it possible to be an intellectually fulfilled atheist."[16]

The basic idea that lies behind Dawkins's statement is that Darwinism makes it possible to see the order that is perceived in nature as only apparent design rather than actual design. Certainly, we do observe what appears to be the adaptation of complex means to achieve ends in nature. However, the basic idea behind Darwinian evolution is that this apparent design can be explained as the result of random variations combined with a process of natural selection, in which organisms that by chance have some variation, which enables them to survive and flourish in their environment better than other organisms, will have an advantage over those others. The favored organisms will be more likely to survive and reproduce, and thus pass on the favorable variation. (Of course, at the time Darwin proposed his theory, the mechanism for variation was not known, but today we know that genetic mutations do provide such variations.) Given a struggle for survival and reproduction between organisms, enough variations with at least some of them being favorable, a long enough period of time, and the existence of stable reproductive mechanisms, Darwin provides a causal story about how such apparently designed systems such as the human heart or the human eye could have developed. As interpreted by the non-believer such as Dawkins, the story requires no intelligent designer. The natural analogues to Paley's watch require only "a blind watchmaker" to explain them.[17]

---

[16] Richard Dawkins, *The Blind Watchmaker: Why the Evidence of Evolution Reveals a Universe without Design* (New York: Norton, 1996), 6.

[17] See Dawkins, *The Blind Watchmaker*.

It is noteworthy that the evolutionary critique of design arguments strikes not only at analogical forms of the argument, such as Paley's, but also at non-analogical arguments such as Aquinas's. For the key element of the criticism is aimed at the claim that beneficial order necessarily requires an intelligent designer, which is fundamental to Aquinas's Fifth Way. Nor does the evolutionary critique aim only at "whole" arguments, as was the case for some of Hume's criticisms, for the evolutionary explanation of order is precisely designed to explain particular biological systems.

Three options present themselves to the proponent of the design argument. The first, and least promising, is to attempt to attack and discredit evolutionary theory. I do not think this strategy, exemplified by advocates of "creation-science," warrants discussion, since it seems to fly in the face of what is today well-accepted scientific theory.[18]

A second, and somewhat more promising, strategy would be to concede that an evolutionary process has occurred, while arguing that the explanation for the process still requires reference to intelligence at certain points.[19] Advocates of such a view may concede what may be called the "common-ancestry" thesis, accepting the claim that animals and plants have evolved from simpler organisms, but reject the idea that the process can be scientifically explained solely as the result of unguided, mechanistic forces. Rather, something intelligent guided the process, either intervening at critical points, or else shaping the whole stream of events in some way, perhaps by ensuring that the right kinds of variations would occur. Perhaps a case could be made for some such view. However, it also faces the difficulty that it is not currently supported by mainstream scientific theory. One concern that dogs the view is the worry that such a view promotes a "god of the gaps," in which divine action is postulated to fill gaps in the scientific account. If the scientific account is extended, as so often has happened, such a "god of the gaps" would be destined to shrink.

[18] For a discussion of the history of "creation-science," see Ronald L. Numbers, *The Creationists: From Scientific Creationism to Intelligent Design* (2nd edn.; Cambridge, MA: Harvard University Press, 2006).

[19] For a good discussion, see Del Ratzsch, *Nature, Design, and Science: The Status of Design in Natural Science* (SUNY Series in Philosophy and Biology; Albany, NY: State University of New York Press, 2001).

The third possible strategy to rehabilitate the argument therefore looks like the strongest option. This third option is to accept the Darwinian account as the best *scientific* explanation of the development of beneficial order, but argue that this scientific explanation is still incomplete. The proponent of the argument will point out that teleological and mechanistic explanations are not always incompatible. Imagine a completely automated factory that produces shoes. One could say in such a case that the shoes the factory turns out are the product of a mechanistic process, and that would be true. But, of course, the machines in the factory work as they do, and the factory turns out shoes that are useful to be worn, precisely because the factory was designed to turn out shoes. A proponent of the design argument who accepts evolutionary theory might simply regard the natural world, with its laws and initial conditions that resulted in an evolutionary process, as the means whereby God chose to realize the ends he wished to realize. An explanation that involves design would in that case be more complete than a scientific explanation that limits itself to the mechanical process.

The critic of the argument might at this point insist that, even if it is possible that God realized the design in nature through an evolutionary process, we lack positive evidence for this. Perhaps if we knew that there was a God, the critic might say, we could interpret the evolutionary process as the means God used to create a certain kind of world. However, the mere possibility that we could interpret the evolutionary story in this way is not a reason to do so.

However, the proponent of the argument has something more to say at this point. The claim that the evolutionary process itself may be something that requires design is not simply an appeal to a bare possibility. For it is a fact that the evolutionary process itself requires a deep kind of orderliness. For Darwinian evolution to occur, for example, there must be stable reproductive mechanisms, and such mechanisms, besides being themselves impressive examples of beneficial order, require natural laws—and laws of a certain kind—to explain their existence. In other words, the proponent of the argument from design may maintain that what we might call surface order, the order that can be observed in nature and that involves the complex adaptation of means to valuable ends, is dependent on a deeper order, the order embedded in the laws of nature that make evolution possible.[20] But it is hard to see why the discovery that this surface order, which seems to cry out for explanation, is dependent on a yet deeper level of order, should dispel and dissolve the mystery of beneficial order. The fact that the beneficial order observed in nature depends on a deep, highly complex order hidden in the structure of nature does not imply that the original beneficial order is an illusion or that it does not point to design. Rather, it might seem to point to a designer who is far more ingenious and powerful than one might have suspected from observing that initial order. A shoe-creator who created shoes by designing and implementing a factory rather than building the shoes by hand certainly seems no less intelligent and powerful. Similarly, a creator God who brought about a complex world by causing a number of natural laws to hold and applying them to the right "initial conditions" seems at least as intelligent and powerful as a being who might bring about such a world in a more messy way.

"FINE-TUNING" ARGUMENTS

The above considerations push the design argument in the direction of what has come to be called a "fine-tuning" argument for God. The basic question where proponents and critics of the argument disagree seems to be whether or not the basic order of the natural universe—the laws of nature that have operated as they have and do to bring about the world as we know it—is a "brute fact." A strong point in favor of the proponent of the design argument is that the laws of nature and the physical constants that govern the universe (the speed of light, Planck's constant, the mass of an electron, and so on) seem very surprising.[21] It looks as if they could have been different, even vastly different than they are, and so it seems implausible to say they are simply brute facts. Of course the critic of the design argument

---

[20] Richard Swinburne provides a good example of a kind of teleological argument that employs evolutionary theory. See his *The Existence of God*, 188–91.

[21] The points made in this sentence and the following ones are adapted from C. Stephen Evans and Zachary Manis, *Philosophy of Religion: Thinking about Faith* (2nd edn.; Contours of Christian Philosophy; Downers Grove, IL: InterVarsity Press, 2009), ch. 6.

can always maintain that they are simply brute and inexplicable facts, but in fact the conditions that make living systems possible seem quite surprising.

Recent developments in theoretical physics seem to support the view that the laws of nature and constants that make living systems possible are indeed surprising. Physicists are now able to show that, had any of a number of laws and physical constants been even minutely different, life as it has evolved would not have been possible.[22] Since the range of other values that are possible seems immense, it looks vastly improbable that the universe *just happened.* The universe looks very much as if it has been "fine-tuned" so as to make life possible, and the evidence for this fine-tuning is impressive enough for life-long atheist Antony Flew to have been recently converted to belief in a deistic God on the strength of the argument.[23]

Non-believers, of course, have responded to such arguments. One strategy for doing so exploits what some have called "the anthropic principle."[24] The anthropic principle rests on the idea that the universe appears to be "just right" for the development of intelligent life; the proponent of the principle affirms that, if this were not so, we humans would not be around to recognize the character of the universe. In some sense the universe then seems "aimed" at the development of humans. On its face, the anthropic principle seems compatible with a design argument, or even to lend support to such an argument. However, the non-believer may argue that it is not really surprising that the universe has the characteristics it must have to support intelligent life, since, if it did not, we could not possibly be here to know about it. But we are here, so the universe must have those characteristics.

By itself the anthropic principle does little to allay our sense of mystery and surprise that the universe is fine-tuned for life. To see this, consider the following analogy. You are facing a firing squad of crack

---

[22] For a clear defense of such a fine-tuning argument, see Robin Collins, "God, Design, and Fine-Tuning," in Raymond Martin and Christopher Bernard (eds.), *God Matters: Readings in the Philosophy of Religion* (New York: Longman, 2003), 119–34.

[23] See Antony Flew and Roy Abraham Varghese, *There is a God: How the World's Most Notorious Atheist Changed his Mind* (New York: HarperOne, 2007).

[24] See John D. Barrow and Frank J. Tipler, *The Anthropic Cosmological Principle* (Oxford: Oxford University Press, 1988).

marksmen. The shooters fire, and, remarkably, all of them miss. You are still alive. Such a fact seems remarkable, highly improbable even if logically possible. You would hardly think it is a good explanation of this remarkable fact if someone were to tell you that the explanation is that you are still alive, and you have to be alive in order to know that the marksmen missed.[25]

However, if the anthropic principle is combined with other considerations, prospects for the non-believer may be better. One strategy is to combine the anthropic principle with some kind of "multiverse theory."[26] The idea is that our universe may be one of many, perhaps even infinitely many, universes. Perhaps only a very few of these universes are suitable for the development of life, but, if there are enough universes, it is not surprising that at least one of them is suitable for the development of adaptive biological systems, including those that make possible intelligent life, and we happen to be part of that friendly universe. In the great universe lottery, we bought the right lottery ticket!

Proponents of the design argument have responded to these multiverse hypotheses in a number of ways. Some have argued that there is little or no evidence for the existence of multiple universes. Others have argued that, even if there are multiple universes, there is still a need to explain the structural order that makes such universes possible; the proposed explanations of the development of the many universes also seem to require fine-tuning. Obviously, a much fuller discussion of these points could be given; here I have wished to say only enough to make the general character of the debate clear.

DOES EVOLUTION IMPLY BENEFICIAL ORDER IS NOT A NATURAL SIGN?

If the beneficial order we observe in nature is a natural sign that points to God, then much of the discussion about whether evolutionary

---

[25] For a version of the firing-squad story, see John Leslie, *Universes* (London and New York: Routledge, 1989), 13–14.

[26] For a good discussion of such cosmologies, see Del Ratzsch, "Saturation, World Ensembles, and Design: Death by a Thousand Multiplications?" *Faith and Philosophy: Journal of the Society of Christian Philosophers*, 22/5 (2005), 667–86.

theory undermines the design argument, or about whether the fine-tuning of the universe supports the argument, takes on a different character. A theistic natural sign, as I have developed the concept, must be something whose reality is widely accessible—something humans across many cultures and times have observed. Such a sign cannot be something that becomes known only as a result of sophisticated scientific discoveries. Hence, it does not appear that the discoveries of the physicists that underlie fine-tuning arguments would be or constitute such a theistic natural sign, however valuable such discoveries might be in providing support for arguments for God's existence. However, for similar reasons it is hard to see why the discovery of a scientific theory such as evolution should undermine the status of beneficial order as such a sign. At least this will be so unless evolutionary theory provides a defeater for—evidence against—the claim that the beneficial order in nature is a natural sign for God, a possibility I will consider below.

Here is how things appear if we take beneficial order as a genuine natural sign for God. The natural world contains many examples of orderly, complex structures where the order seems to be in the service of some good. This order is the result of an intelligent designer, a Mind that is powerful and cares about those good ends. Moreover, God has instilled in humans a disposition to "read" this beneficial order as (correctly) pointing to himself. All of this seems fully consistent with the view that God has chosen an evolutionary process as the means whereby the designs are implemented. Evolutionary theory, if true, entails that the beneficial order that is observed in nature rests on a deeper order, an incredibly intricate process that itself depends on fine-tuned initial conditions and precise laws of nature. There is no reason to think that the fact that the surface order depends on this deeper order implies that the design that is evident to human observation is necessarily only apparent. If God wanted to plant a clue to himself by putting into the natural world things that clearly seem to be the result of intelligence, he could have done so in any number of ways. The fact that he used an evolutionary process would not appear to be a problem, especially if that evolutionary process itself reveals a still more intricate, hidden design.

Let me consider how a critic might respond to this. One might argue that evolution provides a *defeater* for the view that the beneficial order in nature is a theistic natural sign. Some critics have argued that it is highly unlikely that God would have used a Darwinian evolutionary process to bring about a world such as ours.[27] After all, the critic might urge, the Darwinian process is one that is wasteful, taking millions and millions of years and requiring the suffering and death of countless millions of animals. Presumably, an omnipotent God could have created a world full of complex beings by immediate fiat. Hence, the fact that an evolutionary process was involved provides good reason to doubt that the apparent design in nature is genuine design.

This argument against the probability of God employing an evolutionary process seems weak. The main problem is that we have little basis for confidence in a priori speculations about what means a good God would employ to create a world. We simply do not know enough about what it would be like to be God to have any reliable intuitions about such matters. The particular intuitions that underlie the claim that God would not employ an evolutionary process seem particularly dubious. If God is eternal or everlasting, it is not clear what it would mean to say that it is "inefficient" for God to employ a process lasting hundreds of millions of years. It is not as if God has only a certain amount of time to get the job done, and must be careful not to waste it. The claim that it is "wasteful" for God to use a process in which millions of animals' lives are required seems similarly misguided. An omnipotent being does not have a finite stock of power that he must be careful not to misuse or waste.

Perhaps the critic is thinking that what is really important is what comes at the end of the process: we humans and our achievements. What is "wasteful" is taking such a long time to realize what is really valuable. While flattering to our human egos, there is no need to think such a view accurately reflects God's perspective. Even if God does place a special value on humans, there is no reason he cannot regard the whole process as one that has intrinsic value, a grand show in which he takes great delight. God may relish each and every species that passes on the scene of natural history, or even every

---

[27] Paul Draper, "Natural Selection and the Problem of Evil," review in Paul Draper (ed.), *God or Blind Nature? Philosophers Debate the Evidence* (2007), www.infidels.org/library/modern/paul_draper/evil.html.

individual. From the perspective of an omniscient being, nothing may be "wasted."

What about the fact that the evolutionary process, as understood by Darwinians, involves the use of random variations? Can a process that involves chance mutations possibly be one that implements a design? This worry is based on a misconception about the meaning of "random" in evolutionary theory. In this context, to say that variations are "random" is not to say that they are literally the result of chance, or that there is no causal explanation for their occurrence. Rather, to say that variations occur randomly is simply to say that they are unpredictable from the perspective of the biologist. However, it would be quite within the scope of an omnipotent, omniscient being to employ such a process to achieve his ends. This would be so, even if the process literally does include an element of chance in a stronger sense.[28]

But what about the fact that the evolutionary process is one that employs suffering and death for millions of creatures? Would a good God employ such a process? Once more we should be cautious about assuming we know the answer to such questions. We may be inclined to think that, if we were God, we would employ a different method. But how much do we know about the options facing God, about the goods God ultimately intends to realize, or the constraints that those ends may place on God? In effect, the objection to the claim that evolution is a process God would not employ here merges with the problem of evil: the argument that the suffering and evil in the world make it unlikely to be the work of a good God.

A critic might urge at this point that the objection, though related to the problem of evil, is still a specific version of that problem, since it amounts to the claim that the amount of suffering present in the world's history cannot be plausibly regarded as necessary for the origin of species. This raises a question: does the problem of evil, either in general or in this specific form related to Darwinian evolution, undermine the claim that there are theistic natural signs? I shall first discuss the implications of the problem of evil generally for

---

[28] For a defense of this, see Peter van Inwagen, "The Place of Chance in a World Sustained by God," in *God, Knowledge & Mystery: Essays in Philosophical Theology* (Ithaca, NY: Cornell University Press, 1995), 42–65.

the claim that there are natural signs for God, and then say something about the particular claim that the evil that is part of the Darwinian evolutionary process undermines the claim that the perceived order in nature could be such a sign.

It is good to recall at this point that, if there are natural signs for God's reality, the evidence provided by such signs would be defeasible. Even if there are such signs, and even if they do provide evidence, it is possible that a person's epistemic situation is overall one that makes belief in God unreasonable, because the person may have evidence against God's reality that outweighs the positive evidence provided by the signs. That is, it would be possible for a non-believer to admit that there are natural signs that point to God's reality, and thus provide some reason for belief in God, while still maintaining that belief in God is overall unjustified, just as a critic might well think that one or more of the theistic arguments provides some reason for belief in God, but hold that the evidence provided by the argument is overall outweighed by negative evidence.

It seems to me that the best way for the critic to see arguments from evil and suffering is to regard them as providing negative evidence of just this sort. This means that evil and suffering do not imply that beneficial order cannot be a theistic natural sign, but at most would be a defeater for the belief that is supposed to be the outcome of the sign, negative evidence that outweighs belief in God. Could one think of evil and suffering as "negative natural signs" intended to produce disbelief in God? That hardly seems possible. To be a natural sign, an experience or feature of the world would have to be caused by the reality it signifies, and there must be a natural disposition to become aware of that reality and form a belief about it. If God does not exist, there could hardly be a causal relation between a non-existent being and the suffering and evil in the world; nor does it make sense to say that the intended function of suffering and evil is to produce unbelief. Natural signs seem inherently positive in nature; if there are any natural signs of the lack of something, they would surely be parasitic on signs that indicate a positive reality. By experience one might come to learn that, in a particular situation, the object normally indicated by a natural sign is not present, but one would have to know there are such entities in order to have a natural sign of their absence.

It must be conceded that in principle evil and suffering could provide evidence against belief in God that might outweigh any positive evidence provided by natural signs. However, this possibility does not by itself show that there are not natural signs that point to God's reality; that is a question that must be decided on its own merits. Certainly, any overall case for belief in God will have to say something about evil and suffering. The theist might provide either a theodicy (an explanation of why God allows evil), or a defense (an argument that there are possible reasons why God might allow evil, even if we do not know what those reasons are).[29] Alternatively, the theist might provide an undercutting defeater for the argument from evil, an argument that evil and suffering do not in fact constitute powerful evidence against belief in God, or at least not evidence that is powerful enough to offset the positive evidence for belief.[30] A full discussion of the various responses theists have given to the problem of evil lies outside the scope of this book; such a discussion would certainly require book-length treatment. But this much can be said: one way or the other, if belief in God is to be reasonable, the problem of evil must be confronted, and theists believe this is possible.

So far as I can see, the fact that the process of evolution is one that involves pain and suffering for sentient creatures does not make the problem of evil any more difficult. It is abundantly clear, and

---

[29] For theistic responses to the problem of evil, see Swinburne, *The Existence of God*, 236–72; Alvin Plantinga, *God, Freedom, and Evil* (New York: Harper & Row, 1974); Marilyn McCord Adams, *Horrendous Evils and the Goodness of God* (Ithaca, NY: Cornell University Press, 1999); Peter van Inwagen, "The Argument from Evil," in Peter van Inwagen (ed.), *Christian Faith and the Problem of Evil* (Grand Rapids, MI: Eerdmans, 2004), 55–73.

The term "defense" was introduced by Alvin Plantinga, who originally used it in a weaker sense than given above. Plantinga used the term to designate the attempt to give a possible reason why God might permit evil, so as to show that the claim that God could have no such reason is false. It seems to me to be a natural strengthening of this usage to describe a defense as also including reasons for believing not only that there are possible reasons why God could allow evil, but that God actually has a good reason. I thank an anonymous reader for Oxford University Press for pointing out this distinction.

[30] Stephen J. Wykstra provides one version in "The Humean Obstacle to Evidential Arguments from Suffering: On Avoiding the Evils of Appearance," *International Journal for Philosophy of Religion*, 16 (1984), 73–93. See also C. Stephen Evans, *Faith beyond Reason: A Kierkegaardian Account* (Reason and Religion Series; Grand Rapids, MI: Eerdmans, 1998), 126–37.

has always been evident, that the natural world is full of pain and suffering. It is obvious that, if God exists, he has chosen to actualize a world containing a good deal of pain and suffering. It does not seem surprising then that, if God has chosen to create such a world, he might choose to employ a means of doing so that also involves pain and suffering. Indeed, speaking of means and ends here is misleading, since it seems to imply that one can distinguish the reality of the world over time from the process by which it came into being. However, the reality of the universe over time includes the process by which the current state of the universe came into being. If God has good reasons for allowing pain and suffering at all, he must also have good reasons for employing a process of world development and governance that involves pain and suffering as well.

The critic may, of course, claim, not that evil and suffering eliminate the possibility that beneficial order is a natural sign for God, but that evil and suffering might alter our estimate of the character of the intelligent designer the sign points to. This is a major point found in Hume's *Dialogues*. This point seems to be a strong one, and I believe it can be conceded by the proponent of the sign. The natural signs point to God as a real being, but they do not deliver a full or adequate picture of God's nature. Someone who relied solely on the purposive order in the natural world as a basis for belief in God might rightly wonder whether God is completely good. As I have already noted, this is similar to the situation of someone who, on the basis of the experience of design or the design argument, wonders whether God is an all-powerful creator out of nothing, or simply a very powerful designer/builder, who might employ pre-existing material.[31] Beneficial order by itself is not sufficient to settle such questions. It points to an intelligent cause of the natural world that is beyond nature, and thus provides a reason to reject a naturalistic world view. However, to gain adequate knowledge about the nature of that intelligent designer-cause, one would need additional arguments or, even better, some special revelation in which God makes his characteristics more evident.

What about the claim that the suffering associated with Darwinian evolution provides evidence that God is not the cause of this process,

---

[31] See the discussion of this point earlier in this chapter in the section "Hume's Attack on Analogical Teleological Arguments."

and thus a defeater for the claim that the observed beneficial order in nature is a natural sign, caused by God for the sake of pointing humans to God? As noted above, the primary problem with this claim is that we simply do not have enough reliable a priori information about the means a good God would employ to create a world to make such a judgment with confidence. If there is a justification for suffering as part of the world as it currently exists, how could it be known that there is no justification for the prior history of the world as including suffering as well?

I suspect that any lingering dissatisfaction with the claim that God could have employed an evolutionary process to produce the current world may stem from particular theodicies that have been embraced. A critic might think, for example, that the suffering in the current world might possibly be justified by human free will. However, it is hardly plausible to view the suffering of animals that existed before humans as stemming from the wrong use of human free will. So one might think that pre-human animal pain, an inextricable part of the Darwinian story, is a particularly acute problem for theists, and, thus, that Darwinism greatly exacerbates the problem of evil, perhaps even makes it unsolvable. The critic may think that God could surely have brought about a world of morally free, responsible creatures in a manner that involves less animal suffering.[32]

As I have already claimed, I do not think that humans are in a position to know what alternatives God could have employed to bring about the current world, or to understand his reasons for choosing one alternative over another. It might *seem* to us that God could have created the world in a manner that involved less suffering, and that, if he had done this, it would have been better. Well, what alternatives might God have used? One would, of course, be simply to create the world as it currently exists by fiat, with no history whatsoever. Suppose, for instance, that God had created the world five minutes ago, complete with all signs of apparent age, including apparent memories. That would eliminate any pre-human animal suffering, but such an alternative would be problematic, for a number of

---

[32] For a contemporary response to the problem of non-human animal suffering, see Peter Van Inwagen, "The Sufferings of Beasts," in *The Problem of Evil* (Oxford: Oxford University Press, 2006), 113–34.

reasons. In such a case God would be creating a world with "apparent age," and many would argue that such a creation would amount to deception. In a similar way, a world that is only 6,000 or 10,000 years old could be viewed as "massively irregular," to use Peter van Inwagen's phrase.[33]

One might respond that there are surely other alternatives, and this is almost certainly the case. But it is very unclear what those alternatives are and exactly what value and disvalue they might have. Michael Murray has recently argued that there is great intrinsic value in God's creating a world through a process that moves from initial chaos to increasing degrees of order, in a process that is itself nomically regular.[34] It is not at all clear that God could have implemented the world in such a "chaos-to-order" way, employing fixed natural laws, without the kind of suffering that seems intrinsic to evolution. Furthermore, Murray argues that the view that it would be good for God to create the world in this way long antedates Darwinian evolution, extending at least as far back as Augustine, and so it cannot be viewed merely as an ad hoc move made in response to Darwin.[35] In any case, if it were extremely unlikely that God would create a world through a Darwinian process, it is puzzling why there are so many scientists who are also religious believers, and who see no problem at all in believing God has created the world through such a process.[36] It does not appear then that Darwinism significantly exacerbates the problem of evil or presents any insuperable problem for the view that the perceived beneficial order in nature is a natural sign for God.

[33] Peter van Inwagen, "The Problem of Evil, the Problem of Air, and the Problem of Silence," in *God, Knowledge, Mystery* (Ithaca, NY: Cornell University Press, 1995), 78.

[34] See Michael Murray, *Nature Red in Tooth and Claw: Theism and the Problem of Animal Suffering* (Oxford: Oxford University Press, 2008), especially ch. 6, pp. 166–92.

[35] See the discussion of Augustine in Murray, *Nature Red in Tooth and Claw*, 180–1.

[36] For a contemporary example of an outstanding scientist who sees no problem in believing God created the world through an evolutionary process, see Francis S. Collins, *The Language of God: A Scientist Presents Evidence for Belief* (New York: Free Press, 2006). For some surprising examples of early theistic defenders of Darwin, see David N. Livingstone, *Darwin's Forgotten Defenders: The Encounter between Evangelical Theology and Evolutionary Thought* (Edinburgh: Scottish Academic Press, 1987; Grand Rapids, MI: Eerdmans, 1987).

I conclude that evolutionary theory does not undermine the claim that beneficial order is a natural sign that points to God's reality. It also seems to be the case that the "fine-tuning" of the universe is not itself a natural sign either, at least in the sense in which I have explained the concept in Chapter 2. Such scientific discoveries fail the Wide Accessibility Principle test. Natural signs for God need to be things that can be observed by almost anyone at any time in any culture. Of course that does not mean that fine-tuning could not be a natural sign in some other sense, perhaps a clue especially directed at scientifically educated people from the late twentieth and twenty-first centuries. Moreover, the fine-tuning of the universe might well serve as a basis for a design argument. However, if there are features of the natural world or in human experience that we humans have a natural disposition to "read" as pointing to God, it would not seem to be the case that this function would be blocked or advanced by sophisticated scientific discoveries, even though such discoveries might well provide evidence that will figure in arguments that might buttress or defeat the function of the signs.

THE POWER OF THE SIGN: TESTIMONY ON BEHALF OF BENEFICIAL ORDER

Why should we think that beneficial order is in fact a natural sign for God? Perhaps the strongest argument that can be given for this is simply to appeal to the experience itself. It is no accident that people often find an encounter with the natural world to be in some way "spiritual," and that experiences of the natural world frequently seem to produce, in a perfectly spontaneous way, a belief that some kind of purposive intelligence lies behind the beauty and order we find in nature. This is the case not just for religious believers, but also for unbelievers. Contemporary Western culture has a pervasive secular outlook; many intellectuals raised in such an environment will not take full-fledged religious belief to be a live option. Given the fact that natural signs are resistible, their output may be felt and yet blocked by other beliefs. Nevertheless, the felt pull of the sign is still evident. Consider, for example, the testimony of Lewis Thomas, a distinguished physician who wrote movingly about science and many other things:

> I cannot make my peace with the randomness doctrine: I cannot abide the notion of purposelessness and blind chance in nature. And yet I do not know what to put in its place for the quieting of my mind. It is absurd to say that a place like this place is absurd, when it contains, in front of our eyes, so many billions of different forms of life, each one in its way absolutely perfect, all linked together to form what would surely seem to an outsider a huge spherical organism. We talk—some of us anyway—about the absurdity of the human situation, but we do this because we do not know how we fit in, or what we are for.[37]

Thomas cannot help but feel that the natural world, full of organisms that themselves seem perfectly designed, and that link together in intricate and marvelous ways, is no accident. To say that such a world is simply the result of chance seems absurd to him, yet he cannot bring himself to consider in a serious way the kind of religious world view his experience points to.

In Chapter 1 I looked briefly at the responses of Hume and Kant to the purposiveness in nature. Each, after having given what he himself thinks are devastating objections to the design argument, nevertheless proceeds to confess that the experience of design is one that naturally—and properly—leads to belief in God. In the remainder of this chapter, I shall consider these responses in more detail.

Kant

Though it sounds paradoxical to say so, Kant's account of religious belief seems quite consistent with the non-evidentialist account of belief in God that we today associate with Reformed epistemology. Lee Hardy has convincingly argued in some detail for three theses. (1) For Kant belief in God is commonly produced by a "native disposition." (2) This native disposition is what gives rational justification for religious belief. (3) This primary justification is secured independently of any proof or inferential argument, except in cases where an

---

[37] Lewis Thomas, "On the Uncertainty of Science," *Key Reporter*, 46 (Autumn 1980).

individual's disposition to belief has been blocked or defeated by some other belief.[38] (In this sort of case Kant recognizes some kind of argument may be necessary.)

Kant is, of course, famous for his critique of natural theology, in the course of which he argues that the classic arguments for God's existence fail as rigorous proofs. Those arguments do not give us genuine knowledge, because for Kant knowledge does not extend beyond the realm of possible experience, and God as a transcendent being could not be something that is given in sense experience. The theoretical proofs of God's existence illegitimately attempt to apply the categories of the understanding to supersensible realities.

As Hardy points out, however, attention paid to Kant's critique of religious beliefs as knowledge has obscured his claims about the legitimacy of justified religious beliefs. The fact that religious beliefs do not constitute knowledge is not a problem, as Kant sees things, for several reasons. If God were an object of scientific knowledge, God's transcendence of the natural world would be compromised. Second, the standards for scientific knowledge are not reasonable standards for common beliefs, especially common beliefs that have practical import.[39] As Kant himself says, *"It is absolutely necessary that one should convince oneself that God exists; that his existence should be demonstrated, however, is not so necessary."*[40] Most people are aware, of course, that Kant, having rejected the classical theoretical arguments for God's reality, himself gives a moral, practical argument to justify belief in God. However, as Hardy makes clear, Kant does not think reasonable belief in God is dependent on any arguments for most people.

---

[38] See Lee Hardy, "Kant's Reidianism: The Role of Common Sense in Kant's Epistemology of Religious Belief," forthcoming. Hardy speaks of "primary warrant" rather than "justification." However, I think "justification" is the proper term, since "warrant" is used by Reformed epistemologists to refer to a quality that converts true belief to knowledge, and Kant, as Hardy himself points out, regards religious convictions as justified beliefs but not as knowledge.

[39] For a passage in which Kant distinguishes between the kind of proof required for theoretical knowledge and the basis for belief that is necessary for practice, see *Critique of Pure Reason*, trans. Norman Kemp Smith (New York: St Martin's, 1965), A776, B804.

[40] Immanuel Kant, *The One Possible Basis for a Demonstration of the Existence of God*, trans. Gordon Treash (New York: Abaris, 1979).

Kant believes that the most important source of the disposition to belief in God is found in morality, and his views on that issue will be considered briefly in Chapter 5, in connection with my discussion of the experience of moral obligation as a natural sign for God. However, it is clear that morality is not the only legitimate basis for belief in God. Kant reviews what he calls the "universal human concerns" that form the basis for the religious insights of "the great multitude," a group Kant says is "always worthy of our respect."[41] Among those universal concerns, Kant lists "the splendid order, beauty, and providence shown forth everywhere in nature," which in turns leads to "faith in a wise and great author of the world."[42]

It is not surprising, then, that Kant should couple his later criticism of the "physico-theological argument" with praise for the role that design can play in producing reasonable belief.

It would therefore not only be uncomforting but utterly vain to attempt to diminish in any way the authority of this argument. Reason, constantly upheld by this ever-increasing evidence, which, though empirical, is yet so powerful, cannot be so depressed through doubts suggested by subtle and abstruse speculation, that it is not at once aroused from the indecision of all melancholy reflection, as from a dream, by one glance at the wonders of nature and the majesty of the universe—ascending from height to height up to the all-highest, from the conditioned to its conditions, up to the supreme and unconditioned Author [of all conditioned being].[43]

Kant's criticisms of the argument are ones that are directed at claims that through the argument one can achieve an "apodeictic certainty" that would demand "unconditional submission."[44] If we seek merely a "belief adequate to quieten our doubts," then the argument is one he has no objection to.[45]

One might wonder how Kant can object to the argument as a rigorous argument that leads to knowledge, while still commending it as a reasonable argument that leads to belief. The answer, I believe, is that the argument is an articulation of a natural disposition. The argument is not the basis for rational theology as a scholarly

---

[41] Kant, *Critique of Pure Reason*, B xxxii–xxxiii.
[42] Kant, *Critique of Pure Reason*, B xxxii–xxxiii.
[43] Kant, *Critique of Pure Reason*, A624, B652.
[44] Kant, *Critique of Pure Reason*, A624–5.
[45] Kant, *Critique of Pure Reason*, A625, B653.

discipline, but rests on considerations that do provide a basis for what we might call natural belief. Part of the problem with the argument from design is that, insofar as it is empirical in nature, it does not give us a determinate or precise concept of God, but merely leads to a concept of a very great being who is the cause of the design of the universe, not to the theologically precise and significant concept of a greatest possible being.[46] This claim of Kant's mirrors my own earlier contention that the informational output of beneficial order as a natural sign is indeed vague. However, this vagueness is not problematic if the true function of our experience of design is not to be the basis of theology as a scientific discipline, but rather to "prepare the understanding for theological knowledge, and to give it a natural leaning in this direction."[47]

As noted above, Kant believes the main ground for ordinary religious belief lies in our moral experience. The experience of beneficial order, while powerful, supplements the primary basis for belief in God in morality, which provides a rigorous argument for those in need of such a basis.[48] Nevertheless, the experience of beneficial order is one that is rooted in common human experience, and Kant finds the move from that experience to belief in an intelligent designer to be entirely natural. The argument, because it rests on this natural tendency, can lead us to "admiring the greatness, wisdom, power, etc., of the author of the world."[49] Such an outcome is insufficient for scientific theology, but it is quite adequate to support ordinary piety, especially a piety that is rooted primarily in morality. Kant objects to the teleological argument only when the inference it contains is understood as a theoretical argument that is an adequate basis for religious belief and practice. He is especially critical of such an argument when it is alleged to be a strict deductive proof that provides apodeictic knowledge. However, a natural sign makes no pretense to provide such a proof.

---

[46] Kant, *Critique of Pure Reason*, A637, B665.
[47] Kant, *Critique of Pure Reason*, A637, B665.
[48] For Lee Hardy's careful account of the circumstances in which belief in God might require an argument, see "Kant's Reidianism." See also Immanuel Kant, *Critique of Practical Reason*, trans. Lewis White Beck (Library of Liberal Arts 52; New York: Bobbs-Merrill, 1956), 128–36.
[49] Kant, *Critique of Pure Reason*, A629, B657.

It is true that Kant seems to modify some of these claims about design in some of his later writings.[50] For example, in the *Critique of Judgment* Kant gives a critical review of the value of teleological arguments, and he seems to target those that aim not just at "apodeictic certainty," but at any argument that aims to base religious belief on theoretical inferences.[51] Kant here criticizes philosophers who employ teleological arguments, and says it is a mistake to "mingle" such teleological arguments with moral arguments.[52] Kant's purpose here seems to be to stress the importance of his own moral argument, which links religion directly to practical reason. Teleology that is not connected to morality has only a "subjective basis in human reason" rather than a "determinative" basis that is sufficient to provide rational conviction.[53] Nevertheless, even though Kant here says the conviction secured by teleological arguments is an "illusion," he still holds that this illusion is one that is "wholesome in most cases" and that such a proof is "useful to the public."[54]

Despite Kant's criticisms of teleology as a basis for theology in his later writings, I think it is clear that these critical remarks do not undermine the claim that design functions as a natural sign. For even here Kant affirms that there is a natural tendency on the part of human reason (a "subjective basis") to conceive of the world as purposive, however unwilling he is to say that this disposition can ground a theoretically sound argument. Kant's main worry about teleological arguments seems to be that, although we have a natural disposition to see the world as purposive, we cannot scientifically rule out the possibility that the fundamental explanation for this is mechanistic. However, given the Easy Resistibility Principle, the proponent of design as a natural sign could agree with Kant about this. The possibility of a mechanistic explanation simply shows that the sign, like the other natural signs, is

[50] I must here express my appreciation to Karl Ameriks, who read this chapter and helpfully pointed out the relevance of some of Kant's later writings to this issue. An anonymous reader for Oxford University Press also made this point, which led me to revise the material that follows.

[51] See Immanuel Kant, *Critique of Judgment*, trans. Werner S. Pluhar (Indianapolis: Hackett Publishing Company, 1987 (German original published 1790)), particularly pp. 353–9.

[52] Kant, *Critique of Judgment*, 355.   [53] Kant, *Critique of Judgment*, 354–5.

[54] Kant, *Critique of Judgment*, 354–5.

resistible; the sign does not give us a compelling theoretical argument.

In any case, whatever second thoughts Kant may have had about his generous statements about the teleological argument in the *Critique of Pure Reason*, he seems, both in those earlier statements as well as in his later thoughts, to offer testimony that it is in some sense "natural" to view the natural world as purposive. Teleology conceived theoretically may be insufficient by itself to ground proper religious belief, and Kant's own epistemology does not seem to allow any significant role for natural signs for God, since for him God completely transcends the empirical world that is the object of knowledge. But the fact that Kant's overall epistemology pushes so strongly against the recognition of purposive order as a natural sign means that the testimony he offers for such a sign is all the more impressive; it is the testimony of an unfriendly witness, so to speak.

Hume

Despite the objections raised against the teleological argument discussed earlier in this chapter, David Hume offers clear testimony to the power of the experience of beneficial order. In Chapter 1 I looked briefly at Hume's expressions of this in the *Dialogues Concerning Natural Religion*. There Hume acknowledges (on the assumption that Philo here represents Hume's own views) that, despite all the problems with the argument from design, we find it natural to think of the world as the work of an intelligent designer. This is particularly true if we focus, not on the argument itself, but on what we might call our natural and spontaneous impulse to think in terms of a designer when we observe the natural world: "In many views of the universe and of its parts, particularly the latter, the beauty and fitness of final causes strike us with such irresistible force that objections appear (what I believe they really are) mere cavils and sophisms; nor can we then imagine how it was ever possible for us to repose any weight on them."[55]

One might at this point worry that these words, which really come from Hume's character Philo, do not accurately reflect Hume's own

---

[55] Hume, *Dialogues Concerning Natural Religion*, 66.

views. Many of Hume's contemporaries apparently believed he was
an atheist, and lots of later interpreters, both friends and foes, have
followed them in this view.[56] However, it is worth noting that Hume
defended himself against this charge, seeing himself as a latter-day
Socrates, who was convicted of impiety by his fellow citizens even
though he was in reality "the wisest and most religious of the Greek
philosophers."[57] To eliminate any worries that Hume may not share
Philo's sentiments here, I shall take a brief look at Hume's *Natural
History of Religion*.[58]

In this work, Hume actually defends the design argument against
some of the attacks made in the *Dialogues*. When judged by standard
rational canons, the belief in a God who is "infinitely superior
of mankind" is "altogether just," because it conforms to "sound
reason."[59] However, he affirms clearly that belief in God rests not on
any such argument, but on an innate disposition to form a belief in
an intelligent author of nature when humans experience the design in
the natural order. This disposition seems very similar to what Hume
calls in the *Enquiry* an "instinctual belief," a type of belief on which
he puts great stress, since it includes all the beliefs we form on the
basis of cause and effect.[60]

Hume not only claims that we have this propensity to form a
belief in God when we encounter design; he says that we have this
disposition because God has implanted it in us, thus affirming one of
the important conditions required for a natural sign: "The universal
propensity to believe in invisible, intelligent power, if not an original
instinct, being at least a general attendant of human nature, may be

[56] See Lee Hardy, "Hume's Defense of True Religion," forthcoming, for a good
summary of some of these interpreters. I rely heavily on this paper of Hardy's in this
concluding section of this chapter.
[57] See Hume's "Letter from a Gentleman to his Friend in Edinburgh," found in *An
Enquiry Concerning Human Understanding*, ed. Eric Steinberg (Indianapolis: Hackett,
1977), 117.
[58] David Hume, *Principal Writings on Religion: Including Dialogues Concerning
Natural Religion and The Natural History of Religion*, ed. J. C. A. Gaskin (Oxford
World's Classics; Oxford: Oxford University Press, 1998).
[59] Hume, *Principal Writings on Religion: Including Dialogues Concerning Natural
Religion and The Natural History of Religion*, 163, 165.
[60] See Hume, *An Enquiry Concerning Human Understanding*, 30, and also, for
causality, *A Treatise of Human Nature*, ed. L. A. Selby-Bigge (Oxford: Oxford
University Press, 1888), I. iii. 14 (pp. 170, 172).

considered as a kind of mark or stamp, which the divine workman has set upon his work."[61] Since instinctual beliefs such as this are more powerful than intellectual doubts raised against them, we can take seriously the claim of Philo, in the *Dialogues*, that he can explore his intellectual doubts about the design argument without worrying that he will undermine religious faith: "I am less cautious on the subject of natural religion than on any other; both because I know that I can never, on that head, corrupt the principles of any man of common sense, and because no one . . . in whose eyes I appear a man of common sense will ever mistake my intentions."[62] One may justly criticize the arguments presented by natural theologians, but those criticisms do not undermine genuine religious beliefs, since they do not really depend on such arguments: "No man, at least of common sense, I am persuaded, ever entertained a serious doubt with regard to a truth so certain and self-evident."[63]

It is true, as one of the above quotations implies, that Hume does not regard the disposition to form religious beliefs on the basis of our experience of design as a "primary principle of human nature." The reason for this is that the disposition can be overridden. Hume knows that there are in fact atheists. Also, Hume thinks that the output of this disposition is vague. It does not give us a clear picture of the nature of God nor of how we should relate to God. But these qualifications are fully consistent with my claim that beneficial order constitutes a natural sign for God's reality. Such a sign is a clue or pointer that is both widely accessible and resistible. It points us beyond the natural world to an intelligent designer. However, it leaves open the nature and character of that designer, a void that a revelation from God would aptly fill. A natural sign such as beneficial order naturally creates a hunger for more insight into the nature of God, a hunger that the sign itself cannot satisfy.

---

[61] Hume, *Principal Writings on Religion: Including Dialogues Concerning Natural Religion and The Natural History of Religion*, 184.

[62] Hume, *Dialogues Concerning Natural Religion*, 77.

[63] Hume, *Dialogues Concerning Natural Religion*, 13.

5

Moral Arguments and Natural Signs for God

There are probably even more types of moral arguments for God's existence than there are types of cosmological and teleological arguments. There are a variety of ways of classifying moral arguments. One important distinction is between moral arguments that are primarily theoretical in character, and those that are primarily practical. Theoretical moral arguments, like cosmological and teleological arguments, begin with some putative class of facts, such as the claim that humans are morally obligated to act in certain ways. The proponent of the argument tries to show that such facts require an explanation, and that God provides such an explanation. The claim might be that God provides the only possible explanation for the facts in question, or perhaps only that God provides a better or superior explanation for this type of fact than naturalistic rivals. The conclusion of the argument will be that God exists or probably exists.

Practical moral arguments have a different logical structure. The most famous proponent of such an argument was Immanuel Kant. Kant rejected all theoretical arguments for God's existence, as we have seen in earlier chapters, but he held nevertheless that a rational moral agent should believe in God. Kant claimed that a rational moral agent necessarily aims at "the highest good," and he argues that this good consists of a world in which people are both morally virtuous (they do their moral duty) and happy, with their happiness conditioned by their virtue. The highest good is an end that we are obliged to seek, but we must seek it only by following morality. We are not allowed to take any moral short cuts for the sake of happiness. However, in the actual world, it does not appear that doing one's moral duty necessarily makes for happiness, either for the agent or for others. Since we cannot give up our desire for happiness or fail to believe that happiness is a good worth seeking, and yet we can seek it only by moral actions, we must believe, even if it is contrary to all appearances, that the highest good, including happiness, is achievable by moral actions. This requires faith that moral actions will in the long run not turn out to be futile or ineffectual. For Kant this in turn requires faith in providence, a belief that the causal processes that hold in the world are such that moral actions can be effective. Nature is not a blind mechanical system that is indifferent to moral concerns, but must itself be the work of a Moral Being who makes the universe to be a place where moral actions are not absurd.

For Kant "ought" implies "can." What I ought to do must be possible for me to do. I ought to seek to achieve the highest good, but I cannot believe that I can make progress toward such an end unless the causal processes of the natural world are such that moral actions can be effective. This "moral faith" then requires religious faith. The conclusion of the argument is not "Probably God exists" but something like this: "As a rational agent, I ought to believe that God exists."

Some philosophers object to practical arguments such as Kant's on the grounds that such arguments are not aimed at truth but rather try to show that some beliefs should be held because of prudential considerations. The philosophers in question object that we ought to believe only what we have reason to think is true, and the fact that an end that I ought to seek, such as the highest good, cannot be achieved if there is no God is not a reason to think there is a God. I believe that such objections to practical arguments can be met, but I shall not try to do so here.[1] For I think that in most cases it is not difficult to convert such practical arguments into theoretical arguments or at least extract a theoretical argument from them. Kant's argument, for example, can be viewed as implicitly claiming that it would be odd and even inexplicable that there should be moral agents in a universe that is completely indifferent to moral ends. The postulation of God can be seen as a way of lessening this oddity, helping to explain or make

---

[1] See the chapter on Kant in my C. Stephen Evans, *Subjectivity and Religious Belief: An Historical, Critical Study* (Grand Rapids, MI: Christian University Press, 1978), 15–73.

sense of the presence of moral agents in such a world. Hence, I shall in this chapter focus on theoretical arguments, since the natural signs that are my ultimate subject seem to be things that can function as evidence, and evidence provides the basis for a theoretical argument.

Moral arguments for God's existence were quite prominent in philosophy in the nineteenth and early twentieth centuries, being defended by such thinkers as Cardinal Newman, Hastings Rashdall, W. R. Sorley, and somewhat more recently by A. E. Taylor, Austin Farrer, and H. P. Owen. The most well-known use of the argument is found in C. S. Lewis's amazingly popular *Mere Christianity*, a collection of BBC radio talks delivered during the Second World War, which in book form has sold millions of copies worldwide. However, the recent philosophical literature on this type of argument is relatively sparse in comparison with that dealing with the other arguments we have discussed. I will try to say something about why this has been the case in due course, but the influence of Lewis's popular treatment of the argument shows that the argument has continued to be plausible to lay people, regardless of the views of professional philosophers.

The popularity of the argument among ordinary people is easy to understand, since the germ of the argument can be grasped even by a child, and the experience that gives rise to the argument is one that virtually everyone has had. The essence of the argument is expressed vividly by Ivan Karamazov in Dostoevsky's novel *The Brothers Karamazov*: "Without God everything is permitted." Most people are convinced that not everything is permitted. Some acts are morally wrong and are forbidden; other acts are obligatory. Ivan seems to hold that, if there were no God, then such moral obligations would not exist. If one holds that moral obligations do exist, then it is clear that there must be a God, understood as the being responsible for the existence of such obligations.

It will be helpful to put the argument into explicit form, so that different premises can be discussed separately:

1. If there are objectively binding moral obligations, then God exists.
2. There are objectively binding moral obligations.
3. (Probably) God exists.

(1) is, of course, equivalent to the Dostoevskean-type claim that, unless God exists, there will be no objectively binding moral obligations.

By "objectively binding moral obligations" I mean duties that hold independently of the beliefs or desires of the agent. For simplicity I will focus on obligations to perform or refrain from performing various actions, though in principle there could well be obligations to seek to develop or inhibit various character traits, so that a person might have a duty to become more loving or compassionate, or to become less cruel or miserly. Since the argument is obviously logically valid, those who reject it must deny or question one or both of the two premises. I shall proceed to consider each premise in turn. My ultimate purpose is not to defend a moral argument, but to discover any natural signs for God that are embedded in such arguments. However, I believe that important clues to such signs will become clearer if we describe the strengths and weaknesses of the arguments.

Are There Objectively Binding Moral Obligations?

If we define a "proof" as a valid argument with undeniable premises, it is clear that this moral argument fails as a proof, for it is certainly possible to doubt the existence of objectively binding moral obligations. Friedrich Nietzsche provides a pre-eminent example of someone who rejects premise 2. (Although, as we shall see, Nietzsche offers some support for premise 1.) Nietzsche offers us a "genealogy of morals" in which he gives an explanation of how humans came to believe in moral obligations, even though *"there are no moral facts whatever."*[2] For Nietzsche, belief in moral obligations arose from the social relation of creditor to debtor. Those who live in community are indebted to the community for the advantages it brings.[3] This indebtedness developed into an indebtedness to the ancestors (real or mythical) who are thought to have provided the foundations of the community. As Nietzsche tells the tale, these ancestors are magnified to astounding proportions, and in the end some ancestor

---

[2] Friedrich Nietzsche, *Twilight of the Idols*, in *Twilight of the Idols* and *The Anti-Christ*, trans. R. J. Hollingdale, intro. Michael Tanner (Penguin Classics; London: Penguin Books, 1990), 66; emphasis in original.
[3] Friedrich Nietzsche, *On the Genealogy of Morals*, trans. Walter Kaufmann and R. J. Hollingdale (New York: Vintage, 1967), 71.

"must necessarily be transfigured into a *god*."[4] The debt owed to the community becomes the debt owed to god, and the god's will then becomes the source of obligations. When the god becomes the monotheistic God of Christianity and Judaism, those obligations take on the overriding, serious character that characterize what we call "morality."

For Nietzsche, then, what is called "morality" (at least in Western cultures) is dependent on belief in the Judeo-Christian God. He is scathing in his comments on secular moralists who believe that they can hold on to moral obligations without religious foundations, as in this observation, in which Nietzsche probably has utilitarianism in view:

In England, in response to every little emancipation from theology one has to reassert one's position in a fear-inspiring manner as a moral fanatic. That is the *penance* one pays there.—With us it is different. When one gives up Christian belief one thereby deprives oneself of the *right* to Christian morality. For the latter is absolutely *not* self-evident: one must make this point clear again and again, in spite of English shallowpates.[5]

Kant comes in for similar criticism for his attempt to show that moral obligations could be grounded in autonomous reason. He says that "Kant's success is merely a theologian's success."[6] The categorical imperative is the invention of someone "who feel[s] that [he] needs the strongest words and sounds, the most eloquent gestures and postures, in order to be effective *at all*."[7] It is clear that Nietzsche's account of the origin of our belief in moral obligations provides some support for the first premise of the moral argument presented earlier, for Nietzsche holds that the moral beliefs, not merely of Christians, but even of Kantians, utilitarians, and Marxists, depend on belief in God, even if the moralist in question does not recognize

---

[4] Nietzsche, *Genealogy*, 89 (emphasis in original).
[5] Nietzsche, *Twilight of the Idols*, 80 (emphasis in original). By "the latter" Nietzsche here means to refer to the claim that Christian belief is the basis of Western morality, as some other translations make clear.
[6] Nietzsche, *The Anti-Christ*, 133.
[7] Friedrich Nietzsche, *The Gay Science: With a Prelude in German Rhymes and an Appendix of Songs*, ed. Bernard Williams, trans. Josefine Nauckhoff, poems translated by Adrian Del Caro (Cambridge Texts in the History of Philosophy; Cambridge: Cambridge University Press, 2001), 32–3.

this.[8] However, for Nietzsche the claim that there are objective moral obligations is just false, the product of "a shameful act of historical falsification."[9]

Nietzsche's particular explanation of how beliefs in moral obligations came into being might be questioned and yet his conviction that these beliefs are in error still accepted. This is roughly the view of J. L. Mackie, for example, who defends what he calls an "error theory" of morality.[10] On his view, the correct philosophical analysis of our moral beliefs shows that they commit us to moral facts that are both objective and also motivating. Even though this view of morality has, Mackie says, "a firm basis in ordinary thought and even in the meanings of moral terms," that does not show that the moral entities (such as obligations) the beliefs commit us to really exist.[11] Such entities, according to Mackie, would be "queer" kinds of things, like nothing that science discovers, and so he concludes that moral beliefs are simply false. There are no moral facts, and thus no real moral obligations.

The examples of Nietzsche and Mackie—and many others could be given—therefore show that it is possible to doubt the truth of premise (2) of the moral argument. The critic might boldly affirm that there are no objective moral obligations, as Nietzsche and Mackie do, or be content with the more modest claim that we cannot be sure that there are such things. However, the fact that this second premise seems doubtful to some does strongly suggest that this argument fails as a conclusive proof of God's existence. Of course very few, if any, philosophical arguments measure up to such a high standard, and so the fact that this moral argument is not a conclusive proof of its conclusion does not show that it is not a valuable argument that might offer rational support for its conclusion to many people.

The defender of the argument might well point to the high cost of rejecting the second premise. For frequently, as C. S. Lewis astutely observed, the same people who reject objective moral obligations as "illusion" will in the next moment be found "exhorting us to work for posterity, to educate, revolutionise, liquidate, live and die for

[8] Nietzsche, *Gay Science*, 199.   [9] Nietzsche, *The Anti-Christ*, 149.

[10] J. L. Mackie, *Ethics: Inventing Right and Wrong* (London: Penguin Books, 1990).

[11] Mackie, *Ethics*, 32.

the good of the human race."[12] It is hard not to take at least some moral ideals as objectively binding, giving us guidance as to what we ought to do, regardless of how we think or feel about this. Our moral experience often suggests to us (at least to those of us who are not sociopaths) that some acts are really wrong and others are really right. Such experience is far from a proof, but perhaps it does show that, even if the claim that there are objective obligations can be doubted, it is a reasonable belief. Perhaps it is for this reason that many of Nietzsche's and Mackie's atheistic compatriots want to hang on to premise (2) and instead question premise (1) of the moral argument. Contemporary secular utilitarians and Kantians, for example, think that moral obligations are indeed objectively binding, but they deny that such obligations depend on God.

DO OBJECTIVELY BINDING MORAL OBLIGATIONS REQUIRE GOD AS THEIR FOUNDATION?

How might critics of the argument cast doubt on premise (1)? And how might defenders of the argument support the premise? Critics can, I think, cast doubt on the claim that moral obligations require God as their foundation in two ways. First, they might maintain that moral obligations require no foundation at all; true propositions stating that moral obligations hold state brute facts that cannot be explained but that also require no explanation. Second, they might concede that moral obligations require some ground that would explain them, but maintain that something other than God can provide such a ground. Defenders of the argument then face a complex task if they wish to defend premise (1). They must defend the claim that moral obligations require some kind of explanation, and they also need to argue that the proposed non-theistic explanations are inadequate. Since there are a variety of different proposed non-theistic explanations, the second part of the task turns out to be complex in its own right. Besides all this, the defender of the argument needs to explain just how God provides an explanation for the obligations; the defender

---

[12] C. S. Lewis, *Miracles* (San Francisco: HarperOne, 2001), 57.

must offer some positive story about the relation between God and moral obligations that illuminates how God makes moral obligations possible.

Perhaps the position of the critic of the argument who claims that moral obligations are brute facts is the most difficult to attack. Virtually no one denies that some facts are ultimate facts and therefore are themselves inexplicable or "brute" facts. Theists, for example, typically hold that the universe itself is not a brute fact; it is to be explained as the creation of God. God's existence, however, is not to be explained by anything else. Given that there are bound to be some brute facts, why should not moral facts be among these? Given the possibility that moral facts might be brute in this way, it is difficult to see how to demonstrate that someone who simply insists that facts about moral obligations are ultimate and inexplicable is wrong. Erik Wielenberg has recently made such a claim about morality; it is just a brute fact about the universe that some kinds of actions are morally right and others are morally wrong.[13] The possibility of such a position once again shows that the moral argument is not a conclusive proof.

However, even if it is not possible to prove that moral obligations require an explanation, there are certainly considerations that suggest that they do, particularly if we take certain views of the world. George Mavrodes, for example, has argued that moral facts about obligations would be very surprising, indeed downright odd or "queer," if we believed that the universe we live in was a "Russellian universe," a universe that has the qualities Bertrand Russell believed the universe had.[14] Russell himself gave a memorable statement of what such a universe would be like that Mavrodes quotes at some length:

That man is the product of causes that had no prevision of the end they were achieving; that his origin, his growth, his hopes and fears, his loves and his beliefs are but the outcome of accidental collocations of atoms; that no fire, no heroism, no intensity of thought and feeling, can preserve an individual

[13] See Erik Wielenberg, "In Defense of Non-Natural, Non-Theistic Moral Realism," *Faith and Philosophy*, 26/1 (2009), 23–41.

[14] George I. Mavrodes, "Religion and the Queerness of Morality," in Robert Audi and William J. Wainwright (eds.), *Rationality, Religious Belief, and Moral Commitment: New Essays in the Philosophy of Religion* (Ithaca, NY: Cornell University Press, 1986), 213–26.

life beyond the grave; that all the labors of the ages, all the devotion, all the inspiration, all the noonday brightness of human genius, are destined to extinction in the vast death of the solar system, and that the whole temple of man's achievements must inevitably be buried beneath the debris of a universe in ruins—all these things, if not quite beyond dispute, are yet so nearly certain that no philosophy which rejects them can hope to stand. Only within the scaffolding of these truths, only on the firm foundation of unyielding despair, can the soul's habitation henceforth be safely built.[15]

Mavrodes goes on to argue that in a Russellian universe moral obligations would be very odd, and would seem to call out for some kind of explanation. Near the end of his essay, however, Mavrodes considers a position similar to Wielenberg's, one that simply considers it to be "an ultimate fact about the universe that kindness is good and cruelty is bad."[16]

Mavrodes admits, as I have done above, that such a view is not easily refuted: "Since it involves no argument, there is no argument to be refuted. And I have already said that, so far as I can see, its central contention is not self-contradictory."[17] However, Mavrodes points out that a world in which such facts are "brute facts" does not seem very much like a Russellian world. One would think that, in a Russellian world, basically a naturalistic world in which everything reduces to the basic particles of physics, moral facts would not be "deep." Rather, a world in which there are ultimate moral facts seems more like Plato's view of the world than Russell's. And the world as seen by Platonists, though perhaps not necessarily theistic, has usually seemed to be "congenial (especially congenial when compared to some other philosophical views) to a religious understanding of the world." In the Platonic view of reality, whatever moral obligations humans face reflect the basic character of reality itself, and that in turn suggests that the ultimate truth about that universe is not that it is simply "accidental collocations of atoms."[18]

---

[15] From Bertrand Russell, "A Free Man's Worship," in *Mysticism and Logic: And Other Essays* (New York: Barnes and Noble, 1917), 47–8. Quotation in Mavrodes, "Religion and the Queerness of Morality," 215.

[16] Mavrodes, "Religion and the Queerness of Morality," 224.

[17] Mavrodes, "Religion and the Queerness of Morality," 224.

[18] Mavrodes, "Religion and the Queerness of Morality," 224.

Probably it is for this reason that many philosophers who are committed to a naturalistic understanding of morality have not been content with the claim that facts of moral obligations are simply ultimate, brute facts, but have rather tried to give an explanation for those facts. The need for such an explanation can be seen from the fact that philosophers such as Mackie, who are committed to naturalism but do not believe that any such explanation can be given, simply give up believing in any objective moral obligations, and accept an error theory. Alternatively, such philosophers might follow Gilbert Harman and adopt a "relativistic" account of moral obligations.[19] On Harman's account, "absolute" moral values, which would include objectively binding moral obligations, must be rejected because we cannot find a "location" for them in the world as explained by science.[20] Since we cannot explain such moral obligations naturalistically, Harman rejects them altogether, and instead gives an account of moral obligations as grounded in the interests and agreements of concrete individuals. Such obligations are thus not objectively binding. Objective moral obligations, in a naturalistic world, would be surprising, and therefore would be the kind of thing one would expect to be explained.

NATURALISTIC EXPLANATIONS OF MORAL OBLIGATIONS

What alternatives are there for a naturalistic explanation of moral obligations? There are, I believe, at least three possibilities. One is to attempt to show how moral obligations that are binding on humans can be explained by facts about human biology and psychology. I shall call such accounts "naturalistic reductive accounts" of moral obligations. A second strategy is to attempt to show how moral obligations can be explained as the result of a social agreement

[19] See Gilbert Harman, "What is Moral Relativism," in *Explaining Value and Other Essays in Moral Philosophy* (Oxford: Oxford University Press, 2000). I discuss Harman below in looking at views of morality as grounded in social agreements.
[20] Gilbert Harman, "Is There a Single True Morality," in *Explaining Value and Other Essays in Moral Philosophy*, 83.

or contract among human persons. The third is the Kantian-type strategy of attempting to see moral obligations as a kind of demand that humans, as rational beings, make on themselves. I will briefly look at each of these options.

Naturalistic Reductive Accounts of Obligations

One strategy that naturalists often follow to explain moral obligations is to ground them in the value we ascribe to the states of affairs that are the consequences of our actions. If one can identify some natural quality (pleasure or some other experience, for example) as "good" and others as "bad," and if we assume a general "obligation" to maximize good outcomes and minimize bad ones (perhaps on the grounds that it is simply obvious that one ought to seek what is good and avoid what is bad), then it looks as if one might explain obligations as grounded in natural facts. Classical utilitarianism in its various forms, represented by such thinkers as Jeremy Bentham and John Stuart Mill, would be a good illustration of such a strategy.

Contemporary thinkers have developed such a strategy in quite sophisticated ways. Richard Boyd, for example, follows utilitarianism in seeing moral obligations as grounded in the consequences of our actions, but he rejects the idea that the goodness of the outcomes can be measured by some simple property such as pleasure. Instead, Boyd says that the good should be identified with a complex cluster of properties, and he says we ought to rely on scientific inquiry to determine which types of actions are in fact productive of goodness.[21]

Another alternative is to attempt to derive an account of the good from contemporary evolutionary biology that can ground moral obligations. Larry Arnhart attempts this in his book *Darwinian Natural Right: The Biological Ethics of Human Nature*.[22] Arnhart believes that contemporary biology gives us a basis for determining what human desires are "natural" in the sense of being part of human

[21] Richard Boyd, "How to Be a Moral Realist," in Geoffrey Sayre-McCord (ed.), *Essays on Moral Realism* (Ithaca, NY: Cornell University Press, 1988), 181–228, esp. 196–9.
[22] Larry Arnhart, *Darwinian Natural Right: The Biological Ethics of Human Nature* (SUNY Series in Philosophy and Biology; Albany, NY: State University of New York Press, 1998).

nature; such desires are those that we are "hard-wired" to have and cannot be altered without altering our biological nature. Arnhart grants that not everything that humans desire is in fact desirable, but he argues that natural desires that are rooted in our nature must be regarded as desirable by creatures such as ourselves, and thus as good. He goes on to identify at least twenty such desires, and on that basis thinks that we have a guide to what kinds of actions are "right" (conducive to satisfying these natural desires) and those that are not.[23]

There are a host of difficulties that arise in connection with this kind of naturalistic account of moral obligations. First, as G. E. Moore famously argued, the identification of the good with any particular natural property or cluster of properties can always be challenged.[24] Just because human beings (or some human beings) desire some outcome, it does not follow that the outcome is in fact desirable. Arnhart, for example, says that one of our "natural" desires is a desire to dominate and control others.[25] Biologically, Arnhart may be on solid grounds in claiming that this is a pervasive human trait, but it seems highly dubious to infer from this biological fact that domination and control of others is good.

However, a second grave problem is that, even if we concede that we can recognize certain outcomes as good, it is by no means obvious that facts about moral obligations can be derived from facts about what is good. Suppose it is the case that there is someone in my city who desperately needs a kidney to survive. Let us assume that I have two good kidneys, could donate one without significant risk to my health, and that my kidney would be a good match for the one who is in need. In such a situation, if I donate the kidney, the result would seem to be a very good one. And there is no doubt that such a decision on my part would be a morally good thing to do. Few people, however, would argue that, in such a situation, I would have a moral *obligation* to donate the kidney. It looks as if to generate a moral obligation to donate the kidney, we need something more than the goodness of the outcome of the act.

[23] Arnhart, *Darwinian Natural Right*, 17.
[24] See G. E. Moore, *Ethics* (Home University Library of Modern Knowledge 52; New York: Holt, 1912).
[25] Arnhart, *Darwinian Natural Right*, 29–36.

However, the problem is not merely that the goodness of an outcome is not sufficient to generate a moral obligation. Rather, it seems that, in some possible cases, the acts that would bring about the best results are positively immoral and we have an obligation not to do them. Suppose, for example, that a law enforcement officer can prevent a race riot in which hundreds of people would be killed only by surrendering one innocent person to a vigilante mob. Even if a better result would be obtained by such an action, it is anything but clear that the law enforcement officer has an obligation to give up the innocent person. It seems more plausible to say that the officer has an obligation not to do this. Such problems with consequentialist ethics are well known, of course, and consequentialists have attempted to respond in various ways, but the problems still seem daunting to many.

However, even if this kind of problem could be solved, there is one more serious problem that faces any attempt to base moral obligations on a naturalistic account of good. Even the utilitarian or consequentialist typically agrees that one important dimension of moral obligations is a requirement of impartiality. Moral obligations are not simply obligations to produce good results. Morally, we must ask not merely whether the results of our actions are good, but also for whom they are good. Utilitarians and other consequentialists in ethical theory usually insist that our moral duties are to do not simply what benefits ourselves, or even what benefits our family and friends, but what benefits others as well. Indeed, they often insist on a strict impartiality, in which I am morally obligated to consider the needs and desires of other persons, and even sentient animals generally, equally with the needs and desires of myself.

It is to the credit of these moral theories that they acknowledge that at least some of our moral obligations do require us to care about others in this way. The question is how this obligation to be impartial can be explained. It certainly cannot be argued that such impartiality is "natural" in the sense of being the way most people behave most of the time. Consequentialists themselves concede that taking such an impartial moral stance is a difficult achievement that perhaps few people realize in any substantial way. Most of us care more about ourselves, our friends, and our families than we do for others. Many humans, regrettably, seem not to care at all about other persons who are of a different race or religion or sexual orientation (not to mention caring about non-human animals). The naturalistic consequentialist may say at this point that such an impartial stance is simply the viewpoint of a rational person who is looking at things dispassionately. Such a person is taking "the moral point of view."[26] But why should we take such a point of view? What is it that generates our duty to do so?

We can agree that this view of how the good should be sought is how things would look to an impartial "ideal observer." However, we humans are not such ideal observers. The question then remains as to *why* a person ought to take such an impartial "moral point of view." Why should I care how a (fictitious) ideal observer would view my behavior? It might, of course, make a difference if the ideal observer were an actual person (God?) whose evaluation mattered to me. But it is not obvious why I should care about the views of an ideal observer if there is no such person. Perhaps it is true that a person who looks on the world from a moral standpoint will look at things in such an impartial way. But it seems all too obvious that this is not the only way humans can look at things, and difficult to see what answer the naturalist can give to the question as to why human persons *should* adopt such a moral standpoint. One of the most basic features of moral obligations then seems not to be explained by the view that our duties are simply to maximize good consequences.

We could, of course, attempt to explain moral behavior in various ways by looking for the natural causes of such behavior. Various attempts have been made to show that altruistic, impartial behavior is somehow grounded in our nature, as understood by evolutionary biology. For example, some have theorized that altruistic behavior has a genetic basis.[27] However, even if these theories succeed in explaining why humans sometimes behave in moral ways, it is completely mysterious as to how such facts could explain the existence of genuine moral *obligations*. For, whatever an obligation may be, it is not simply a tendency to behave in some particular way, and no

---

[26] Kurt Baier, *The Moral Point of View: A Rational Basis of Ethics* (Contemporary Philosophy; Ithaca, NY: Cornell University Press, 1958).

[27] Frans de Waal, *Good Natured: The Origins of Right and Wrong in Humans and Other Animals* (Cambridge, MA: Harvard University Press, 1996), 135–6.

biological explanation of why humans might care about other humans seems capable of explaining why they *should* care about them.

Social Contract Theories

Those who think it is difficult or even impossible to explain moral obligations as stemming from natural facts about human desires may be attracted by a different strategy: perhaps we can explain moral obligations as the result of an agreement or contract that human persons have made with each other. Moral obligations, while not reducible to biology or other natural facts, are things humans have constructed, and no appeal to God is necessary to explain them.

If one asks why humans should make such an agreement, the best answer seems to be that it is in our self-interest to do so. Human persons who lived in what we might call a moral "state of nature" in which there are no moral obligations would find their situation to be undesirable in many ways. Thomas Hobbes famously described a political state of nature as one in which humans are at "war" with each other, and in which life is "solitary, poor, nasty, brutish and short."[28] In a similar way, in a moral state of nature, humans would be free to pursue their own individual desires at the expense of others, but in such a society the goods that cooperative action makes possible would be severely imperiled. It is true that our moral duties often forbid us to do what is to our advantage, but the defender of the social-agreement view of morality argues that, in the long run and on the whole, the "acceptance of duty is truly advantageous."[29]

The social agreement that is the ground of morality on this view is one in which people agree to accept certain constraints on their behavior so long as others agree to those same constraints. I will not lie to you or steal from you or break my promises to you, on the condition that you do not lie to me, steal from me, or break your promises to me. It is important to note that the agreement is reciprocal and conditional on what others do. For it would not be rational to give up my rights to privilege my own well-being if other

---

[28] Thomas Hobbes, *Leviathan*, ed. Richard Tuck (Cambridge Texts in the History of Political Thought; Cambridge: Cambridge University Press, 1996), 89.
[29] David Gauthier, *Morals by Agreement* (Oxford: Oxford University Press, 1986), 2.

people continue to privilege their own well-being and refuse to take my well-being into account. David Gauthier, who defends this kind of account of morality, says that the person who promises to keep the agreement should not be a "dupe." Instead, such a person should comply with the agreement only if others do so as well. In that way "she ensures that those not disposed to fair co-operation do not enjoy the benefits of any co-operation, thus making this unfairness costly to themselves, and so irrational."[30]

The social-agreement explanation of moral obligations has a degree of plausibility, for we do recognize that it is often the case that morality "pays off." Even a dishonest shopkeeper may be deterred from cheating customers by the worry that the dishonesty might be recognized and could cost the shopkeeper business. However, there are basic problems with the social-agreement view as an account of morality. Some have to do with whether such an account can adequately explain all of the actual obligations we have, and I will discuss these a little later. However, some basic problems have to do with the nature of the agreement itself.

Let us first examine the nature of the agreement. Is the social agreement supposed to be an actual agreement people have made, or is it merely a hypothetical agreement, one that people would accept if, finding themselves in the right circumstances, they had the opportunity to do so? Either option presents problems.

Let us first consider the agreement as an actual agreement individuals have entered into. One might object by asking when the agreement is supposed to have been entered into, and how it was created. Someone might wonder if he or she was not informed about the meeting! However, perhaps this problem can be solved by noting that agreements can be tacit and implied; perhaps no explicit agreement is necessary. There are more serious problems. First, has everyone in fact made a commitment to such an agreement? What about the person who is a hit man for the Mafia, or the individual who is a racist and believes he can behave as he wishes towards members of some other race? Second, if the moral rules that govern our lives together rest on actual agreements, why should we think that there is only one such agreement? Surely different communities can and

30 Gauthier, *Morals by Agreement*, 179.

will opt for different rules. If the rules are to be such that everyone in the community will accept them, then they most likely will reflect the differences in resources and status and power that different individuals have. Those who are rich might well agree with a rule that no one should steal from others, but reject a rule that those who are well off should offer assistance to those who are disadvantaged.[31] If different groups of people agree on different sets of moral rules, it looks as if moral obligations will not really be objective, but relative to the communities that have made the agreements.

Furthermore, it is not clear why the agreement should be viewed as one that is binding in the way moral obligations are supposed to be binding. After all, most agreements that people enter into are not open-ended, but valid for a particular period of time, and many agreements have provisions that allow individuals to "opt out" if they choose to do so. It is hard to see why it would not be reasonable for individuals to choose to opt out of any agreement to live by the rules of morality in cases where following those rules might seriously disadvantage them. And there seems little reason to doubt that there are times when a person's doing what is moral does disadvantage that person, at least when judging advantages by the criteria appropriate to a naturalistic world view, which would presumably include achieving such things as wealth, health, and reputation. (Someone wishing to defend the claim that morality can be naturalistically explained could hardly appeal to something like the advantage that God approves of one's conduct in order to show that moral actions are really advantageous after all.) However, one of the features of moral obligations that most requires explanation is the fact that they are objectively binding; they are applicable to everyone and at all times. Moral rules that hold because of an agreement that I can opt out of would lack just this feature.

Another set of problems pertains to the scope of any actual agreement that might be made. Since the motivation for the agreement

---

[31] Gilbert Harman argues that the principles of morality are relative in just this way, and thinks that this is due to the fact that they are grounded in actual agreements humans have made, agreements that reflect the different bargaining positions different people bring to the table, so to speak. See Gilbert Harman and Judith Jarvis Thomson, *Moral Relativism and Moral Objectivity* (Great Debates in Philosophy; Cambridge, MA: Blackwell, 1996), 23.

is self-interest, it looks as if it is reasonable to make such an agreement only with those who might benefit me, or at least not harm me, as a result of the agreement. However, there are surely many persons, perhaps those with mental or physical challenges or those who live in desperately poor countries, who cannot realistically be expected to benefit me in any way, nor pose any kind of threat to me. It would seem logical then to see such people as outside the scope of any such social agreement. However, those who believe in the reality of objective moral obligations usually believe that we have obligations toward those who are ill or severely handicapped, and even that our obligations toward such people are especially important ones. Furthermore, though there may be honest differences over what exactly those who reside in prosperous countries might owe those in very poor countries, it surely must be true that those who reside in poorer countries should at least be subjects of moral concern for those with financial resources. It is hard to see how any such obligations could be the result of an actual agreement motivated by self-interest.

Perhaps we should then consider the other possibility, in which the agreement is seen not as an actual agreement but as a hypothetical agreement, one that individuals would accept if certain conditions were satisfied. For example, one might claim that the rules of morality are the rules that people would accept if they were ignorant of their status in society. Suppose that I were going to choose the moral rules for humans to live by, and that I do not yet know what my situation in life will be. I do not know whether I will be male or female, rich or poor, what area of the world I will live in, and so on. In that case, it might be argued, the rules I would accept would be more likely to be fair and impartial to all, since it would be risky to favor rules that might be to the disadvantage of some group that might include me.

It does seem plausible that such a hypothetical agreement would be more likely to include rules that are fair and impartial than would be the case for an actual agreement. However, different problems emerge at this point. Most fundamentally, it is difficult to see how *actual* obligations could be grounded in an agreement that is only hypothetical, an agreement that I would make (or would be rational to make) if certain conditions were the case, even though those conditions do not in fact hold. To see this, consider the following scenario. It might be true that, if I were to go and hear my local symphony play, and afterwards hear an appeal for funds to make it possible for the symphony to continue, I would promise to make a substantial contribution. And, if I were to make such a promise, it seems reasonable to think I would be obligated to make the contribution. However, it is hard to see how the hypothetical fact (assuming it is a fact) that I would make such a promise in a certain situation (one that does not hold) obligates me to make a contribution. It might be good for me to make such a contribution, but it surely is not something I have a duty to do. Nor is a duty created merely by a hypothetical fact about a promise that I would make in a certain situation, when no such agreement has been made, and the actual situation is quite different.

In a similar way, perhaps there are rules that all humans would agree to live by if they were to meet under a "veil of ignorance" (as in John Rawls's famous proposal), not knowing what positions they would have in life.[32] But it is difficult to see how the fact that those humans would make such an agreement creates obligations for us as actual persons. For we are not those fictitious persons.

Both actual agreements and hypothetical agreements face some other formidable difficulties. One stems from the fact that the agreement is a conditional one, in which the individual promises to live by certain rules *if* others do so as well. The problem is that we have good empirical reasons to think that others will not always do this. Take the example of academic cheating. Let us suppose that a community where cheating does not occur is in many ways better off than a society in which there is rampant cheating. Even though an individual might be tempted to cheat to secure some good (a better job, admission to a school, and so on), one might argue that it would be reasonable for a person to agree to refrain from cheating if others will do so as well, because, if cheating is widespread, there will be many undesirable consequences. The problem is that, in the actual world, cheating is in fact very widespread. Hence, even if a person promised (or would be willing to promise) not to cheat *if* others also agreed, no obligation not to cheat would result. If I know that others will in fact cheat, then the condition for my agreement to the rule has vanished. If I do not want to be a "dupe," I may reason that,

---

[32] John Rawls, *A Theory of Justice* (Cambridge, MA: Belknap Press, 2005), 136–42.

since others are cheating, not to do so would be to place myself at a disadvantage.

Another difficulty is the problem posed by "free-riders" and "parasites." From the perspective of self-interest, it might well make the most sense for an individual to agree to live by the rules of morality, if others do the same, but nevertheless selectively break those rules. One might object that, if I break the rules, I will be punished by others, and this is possible. However, there clearly are going to be some cases where a violation of moral rules will be undetectable and in those cases no punishment will happen. Hence, it appears that the best strategy for an individual would be to agree to the rules of morality, and to keep them in all cases where there is some likelihood that violations would be detected, but to deviate from those rules in cases where this cannot be detected and some significant advantage can be secured. In this way an individual will have the best of both worlds: a reputation for being morally good while enjoying the possibility of acting immorally in some cases where this would be advantageous.

Self-Legislation Theories

The final option I will consider for explanations of moral obligations is to see them as self-imposed. This is, famously, the kind of view developed by Immanuel Kant, who saw moral obligations as laws that we humans autonomously legislate for ourselves. On such a view we are both authors of the moral law as well as the subjects of that law. Kant is often interpreted by contemporary philosophers as developing an account of morality in this way that makes God unnecessary for morality, and this is the kind of view that I want to consider in this section.

However, it is worth noting that the historical Kant may not have held such a view, since he thought that belief in moral obligation was linked to belief in God in a number of ways. First of all, as I noted at the beginning of this chapter, Kant famously argued that a commitment to morality required an individual to believe in God as what he called a "postulate of practical reason."[33] Perhaps even more

---

[33] Immanuel Kant, *Critique of Practical Reason*, trans. Lewis White Beck (Library of Liberal Arts 52; New York: Bobbs-Merrill, 1956), 128–36.

significantly, Kant did not think that humans create or invent the moral law by their legislation. Rather, what they do is add something like their own reflective endorsement to a principle that is in some sense objective. One way of seeing this is that Kant held that to be a moral being is to be a member of what he called the "Kingdom of Ends," and he also taught that God was the "head" of this kingdom.[34] As head of the Kingdom of Ends, God is also in a profound sense the author of the moral law. So, despite holding that the moral law was a principle that reason autonomously endorsed, Kant also held that it was proper and correct to see the moral law as a divine command.[35]

When Kant's notion of self-legislation is interpreted in a secular way that sees no significant role for God in the Kingdom of Ends, at least two types of difficulties emerge. One type of issue concerns the character of the moral law as self-commanded, and the other concerns the content of the moral law. I shall briefly look at each type of problem.

The first type of difficulty is memorably described by Kierkegaard:

Kant was of the opinion that man is his own law (autonomous)—that is, he binds himself under the law which he himself gives himself. Actually, in a profounder sense, this is how lawlessness or experimentation are established. This is not being rigorously earnest any more than Sancho Panza's self-administered blows to his own bottom were vigorous.[36]

Kierkegaard's thought here is clearly that a law, especially a moral law, must be able to bind us if it is to be a genuine law. However, a self-given law lacks this binding force, since, if the self has the power to enact the law, it must also have the power to rescind it, and will probably be tempted to do just that when morality goes against what a person wants to do. Kierkegaard's intuition here is shared by Elizabeth Anscombe, who argued, in a well-known article, that "the concept of legislation requires superior power in the legislature." Anscombe claims that the idea of "legislating for oneself" is like claiming that

[34] Kant, *Critique of Practical Reason*, 135–6.
[35] Kant, *Critique of Practical Reason*, 134.
[36] *Søren Kierkegaard's Journals and Papers*, ed. and trans. Howard V. Hong and Edna H. Hong (Bloomington, IN: Indiana University Press, 1967), vol. i, entry 188, p. 76.

every decision a person makes is a "vote" that always turns out to be a majority of 1–0.[37]

The other type of problem that afflicts this Kantian-inspired move is determining the content of the moral law. If we interpret the self-legislation model as in the previous paragraph, in which the individual invents the moral law, then any content appears arbitrary.[38] Kant himself, of course, did not think the moral law was in any way arbitrary, but that the categorical imperative could be derived merely from the rational form of the concept of law, which he saw as universality: "I ought never to act except in such a way that I can also will that my maxim should become a universal law."[39] However, almost from the beginning Kant's critics have objected that this requirement is so formal and abstract that it fails to specify any determinate content; human persons can consistently will almost anything as a universal law without contradicting themselves.

Kant, of course, gives several versions of the categorical imperative, which he claims are equivalent to the original version, a claim that seems very doubtful to many philosophers. However, perhaps one of the other forms of the principle is more promising, particularly the form in which Kant urges that we should "act in such a way that you always treat humanity, whether in your own person or in the person of any other, never simply as a means, but always at the same time as an end."[40] Kant thought that a rational being necessarily valued himself or herself as an end, and that rational consistency required that a rational being necessarily value other rational beings as well. This principle does, I believe, have a better chance of delivering moral content than Kant's purely formal version of the categorical imperative.

Probably it is for this reason that contemporary Kantian Christine Korsgaard relies on a version of this principle when she attempts to develop a contemporary account of how we humans can ourselves

---

[37] Elizabeth Anscombe, "Modern Moral Philosophy," *Philosophy*, 33 (1958), 1–19.

[38] See Alasdair MacIntyre, *After Virtue: A Study in Moral Theory* (London: Duckworth, 1981), 40–5, for a critique of the idea of "radical choice."

[39] Immanuel Kant, *Groundwork of the Metaphysic of Morals*, trans. H. J. Paton (Harper Torchbooks, The Academy Library; New York: Harper & Row, 1964), 402 (p. 70).

[40] Kant, *Groundwork of the Metaphysic of Morals*, 429 (p. 96).

be the ground of the moral law. Though Korsgaard follows Kant in seeing the source of normativity to be the lawlike, universal "form" that is constitutive of our "reflective endorsement" of a possible way of acting, she admits that this universal form cannot give fully determinate content to the moral law.[41] She makes a distinction, one Kant himself does not clearly make, between the categorical imperative and the moral law.[42] The categorical imperative rules out some maxims as possible laws, because not every principle can be consistently willed as a universal law. However, for Korsgaard, the particular maxims that have authority for an individual ultimately stem from the identity of that individual, since "a view of what you ought to do is a view of who you are."[43] Since it is clear that people can and do conceive of their identities very differently, it follows that people who conceive of their identities in different ways will see themselves as having different obligations, and on Korsgaard's view will actually have different obligations.

Korsgaard attempts to limit the relativistic implications of this by arguing that whatever practical identity a person takes must include a recognition of his or her own value as a human being. Essentially, "our identity as moral beings—as people who value themselves as human beings—stands behind our more particular practical identities."[44] If we assume that valuing ourselves in this way implies we should value other humans as well, then we are close to the Kantian formula that persons must be valued as ends in themselves, never only as means.[45]

I agree that such a formula captures something deep about our moral obligations, and I will argue later in this chapter that our recognition of the value of human persons is in fact a natural sign for God, one of the ways our moral experience points us toward God. The question does not concern the truth of the claim that human persons have intrinsic worth and dignity, and therefore should be valued as ends, but the reason why this is true. Korsgaard sees herself as developing a "constructivist" account of morality, in which moral

[41] See Christine Korsgaard with G. A. Cohen et al., *The Sources of Normativity* (Cambridge and New York: Cambridge University Press, 1996), 92–8.
[42] Korsgaard, *The Sources of Normativity*, 98–100.
[43] Korsgaard, *The Sources of Normativity*, 117.
[44] Korsgaard, *The Sources of Normativity*, 121.
[45] Korsgaard, *The Sources of Normativity*, 121.

truths are the product of human reflection and deliberation, and this constructivism is seen as an alternative to "substantive realism" about morality, which sees moral properties as intrinsic to objective entities and states of affairs.[46] However, recognizing all human beings as creatures who possess intrinsic worth and dignity seems suspiciously like substantive realism.

For Korsgaard the ground of obligation is our "practical identity," and the moral law is rooted in a legislative affirmation of our identity as human beings, one shared with all other humans. However, it is painfully obvious that not all human persons conceive of their practical identity in this way, seeing all other humans, like themselves, as beings with intrinsic worth who must be valued as ends in themselves. From time immemorial, many humans have been all too willing to affirm that we should "love our friends and hate our enemies," treat with respect those we care about (such as friends and family members), but act as we wish toward the "others," whether the others be members of a different clan, different tribe, different race, different religion, different gender, or sexual preference, or whatever.

This sad fact raises a dilemma for a view such as Korsgaard's. It seems obvious that people have some choice about how they define their identity. When people do not construe their practical identity in the way Korsgaard (and Kant) think they should, are they making a mistake? If so, it looks as if moral realism is right after all, since those who dehumanize other persons seem to be failing to recognize an objective truth: that all human persons have intrinsic worth. If they are not making a mistake, then it appears that to opt for an identity that sees human persons as having worth is just a "radical choice," similar to the "existentialist" move that sees morality as grounded in a contingent choice. Perhaps Korsgaard would try to avoid this dilemma by arguing that, although any identity that does not affirm the value of humanity is a kind of mistaken identity, the mistake is one not of failing to recognize some substantive moral truth, but of failing to solve a practical problem in the "right" way, the way that "reason" requires. However, it is hard to see why other solutions can be "wrong" if it is not the case that humans as such have the value that morality presupposes they have. Surely, the many cultures

---

[46] Korsgaard, *The Sources of Normativity*, 112.

that have failed to recognize the intrinsic worth of all humans are not fundamentally lacking in rationality. It is worth recalling here that even so great a philosopher as Aristotle, the man who virtually invented logic and defined the Western conception of rationality, saw women and slaves as naturally inferior beings, who lacked the fundamental rights that a Kantian believes all humans possess. This strongly suggests that the Kantian principle of valuing all human persons is not an inescapable result of practical reasoning *per se*, but rather seems practically rational only to those who recognize the intrinsic value of human persons.

That one's personal identity is ultimately contingent is something Korsgaard implicitly admits, when she concedes that our identity as a moral agent "does not always swamp other forms of identity," which means that it is not the case that moral obligations always trump other kinds of obligations.[47] Perhaps Korsgaard or someone defending a similar view might respond that the value we ought to attribute to human persons simply derives from the value we necessarily place on our own reason. If we reflectively attempt to decide how we should live our lives, we cannot help but value reflection itself, and our lives as reflective beings, and reason will require that we value other persons as reflective beings as well.

There are two kinds of problems with such a response. One concerns whether it is true that our value as humans does in fact depend on our capacity to engage in rational reflection. I will argue later in this chapter that this is not the case: humans who are not capable of rational reflection—infants, the severely mentally ill, those suffering from senility—are creatures to whom special moral duties apply. They have intrinsic worth and dignity that cannot be grounded in a capacity for reasoning. The second problem is that, even if we assume that human worth is grounded in rationality, there is no reason why all humans must be valued. Many human persons have often thought of other human beings as not fully rational. Those who dehumanize slaves, women, or people of some other race all too commonly deny that those who are dehumanized are really capable of rational reflection. If these people are making a mistake, then again it seems that substantive moral realism is true.

---

[47] Korsgaard, *The Sources of Normativity*, 125.

TWO NATURAL SIGNS FOR GOD EMBEDDED
IN MORAL ARGUMENTS

It is now time to take stock of what we have achieved so far. If we define a proof of God's existence as a valid argument with undeniable premises, it is clear that the moral argument as I have developed it is not a proof. For not only is it possible to doubt the existence of objective moral obligations, and thus cast doubt on premise (2) ("There are objectively binding moral obligations"); we have now seen a variety of ways in which critics might doubt premise (1) ("If there are objectively binding moral obligations, then God exists") by looking at three possible explanations of moral obligations that explain them without positing a God. However, we have also looked in some detail at the liabilities of these attempts to undermine the argument, and it is clear all come with a cost. Error theories such as those given by Mackie and Nietzsche carry the cost of a denial of many deeply held moral convictions. Reductivist, social contract, and self-legislation theories each carry their own costs, and in many cases seem not to explain adequately some important features of morality. The result is that moral arguments, while certainly failing to reach the standard of proof, seem to have genuine force, at least for those who accept a certain conception of moral obligations.

In the remainder of this chapter, I shall try to show that the reason moral arguments have this force lies in the natural signs for God that the arguments rest on. I shall focus on two such signs: (1) our experience of ourselves as responsible and accountable moral beings; (2) our perception of the special value and dignity of human persons. Before giving an account of these, I shall first give a brief explanation of a "divine command theory" of moral obligation. If such a theory is the correct account of moral obligation, it will be easy to see that moral obligations function as natural signs for God. Ultimately, however, the case for recognizing these natural signs for God does not depend on accepting such a theory. Even for those who reject a divine command theory, however, laying out the theory will highlight some possible ways moral obligations might point to God.

Divine Command Theories of Moral Obligation

The account of a divine command theory of moral obligation I shall give is heavily indebted to Philip Quinn and Robert Adams, both of whom did pioneering work in developing such a view in the contemporary philosophical world.[48] I shall try to give a very brief and concise account of such a view, but the particular form I shall give to it is my own.

First of all, a divine command theory (DCT) as I shall expound it is limited to moral *obligations*. It is not a general account of ethical concepts; in fact, as we shall see, it presupposes several other ethical concepts, especially some concept of the good. The assumption that lies behind a DCT of obligation is that the concept of obligation is not reducible to any concept or concepts outside what we might call the obligation family. To say that an act is forbidden or obligatory is not, for example, simply to say that the outcome of that act is bad or good, or even that it is the best or worst outcome possible. An analogy might help. It would not be good for me to drive at 110 miles per hour on a German autobahn, because I am not that good a driver. Nevertheless, I have no legal obligation not to drive at that rate of speed, because there are no legal speed limits on the autobahn. In a similar way, the proponent of a DCT of moral obligation holds that the goodness and badness of the consequences of our actions does not by itself mean that those actions are obligatory or forbidden or permissible (neither obligatory nor forbidden).

Second, a DCT rests on what Robert Adams has called a social theory of obligations. There are obligations of various kinds: moral, legal, familial, obligations of etiquette, and many others. Although these different obligations overlap in various ways, they are conceptually distinct. All of these different kinds of obligations are grounded in social relationships of various kinds; the obligations are best thought of as constitutive of the relationships. If I get married, I thereby incur certain obligations to my spouse, for those obligations are part of what

---

[48] See Philip L. Quinn, *Divine Commands and Moral Requirements* (Clarendon Library of Logic and Philosophy; Oxford: Oxford University Press, 1978); Robert Merrihew Adams, *The Virtue of Faith and Other Essays in Philosophical Theology* (New York: Oxford University Press, 1987).

it means to be married to someone. Similarly, I incur particular legal obligations by being part of a society governed in a particular way.

A proponent of a DCT holds that God is an actual person and that all humans have a relationship with God by virtue of being God's creatures. This Creator–creature relationship, like other social relationships, can be the ground of obligations in a variety of different ways. First, God, simply by virtue of being who he is, seems entitled to respect and admiration, since God is supremely loving, supremely knowledgeable, and supremely powerful. Second, as the creator, God has given to every human person the gift of life, as well as every other good that a person may enjoy. Humans thus owe God an enormous debt of gratitude, greater by far than that owed to any human. Third, the proponent of a DCT may hold that God intends every human to enjoy a life of eternal joy and blessedness, which is in turn made possible by an enhanced relationship to God, one in which humans experience God's love and love him in return, enjoying friendship with God. For all these reasons (and doubtless more) God's commands (or requirements or expectations, if someone objects to the language of commands) are ones that humans should strive to fulfill. If God asks me to perform a certain act, I now have a reason to perform that act that I would not otherwise have. Perhaps I should perform the act out of gratitude to God. Perhaps I should perform the act because it will enhance my friendship with God, something that is good in itself but that will also lead to my own eternal happiness. Perhaps I should perform the act because I know that God will approve if I do, and I value his approval, both because I am his friend and because I know he is supremely loving and wise.

The proponent of a DCT holds that the obligations generated by God's commands are precisely the obligations we call moral obligations. God's status as all-wise and all-good creator gives him the authority to make moral laws, just as a good government powerful enough to control its territory has the authority to make governmental laws. Identifying moral obligations with God's laws explains many features of moral obligations that rival, naturalistic accounts do not explain or do not explain so well. For example, we can explain why moral obligations are overriding. I might live in a racist state, in which I am legally obligated to treat members of a minority race in a degrading way, but morality requires that I do otherwise. When legal and moral obligations conflict, morality has the trump card. If moral obligations are generated by my relationship to God, we can understand why this should be so, because no social relationship has more value and importance than the relationship to God.

Seeing moral obligations as divine commands also explains their objectivity. There is a fact of the matter about whether God has commanded or forbidden an act or not, and we can therefore be right or wrong in our beliefs about moral obligations. But this realism about moral obligations, unlike some forms of moral realism, does not make it mysterious why moral obligations should be motivating. On the contrary, a DCT gives an excellent account of why we should care about our moral obligations, since they are linked to a relation that is inherently valuable.

The DCT can also explain why we have moral obligations that extend to all human persons, including people who can offer us no reciprocal benefits, and those who are senile, or who suffer from mental handicaps that make them incapable of reasoning. For God has created all human persons in his image. Even those who in this life are unable fully to actualize the possibilities God has for them will be able to enjoy those possibilities in eternity. It therefore seems eminently reasonable that one of the things God would command is that we should respect the worth and dignity of all those creatures made in his image. Of course, Judaism and Christianity hold that one of God's most important commands is a command to "love our neighbors as ourselves," and, as the parable of the Good Samaritan makes clear, the neighbor cannot be restricted to friends or family or members of one's own ethnic or racial group.

A DCT as I have explained it is an ontological or metaphysical claim, not a semantic claim. It is a claim not that "moral obligation" means "divine command," but that moral obligations are in fact divine commands, just as it can be true that "water is H_2O" even though "water" and "H_2O" do not have the same meanings.[49]

---

[49] For simplicity of exposition I am here assuming that divine commands are identical with moral obligations. Other versions of DCT might hold that moral obligations supervene on divine commands, or perhaps are caused to exist by divine commands. Everything I wish to say about divine commands and moral obligations could be said using the language of these alternative versions of a DCT, but the points would be much more cumbersome. In any case, one might well know that some form

An important part of a DCT will be an account of how the divine commands are promulgated. How does God make it possible for humans to know what his requirements are? Here a variety of options present themselves. One would be to hold that God makes his laws known only through special revelations. However, such a view would have awkward consequences. One could hardly hold persons responsible for obeying a law that they could not possibly have known about, so, if God's laws are made known only through special revelation, then this would imply that those who have no access to that revelation would not be responsible for living in accordance with moral obligations (assuming that they are in fact divine commands). So it seems much more plausible for a proponent of a DCT to hold that special revelations, while doubtless one way God could reveal his expectations, would not be the only way. One might think, for example, that God could make his expectations known through conscience, a special moral faculty. Such a moral faculty would not have to be infallible in order to be valuable, and of course it would necessarily operate in a cultural context that would inevitably color and perhaps distort its outputs. But conscience might still be effective in helping humans to know about at least some of their moral responsibilities.

Let me conclude this discussion of a DCT by raising and answering one important and common objection to this kind of theory. It is often alleged that a DCT falls victim to a problem similar to one found in an argument developed by Socrates in Plato's *Euthyphro*. Socrates argues that, if piety is identified with what the gods love, piety as a quality will be arbitrary, and the love the gods have for pious actions will be unmotivated. Anything the gods love would be by definition pious, and so one cannot say that the gods love pious actions because they are pious. Similarly, one might think that, if a moral obligation is simply whatever God commands, then God's commands will be arbitrary. God cannot command a person to do something because it has the quality of moral rightness if whatever God commands will be morally right.

Certainly, if moral obligations are divine commands, one cannot say God commands an act because it is morally obligatory. However, this does not imply that God's commands are arbitrary. A DCT as developed by Robert Adams holds that only the commands of a good and loving God would constitute moral obligations. Since God is essentially good and loving, his commands will be grounded in his understanding of the good and love for the good. The actions acquire the status of being moral obligations by being commanded by God, but they will have the status of being good antecedently to those commands (just as legislators enact laws and thereby make some acts illegal, but are supposed to be guided by their understanding of how those laws serve the common good).

We can in fact distinguish two aspects of a DCT, only one of which is essential. One aspect is what we might call the Modal Status Thesis, which is a claim that an act acquires a special moral status by virtue of being commanded by God. The second aspect of a DCT is what I would call the Discretion Thesis, which is the claim that, with respect to at least some of God's commands, there are alternative commands that God could have made, just as, in many cases, human legislators guided by a quest for the common good often have alternative ways of pursuing that good. The Discretion Thesis is commonly held by thinkers regarded as divine command theorists, such as Duns Scotus. However, it is important to note that not even Scotus held that God has discretion with respect to everything God commands. For example, taking the Decalogue as a summary of God's commands, Scotus held that some of what God commands, such as the command to worship God, he commands necessarily.[50] Other commands, such as the command to honor the Sabbath, while directed at the good, do allow for some discretion. There might be other ways in which God could have allowed for the human need for rest.

It is not clear, however, how many of God's commands are such that he might have had alternatives. In fact, it seems possible that there might be no cases of this sort: perhaps all of what God commands

---

[50] "The Decalogue and the Law of Nature," in *Duns Scotus on the Will and Morality*, selected and translated with an introduction by Allan B. Wolter, OFM (Washington: Catholic University of American Press, 1986), 268–87. This section is a translation of Scotus, *Ordinatio* III, suppl. dist. 37, according to Wolter. Wolter also provides a helpful discussion of this section of Scotus on pp. 60–4 of the volume.

he commands necessarily. It is important to realize that even those actions that God necessarily commands or forbids still acquire a new moral status by virtue of God's commands. The Modal Status Thesis could still hold, even if the Discretion Thesis were false. We might, therefore, consider the case of a philosopher who holds only the Modal Status Thesis but not the Discretion Thesis as a kind of limiting case of a DCT, a minimal DCT. It is in fact plausible to think of Kant as a proponent of such a view.

TWO NATURAL SIGNS FOR GOD IN MORAL EXPERIENCE

We are now finally in position to describe the natural signs for God that moral arguments for God attempt to capture. I shall discuss two distinct signs of this type. The first lies in our experience of being morally accountable or responsible. The second lies in our perception of human beings as having a special value and dignity.

In Chapter 2 I tried to show that theistic natural signs, like Reidian natural signs, could be of two types. Certain experiences or mental states could point us to God, in a way analogous to the way sensations point to perceptual objects in Reid. However, actual features of the world might be theistic natural signs as well, just as for Reid some perceived objects, such as facial expressions, can be natural signs for mental states. The two natural signs connected with morality could be understood in both of these two ways. Perhaps it makes most sense to descsribe the first type of moral sign I shall discuss as an experience, the sense of being bound or obligated. If construed in this way, the sign is, like a Reidian sensation, something mental. However, if the moral obligation that is perceived is an objective reality, then one might argue that this sign is more like a facial expression for Reid, something perceived that is in turn a sign for something else.

The second moral sign, our experience of humans as having a special worth and dignity, is similarly capable of being interpreted in more than one way. I think that it is most plausible to think of this sign as a perception of an actual feature of the world: human beings as possessing certain qualities. But perhaps it would also be plausible to think of the sign here as residing in our experience; it is our awareness of humans as having this special worth that is the sign.

Moral Accountability as a Natural Sign

If a DCT provides the correct account of morality, then our awareness of moral obligations simply is an awareness of God's commands (or requirements or expectations), or else it is an awareness of something that directly stems from an activity of God that grounds our moral obligations (in case we think of moral obligations as supervening on God's commands or being caused by them). It seems clear, then, that the truth of a DCT would imply that moral obligations would count as natural signs for God. They would be phenomena that are caused by God, and it certainly seems that part of their intended function would be to point us toward God as moral lawgiver and thus make possible an enhanced relationship to God. Furthermore, if a DCT is true, it seems plausible that experiences of moral obligation often actually do function in this intended manner. Human persons who sense that they are morally obligated to perform or refrain from performing an action commonly see themselves as accountable or responsible in some way, and they frequently interpret this accountability as actual responsibility to God.

It is not hard to see why this should be so. It seems reasonable to think of accountability as a social concept. If that is correct, then I cannot just be accountable; rather I must be accountable to some person or community. If God is the source of our moral obligations, then God will be among the ones to whom I am accountable; indeed, God will be the primary one to whom I am accountable. It is, of course, common to interpret this accountability with reference to divine sanctions, in which God punishes the guilty and rewards the good. Popular pictures of heaven and hell, with streets of gold and tormenting fire, do not have to be accepted as part of the story, however. The "holding accountable" does not have to be understood in terms of heaven and hell, as they are popularly understood. For the person who loves God, God's approval and disapproval may be what is crucial. Most theological accounts of heaven and hell see heaven as consisting of a blissful experiential relationship to God and others who love God, while hell is seen as a loss of this good. If this is right, then the primary sanction that stands behind moral obligation is simply this: obedience to moral obligations understood as divine commands facilitates the friendship with God that is the chief good for humans; disobedience is a barrier to the achievement of this good. So, if God is the source of moral obligations, and we have a natural tendency to see moral obligations as stemming from God, then our awareness of moral obligations will be a theistic natural sign.

However, in order for moral obligations to function as natural signs for God, it is not necessary that a full-fledged DCT be true. At the very most one would need only what I called in the previous section a minimal DCT. For what is important in this context is the Modal Status Thesis, not the Discretion Thesis. The Modal Status Thesis implies that actions that God commands thereby acquire a new moral status that they would otherwise not have. Actions that perhaps (or even certainly) would have been good or bad even independently of God's commands are now important for a new reason. If I do what is morally forbidden or fail to do what is morally required, I disappoint God, who has a rightful claim on my obedience. Even if what God commands he commands necessarily, this will still be the case. Moral obligations on this view can be things that bind me in a way that is analogous to the way in which a human law can bind me. This sense of accountability could come through a number of different types of experiences, including the basic sense that I "must," or "ought to," act in a certain way, a sense of guilt when I fail to do so, and a sense of satisfaction or happiness over having fulfilled a moral requirement. (An emphasis on such experiences would suggest that the sign in this case is, like a Reidian sensation, something subjective.)

We can go even further than this in decoupling a sense of account-ability from a DCT as a theistic natural sign. Although a DCT is still valuable in giving us a kind of model of how humans might relate to God through moral experience, a sense of moral accountability could be a natural sign for God even if a minimal DCT fails to hold. Some critics argue that a DCT is false, because not all moral obligations are rooted in divine commands. For example, one might argue that the obligation to obey God is itself a moral obligation, and that such an obligation must be presupposed by divine commands and cannot be generated by a divine command. If such a criticism, or some other criticism of a DCT, is true, this still does not mean that the experience of accountability is not a theistic natural sign, because the claim that some moral obligations can be natural signs for God does not require the truth of a DCT, even in its minimal form. That is, it need not be the case that all moral obligations are God's commands or even that all moral obligations depend on divine commands. All that is needed in order for it to be true that there are natural signs for God in our moral experience is that *some* moral obligations be divine commands or depend on divine commands in the relevant way. It certainly seems reasonable to think that, if God exists and has created human persons, God's expectations of us would create *some* obligations. So, even if it is not generally true that moral obligations depend on God, it could well be the case that our moral experience will include natural signs that point to God.

Of course, religious believers will naturally "read" this experience of being bound or obligated by morality as a natural sign for God, because they will see their moral duties (or at least some of them) as divine commands. However, even the non-believer can and does feel the force of this sense of obligation. The very language of the "moral law" suggests that our situation is such that it is *as if* there is an authority to which we are responsible. The fact that secular thinkers acknowledge the force of the law is shown by the energy devoted to finding an alternative explanation for the ground of the law, the weakness of those alternative explanations, as explored earlier in this chapter, notwithstanding. This can be clearly seen in the existentialism of Jean-Paul Sartre, who affirms the Dostoevskean principle that "everything is permissible if God does not exist."[51] Sartre recognizes that his own account, in which each individual human chooses what is right and wrong, is vulnerable to the charge that it makes morality arbitrary, but he thinks that he has no choice, since he accepts the Nietzschean dictum that "God is dead." "My answer to this [the charge that values are arbitrary] is that I'm quite vexed that that's the way it is; but if I've discarded God the Father, there has to be someone to invent values."[52]

---

[51] Jean-Paul Sartre, *Existentialism and Human Emotions* (New York: Philosophical Library, 1957), 22.
[52] Sartre, *Existentialism*, 49.

It is important to recall the "Pascalian constraints" that I argued will limit any natural signs for God. One is that the signs will be widely accessible. The other is that the signs will be easily resistible. The experience of moral accountability certainly satisfies both of these conditions. Moral accountability seems to be a prominent element in virtually every culture, and it is certainly common and arguably natural for humans to interpret this experience as pointing to God. However, the sign is certainly resistible. Not only is it the case that some deny the reality of objective moral obligations, as Nietzsche did. Many others, who cannot bring themselves to deny the reality of moral obligations, look for alternative explanations of the phenomenon, with varying degrees of success. Seeing moral accountability as a natural sign for God explains both the appeal and force of moral arguments for God as well as the lack of conclusiveness of such arguments.

The Intrinsic Worth of Human Beings as a Theistic Natural Sign

In looking at Christine Korsgaard's "constructivist" attempt to account for moral obligations, I noted her reliance on the Kant-inspired formula of the moral law as requiring that we treat all human beings as ends in themselves, creatures that have intrinsic worth and dignity. Humans, of course, have all kinds of worth. Many of the kinds of worth we have are kinds that can be possessed in degrees. Some people have the worth of being excellent philosophers, and some of them, such as Korsgaard herself, have this excellence to a higher degree than some other philosophers. Some, like Tiger Woods, have the worth of being excellent golfers, Woods certainly having an exceptional degree of this worth. In addition to these kinds of worth, Korsgaard holds that every human being possesses a certain basic worth, just as a human being, and this kind of worth is not a matter of degree. Some may be better human beings than others in various respects, but all are equally human.

In my earlier discussion in this chapter I agreed with Korsgaard that humans do indeed possess this kind of value, but questioned whether such a claim is really consistent with a constructivist account of morality. It seems rather that the principle of treating human beings as ends in themselves depends upon the recognition that human beings as human beings have a special kind of intrinsic worth, and that this is an objective fact about them, not the outcome of a decision that humans make as rational agents.

Of course not every human person accepts this claim that all humans possess this kind of worth. The Nazis did not agree that Jews and gypsies and homosexuals had intrinsic worth as humans. White racists do not regard people of color as having such value. As I have noted before, it is all too common for human beings to draw a line separating "us" from "them," whether the "us" be defined as friends and family, members of the same community, race, ethnic group, or religious group. In every case the "outsiders" are those who do not fit into the favored group. Sadly, even some of those who profess to hold that all human beings have intrinsic value often fail to live up to that ideal. However, despite these failures, I would argue that this belief in the value of human beings as human beings embodies an ideal that is affirmed by the best humans in their best moments. I agree with Nicholas Wolterstorff that such a belief undergirds the conviction that humans possess "natural rights" as humans.[53] Not only is it wrong intentionally to kill my fellow citizens; it is also wrong to kill innocent human beings who have no natural ties to me, other than that they are fellow humans. All humans possess a right to life, as well as other natural rights. Nazis and white supremacists may not agree, but it is precisely because Nazi ethical beliefs and practices contradict this ideal so flagrantly that Nazism has become the paradigm of an evil system.

Some have argued that this conception of human beings as possessing an intrinsic worth and dignity that grounds natural human rights is a product of Judaism and Christianity, both of which claim that human beings are not only creatures of God, but are made in the image of God.[54] Nicholas Wolterstorff has recently argued that the concept of humans as having a kind of intrinsic worth that is the ground

---

[53] Nicholas Wolterstorff, *Justice: Rights and Wrongs* (Princeton: Princeton University Press, 2008), 316–19.

[54] Nicholas Wolterstorff draws on the work of a number of historians to make a strong case that the historical roots of this conception lie in the Hebrew Bible and the New Testament, with the concept of "natural rights" fully developed by the medieval period. See his *Justice*, chs. 2–5.

of rights was not only historically produced by Jewish and Christian conceptions of human beings, but that even now there is no plausible alternative to this religious framework to provide a "ground" for natural human rights.[55] Wolterstorff argues, for example, that the worth of humans that is the ground of natural human rights cannot be grounded in some ability or excellence such as the power of reason, because many of those who possess human rights have no such power to reason. Infants, those with Alzheimer's, and those born with severe mental impairments lack any such rational powers, but they surely still have whatever inherent dignity and worth belongs to humans as humans. If Wolterstorff is right, then a belief in human rights may be fragile, and difficult to sustain without a belief that humans are created by God in the image of God. Nevertheless, those who believe that natural human rights are an important part of the moral fabric of a humane society may at least hope that such a belief can survive, at least for a time, without any religious foundation.

Such a hope does not appear to be completely without foundation. The *Humanist Manifesto II*, while rejecting any transcendent religious framework as a basis for understanding human nature, clearly affirms that every human person has inherent worth by endorsing "the preciousness and dignity of the individual person."[56] It is not surprising, then, that later on the same document endorses the United Nations' "Universal Declaration of Human Rights." Nor is this Humanist document unusual. Many secular philosophers who would not accept any kind of theistic belief nonetheless continue to believe that all humans have inherent worth, and look for some way to explain or ground that worth.[57]

One might say that, whether or not they have an adequate explanation of the inherent worth a human person possesses, it is somehow evident to these secular thinkers *that humans do have such worth.* I

[55] See Wolterstorff, *Justice*, ch. 16, "A Theistic Grounding of Human Rights."

[56] See *The Humanist Manifesto II*, www.americanhumanist.org/who_we_are/about_humanism/Humanist_Manifesto_II.

[57] Besides Christian Korsgaard, I would cite Alan Gewirth, *Human Rights: Essays on Justification and Applications* (Chicago: University of Chicago Press, 1982), and Ronald Dworkin, *Taking Rights Seriously* (Cambridge, MA: Harvard University Press, 1977), as contemporary examples. See Wolterstorff's discussion of them in *Justice*, ch. 15.

believe it is plausible to interpret such a recognition as a perception of what Christian theologians have traditionally called the "image of God" in humans, and to see this perceived value as a theistic natural sign. I shall try to defend these claims through a discussion of Søren Kierkegaard's *Works of Love*, which consists of a series of reflections on the great command, common to Judaism and Christianity, to love one's neighbor as oneself. Kierkegaard understands this command, drawing on the parable of the Good Samaritan, as implying that every human is in fact the neighbor of every other.

It is true that Kierkegaard affirms that this injunction is a divine command. However, as I noted in looking at divine command theories, God's commands are not arbitrary but directed at the good. In fact, for some (or even all) of God's commands, the good of the end commanded may be so overwhelming that God's commands are necessary. For example, as I noted above, according to a divine command theorist such as Duns Scotus, God necessarily commands humans to worship him alone, because God is the only one worthy of worship and a relationship to God is the supreme good. If humans are made in God's image, perhaps God also necessarily commands humans to recognize and honor other humans; one can hardly love God without also loving what God has made, especially if what God has made bears a resemblance to God.

Kierkegaard tries to express this idea that humans have a special worth in two ways: by speaking of an "inner glory" that all humans possess and by use of the image of a "common watermark." He compares human life to a play.[58] In a play all the actors wear various costumes that befit their roles. One may play a beggar, while another plays a king. "But when the curtain falls on the stage, then the one who played the king and the one who played the beggar, etc., are all one and the same—actors."[59] Human life also contains a great "multifariousness," and some are indeed beggars and others are kings. However, "when at death the curtain falls on the stage of actuality . . . then they, too, are all one, they are human beings."[60] Each person, whatever his or her earthly differences, possesses an

---

[58] Søren Kierkegaard, *Works of Love*, ed. and trans. Howard V. Hong and Edna H. Hong (Kierkegaard's Writings; Princeton: Princeton University Press, 1995), 86–9.
[59] Kierkegaard, *Works of Love*, 87.   [60] Kierkegaard, *Works of Love*, 87.

"inner glory." Every human being, according to Kierkegaard, can be compared to a fine piece of stationery:

Take many sheets of paper, write something different on each one; then no one will be like another. But then again take each single sheet; do not let yourself be confused by the diverse inscriptions, hold it up to the light, and you see a common watermark on all of them. In the same way the neighbor is the common watermark, but you see it only by means of eternity's light when it shines through the dissimilarity.[61]

Perhaps Kierkegaard can be taken as suggesting that, when we see our fellow humans as our neighbors in this special sense of "neighbor," we are sensing this "inner glory."

The religious believer can clearly make sense of this perception of humans as possessing this "inner glory," because the believer sees humans as made in God's image. However, perhaps it is possible for someone who is not a believer, or who is not yet a believer, to perceive this basic human worth as well. Such a person can see the "light of eternity" that illuminates the "common watermark." In that case, perhaps the person is seeing the image of God in the person, is recognizing the person as made in God's image, even if the person does not realize that this is what the person is seeing. In this way the person would be perceiving a natural sign for God: perceiving something that God created and intended to function as a pointer toward God, something that does indeed point toward God as the transcendent ground of the mysterious value we see in ourselves.

Such a natural sign is particularly valuable, for a number of reasons. First, it does not depend in any way on a divine command account of moral obligation, not even in the attenuated sense in which seeing the experience of accountability as a theistic natural sign assumes that a DCT at least provides us with a model for how humans might relate morally to God. However, it is important to recognize that seeing human beings as having an intrinsic worth that is a natural sign for God is fully compatible with a divine command theory of obligation; the value of humans supplements a DCT by providing an explanation of why God commands us to love and value humans. Clearly, such a command is rooted in the goodness God has placed

---

[61] Kierkegaard, *Works of Love*, 89.

in humans. Recognizing humans as having this intrinsic worth also appears to meet the Pascalian constraints on a theistic natural sign. Again, we have something that is widely available; many people, including religious non-believers, are able and willing to perceive humans as having this kind of unique value and worth. Again, we have a resistible sign, in that it is possible to explain or interpret the value in some other way, or even to see the apparent value simply as an illusion.

Still, it is plausible to see the sign as having some genuine force. Since the sign in this case lies in our own nature, it is hard to miss. The fact that people continue to affirm the value of humans even when they lack any plausible account of why humans have such value shows the force of the sign, as does the energetic efforts of philosophers to find a non-theistic explanation of the value.

CONCLUSION

In Chapter 2 I noted that theistic natural signs point to God, but differ in what we might term their informational payload. They function to make people aware of God's reality, but, even when they do this successfully, those who rely on the sign may have widely differing beliefs about God, with many of those beliefs false. The cosmic wonder examined in Chapter 3, which I argue lies at the base of cosmological arguments, points to some kind of transcendent ground of the natural world, but does not tell us very much about the nature of that ground. The purposive order examined in Chapter 4 offers somewhat more content, since it seems to point to a God who is intelligent and cares about value. However, in my view, the two theistic natural signs that lie in our moral experience, and that help make moral arguments for God plausible, not only point to God in a more powerful way, but also offer more insight into God's nature. For they point to a God who is essentially good, and who desires a relationship with human persons. Someone who comes to know God as the ground of moral obligation does not know merely an abstract metaphysical reality but a personal reality who makes a claim on the life of humans. Someone who knows God as the source of the inherent value that is present in human persons also knows God as a personal being, and as the one who pre-eminently possesses the worth and value we see in human beings.

Of course it is one thing to show that these theistic natural signs are putative evidence for God. It is another to show that they constitute good evidence. It is to that task that I shall turn in the final chapter.

6

Conclusions: Can We Rely on Natural Signs for a "Hidden" God?

I have examined a number of theistic natural signs, patterning the concept of such a sign on the Reidean natural signs explained in Chapter 2. The experience of cosmic wonder is, I suggested in Chapter 3, a natural sign for God that lies at the core of cosmological arguments for God's existence, and the force of this natural sign partially explains the continued appeal of this argument. I argued in Chapter 4 that the purposive order that can be observed in nature is also a natural sign, one that lies at the heart of teleological arguments for God's existence. This observed order points to a designer of the natural world, and evolutionary theory is not a defeater for the reliability of such a sign. In Chapter 5 I looked at moral arguments for God's existence, and claimed that two distinct natural signs for God come into view when we examine such arguments: the sense of being obligated or bound by moral obligations and our awareness that human beings as human beings possess an intrinsic worth or dignity.

I could attempt to expand this account by looking at still other theistic natural signs. For example, other natural signs for God could be discussed that are not commonly associated with the classical arguments of natural theology. A deep sense of gratitude that a person may feel for one's life could plausibly be viewed as such a theistic natural sign. It is not uncommon even for atheists to be filled with a profound sense of joy over the sheer fact that they are alive, and spontaneously to feel a deep sense of thankfulness for their lives, with all that those lives include: friends, family, a beautiful world full of beautiful and awe-inspiring things. It feels, in such situations, as if one's life is a *gift*, and it is natural to feel gratitude for this gift. Perhaps this sense that life is a gift is literally true, and the emotion in question is a perception of the goodness of that gift. Of course, gratitude seems to be the sort of thing that requires an intentional object. One is not just grateful. One is grateful *to* somebody *for* something. This kind of gratitude may therefore be yet another theistic natural sign.

However, rather than attempt an exhaustive catalogue of types of theistic natural signs, I would like to tackle the questions raised by the natural signs for God I have discussed. I have tried to show that these signs can plausibly be viewed as evidence—that is, putative evidence—for God's reality. But is it possible to show that they provide genuine evidence—good evidence—for belief in God's existence, or at least for doubts about the naturalistic world view so often taken for granted by philosophers in the contemporary Western world?

Of course this question raises others, including some of the most vexed and contentious questions in philosophy. What is evidence? How do we decide whether something that is alleged to be evidence is genuine evidence? Here we find huge disagreements. In law or medicine evidence is often taken to be physical in nature. In a criminal case the police look for blood on the knife, or a fingerprint on the gun. A physician looking for evidence of a disease looks for a certain molecule in the blood, or a lump in the abdomen. However, many philosophers have viewed evidence as consisting of something mental: beliefs, knowledge, occurrent thoughts, sensations.[1] Even among philosophers who see evidence as residing in "internal" mental states, there are seemingly intractable disagreements. Earl Conee and Richard Feldman claim that a person's evidence consists of the person's occurrent mental states, including false beliefs the person may have.[2] Timothy Williamson, however, says that evidence consists of the totality of what a person knows; since one can know only what is true, false beliefs are disqualified.[3]

---

[1] For a good discussion of this point, see Thomas Kelly, "Evidence," in *The Stanford Encyclopedia of Philosophy* (Stanford, CA: Stanford University, 2006), 1–2.

[2] Earl Conee and Richard Feldman, *Evidentialism: Essays in Epistemology* (Oxford: Oxford University Press, 2004).

[3] Timothy Williamson, *Knowledge and its Limits* (Oxford: Oxford University Press, 2000).

Perhaps more progress can be made if we try to say what evidence is by saying something about its function or value. Evidence is often described as what justifies belief or makes a belief more reasonable, and also as what makes a belief more likely to be true. However, it is not obvious that these two functions coincide. What I am justified in believing or what it is reasonable for me to believe is surely determined by what else I believe, and thus is relative to the believer's epistemic state. Defining evidence along these lines tilts it strongly toward the individual's subjective history, for what it will be reasonable for me to believe will surely vary from what would be the case for another person with a different history and different past experiences. A connection to truth, however, seems more objective. If evidence is what makes a belief more likely to be true, then evidence should be connected in some way with what is the case, and this pushes in the direction of a view of evidence as a sign or marker of truth, something that should not vary from person to person. In any case, even if we agree that evidence is what justifies a belief, or makes a belief more likely to be true, we have made little progress in finding out what actually counts as evidence, unless we can say, concretely, when our beliefs are justified, or when they are more likely to be true.

A KANT-INSPIRED OBJECTION TO NATURAL SIGNS FOR GOD

Let us begin by thinking of natural signs as evidence in the objective sense of being a marker for the truth. In this sense, red spots of a particular kind on a human body are a sign of measles, a reliable (though not infallible) indicator that the disease is present in a person. It seems plausible that such signs presuppose some kind of natural regularity, and also plausible that we come to know about such regularities by experience. The physician knows that the particular red spots are a sign of measles because he or she has observed the spots before and then confirmed that the persons with the spots were usually ill with measles.

If we think of natural signs for God along these lines, those who are influenced by Kantian views of experience may object that we cannot know that there are natural signs for God. For to know that one thing A is a sign for another B, I must have experience of both A and B, so as to establish that they are regularly connected. However, many people, including some theologians, are inclined to agree with Kant's claim that our human experience is limited to experience of the spatio-temporal world given to us by sensation.[4] If we suppose that to know that something, such as an experience of cosmic wonder, is a natural sign for God we would have to have experiences of both the cosmic wonder and of God so as to come to know they are regularly connected, then this implies we could never know that cosmic wonder is a natural sign for God. One cannot know that A and B are regularly connected in our experience if it is impossible to have any experience of B. And one might think that, if this were not the case and one did have experiences of God, that natural signs for God would not be necessary, or would at least be less important, since, if God can be known through direct experience, theistic natural signs would not be essential.

One could respond to this objection by challenging the Kantian claim that experience of God is impossible. Kant's reasoning seems to be that, since God is not a spatio-temporal object, he cannot be the object of human experience. God possesses such qualities as infinite power and knowledge, and being omnipresent, and it is not possible for humans to experience such qualities. However, even if it is not possible to experience some of God's qualities, that does not mean it is impossible to experience God. God may be experienced as powerful, or as wise, even if it is not possible to experience qualities such as omnipotence or omniscience. God can be experienced as doing things—speaking to someone, forgiving sin, comforting in grief—even if one cannot experience the property of being "all-good."

The Kant-inspired critic might object that qualities such as power, knowledge, and goodness, as well as the action types just mentioned, cannot be analyzed in terms of "phenomenal qualities," qualities that are composed out of sensory qualities such as color and sound. However, precisely the same thing is true of ordinary, non-religious perception. As William Alston reminds us, "we typically attribute to

---

[4] See Immanuel Kant, *Critique of Pure Reason*, trans. Norman Kemp Smith (New York: St Martin's, 1965), A603–14, B631–42.

external objects, on the basis of perceptual experience, objective properties that go beyond anything that is displayed in that experience, for example, being a dog or being very powerful."[5] No plausible account of ordinary perceptual experience limits what one can experience to phenomenal qualities. How do we find out what it is possible for humans to experience? One would think that this question must be answered from experience, and not by an a priori pronouncement. And the Kantian claim that it is not possible to experience God seems to be such an a priori claim, one that is contradicted by the millions (perhaps billions) of people who claim to have had experiences of God. Recently, a good deal of rigorous argument has been developed to defend the possibility of religious experience, and it would seem rash to dismiss the possibility of this in a peremptory fashion.[6] Hence, even if we did require experience of God as a basis for recognizing natural signs, it is not clear that this would make the task of defending such signs impossible.

However, this Kant-inspired line of objection that experience of God is impossible can be met in a different way, for it rests on a misunderstanding of the nature of a natural sign. To see this, we need to recall the nature of a Reidean natural sign. For Reid, some natural signs, particularly some sensations but also some facial expressions, are "original" signs. They are the means whereby we come to know such things as that there are external physical objects and other people with minds. The conception of these things through the sign is psychologically immediate and not the result of any inference. It is not that I have discovered that the sensation I get when I touch a physical object is normally linked to the presence of a physical object, and so I can properly take the sensation as reliable evidence for the object. For it is precisely by means of such sensations that we are able to come to know that there are physical objects. The view that we need empirical evidence of a regular connection between the sensation and the physical object in order to rely upon the sensation as evidence for the physical object would make it impossible to have

---

[5] William Alston, *Perceiving God: The Epistemology of Religious Experience* (Ithaca, NY: Cornell University Press, 1991), 48.
[6] Perhaps William Alston's *Perceiving God* is the most outstanding example of this work.

any knowledge of the physical world at all. Berkeley's arguments for idealism are sound, if one assumes, as Berkeley did, that all we are directly acquainted with are sensations. Reid, of course, claims that we are directly acquainted with physical objects. Reidean natural signs are one of the means whereby we obtain our basic knowledge of such objects. From the Reidean perspective, if we do not begin by trusting such basic sources of knowledge, we will end up as skeptics.

My proposal is that theistic natural signs may be similarly "original" in character, providing non-inferential knowledge of God. If this is the way that humans become aware of God's reality, then it is a mistake to view the sign as providing evidence for an inference. It is wrong to think that, in order to know God by way of a natural sign, one must first establish some natural regularity between the sign and God. Rather, the sign should be seen as a source of basic knowledge. The proposal is that there is a connection between the sign and God; God has instituted the signs so as to make it possible for people to become aware of his reality. And there is a "hard-wired" natural tendency to "read" the sign in this way, to see it as pointing to God.

There are, of course, significant disanalogies between theistic natural signs and Reidean natural signs. Reidean natural signs seem to be virtually universal in their operation, and some of them, according to Reid, are irresistible, though others can be modified, altered, and even blocked from operating by other experiences or beliefs. One might think that the universality of Reidean signs makes it reasonable to trust them as a source of basic knowledge. Theistic natural signs seem far less universal and far less powerful. Surely, one might think, we need some reason to trust such signs. How do we know that they do not produce what we might call a natural illusion?

THE REASONABLENESS OF PASCALIAN CONSTRAINTS

The most important difference between Reidean natural signs and theistic natural signs lies in the fact that the latter are more susceptible to being influenced by other beliefs, including those one holds as a result of a cultural context. This malleability goes hand in hand with the fact that theistic natural signs are also more easily resisted than

Reidean natural signs. (Although the differences are not absolute; many Reidean natural signs are also resistible to some degree and subject to modification in light of other experiences and beliefs.) In introducing theistic natural signs, I argued in Chapter 1 that they should plausibly be seen as subject to two "Pascalian constraints," the Wide Accessibility Principle and the Easy Resistibility Principle. The Wide Accessibility Principle implies that genuine natural signs will be relatively widespread, cross-culturally present, with some tendency to form beliefs about God on the basis of the sign as a "hard-wired" human trait. The Easy Resistibility Principle implies that this tendency can be overridden by various factors, because of the fact that God has good reason not to make theistic natural signs overpoweringly strong.

One way to reflect on the reasonableness of theistic natural signs is, therefore, to reflect on these Pascalian constraints. Here there are two different kinds of questions to ask. One is whether the theistic natural signs I have discussed in Chapters 3–5 actually satisfy these Pascalian constraints. The other type of question is whether those constraints are themselves reasonable. If theistic natural signs do satisfy these constraints, is this a strong point in their favor? If so, how strong? I shall first address the question of whether the natural signs actually do satisfy these Pascalian constraints.

The fact that belief in God or gods is so prevalent certainly supports the claim that there are *some* natural mechanisms that produce belief in God. And such beliefs are clearly very widespread.[7] E. O. Wilson, for example, affirms that "religious belief is one of the universals of human behavior, taking recognizable form in every society from hunter gatherer bands to socialist republics."[8] This near-universality increasingly leads cognitive scientists to think that belief in God or gods, as well as moral beliefs, results from in-born predispositions in humans to develop such beliefs. Although the particular content of those beliefs varies with cultural contexts,

---

[7] Currently there is no reliable research on the percentage of believers in God worldwide, although researchers at the Institute for Studies of Religion (ISR) at Baylor University plan to add questions on this to the Gallup World Poll. According to Byron Johnson, Director of ISR, there are some data to support the claim that the percentage of people who self-identify as atheists worldwide is under 10%.

[8] Edward O. Wilson, *On Human Nature* (Bantam New Age Books; New York: Bantam Books, 1976), 176.

there does seem to be a conceptual core that humans are hard-wired to develop. Anthropologist Scott Atran, for example, claims that "supernatural agency is the most culturally recurrent, cognitively relevant, and evolutionarily compelling concept in religion. The concept of the supernatural is culturally derived from an innate cognitive schema."[9]

However, even if religious belief is nearly universal and even if this is explained by innate cognitive tendencies, are those tendencies actuated by the particular theistic natural signs I have discussed? First, it should be noted that I have nowhere claimed that theistic natural signs are the only way that belief in God could be produced. Nor have I argued that the theistic natural signs I have discussed are the only ones that operate; I have selected the ones I have discussed partly because of the role they have played in classical theistic arguments. So, if it turns out that belief in God is activated by other factors, including other natural signs, this is not necessarily a problem. It will mean only that there are other theistic natural signs than the ones I have discussed, and perhaps some other means of producing belief in God than natural signs.

However, there is reason to think that the theistic natural signs I have discussed, such as cosmic wonder and purposive order, are among the things that typically trigger belief in God or gods. Some psychologists have discovered experimental evidence that young children do naturally view the world as purposefully and intelligently designed, and that this tendency is linked to religious beliefs. Psychologist Deborah Keleman, for example, says that children are "intuitive theists" prone to "promiscuous teleology."[10] The very widespread and natural way that humans link their moral experience with religious beliefs in many cultures also supports moral obligation as a natural sign. Moral guilt is typically seen as requiring not only some kind of human forgiveness but divine forgiveness as well.

Certainly more research could be done on the ways the natural signs I have discussed give rise to religious belief. Studying such

---

[9] Scott Atran, *In Gods We Trust: The Evolutionary Landscape of Religion* (Evolution and Cognition; Oxford: Oxford University Press, 2002), 57.

[10] Deborah Kelemen, "Are Children 'Intuitive Theists'? Reasoning about Purpose and Design in Nature," *Psychological Science*, 15 (2004), 295–6.

questions raises formidable methodological issues, since the grounds of beliefs are often complex and murky. But in principle such research could be done, and I would be delighted if this book inspired some scientists to do such work. But, even without this research, a case can be made for the importance of these signs, appealing to the intuitive connections between the signs and religious belief and the role the signs have played in the classical theistic arguments. It is particularly significant, I think, that it is often the case that those who reject the arguments—even atheists in some cases—offer testimony to the force of the signs. So it seems very reasonable to see these theistic signs as meeting the Wide Accessibility Principle; they make belief in God possible for many people in a vast range of cultures and historical periods.

Nevertheless, it can be argued that the fact that these signs meet the Wide Accessibility Principle is not all that significant. After all, most of the scientists—anthropologists, psychologists, and cognitive scientists—who have led the charge for the view that humans are hard-wired to believe in God are themselves atheists. While they hold that religious belief is very widespread and in one sense natural, they also hold that it is a kind of natural illusion, a by-product of evolution if you will, giving us beliefs that are false but stemming from a faculty that had some survival advantage for our ancestors. Such a view is certainly possible, and I would not want to claim that one can infer the reliability of these theistic natural signs merely from the fact that they seem to be almost universally present. I would want to argue only that the fact that religious beliefs have such a biological basis should not count against their truth, as some thinkers seem to assume.[11] For in fact this hard-wired propensity to form beliefs in God is something that must be the case if belief in God is founded on natural signs; if religious beliefs are based on natural signs, then such a natural propensity to believe in God cannot be evidence *against* the reality of God.

What about the Easy Resistibility Principle? It is not hard to show that the theistic natural signs I have discussed satisfy this constraint

---

[11] Daniel Clement Dennett, *Breaking the Spell: Religion as a Natural Phenomenon* (New York: Viking, 2006), 97–114; Richard Dawkins, *The God Delusion* (Boston: Houghton Mifflin, 2006), 190–240.

as well. The fact that many people, including many philosophers, are aware of things like moral obligation and cosmic wonder, but do not form a belief in God, shows this must be true. That the signs are resistible can also be seen from the discussion of the theistic arguments given in the previous three chapters. For example, when moral obligation is made into the basis of a moral argument for God, the argument can be disputed, either by rejecting the existence of objective moral obligations, or by accepting such obligations but attempting to give a non-religious explanation of their reality.

It seems then that the theistic natural signs I have described do satisfy the Pascalian constraints. However, perhaps this is not all that surprising. The question as to the reasonableness of those constraints seems more interesting. Is it plausible to think that any natural knowledge of God would conform to those constraints? If so, then the fact that the theistic natural signs do so will take on some added weight.

Of the two constraints, the Wide Accessibility Principle seems relatively non-controversial. It is hard to see why anyone would doubt that God, if God is real and desires humans to have a relationship with him, would make knowledge of God widely available to humans. It seems implausible to think that the knowledge of God would depend solely on some esoteric philosophical argument requiring great skill in symbolic logic, or on the discovery of some exotic scientific theory. Nor does it seem plausible that the knowledge of God would be limited to some narrow time period or particular geographical region. If any criticism of the principle could be made, it would seem to be that the principle is too weak. Would not God want the knowledge of God to be universal, rather than just widely available?

The natural answer to this objection that the Wide Accessibility Principle is too weak is to claim that it could not be strengthened without undermining the Easy Resistibility Principle. Whatever God might do to make the knowledge of God truly universal would make such knowledge impossible to resist. So, if the Easy Resistibility Principle is sound, there will at least be some reason to doubt that the Wide Accessibility Principle needs to be stronger. But is the Easy Resistibility Principle sound? Some may wonder whether the Easy Resistibility Principle simply provides the theist with an easy way to wiggle out of some tough objections. One might think that God can and should provide evidence for his reality that is clear and undeniable. When non-believers find that the signs fall short of this standard, the theist can simply respond by citing the Easy Resistibility Principle. It may then appear to the non-believer that alternative interpretations of the signs or explanations of them are not taken sufficiently seriously.

A particularly forceful version of this kind of objection can be found in the work of J. L. Schellenberg, who has developed an objection to belief in God that is grounded in the problem of "divine hiddenness."[12] Schellenberg, as I noted in Chapter 1, would accept a weaker version of the Easy Resistibility Principle. He agrees that God, if he exists and is loving, would want humans to have a relationship with God that is grounded in a free response on the part of humans. Hence Schellenberg agrees that God would not provide evidence of his reality that is so overwhelming that it would be necessary for a human who wished to have nothing to do with God to believe in God. "For a loving God, out of respect for our freedom, might well allow us to shut him out altogether—not only to fail to respond to his overtures, but also to put ourselves in a position where these were *no longer noticed.*"[13] However, Schellenberg insists that, if this were to happen, the people who refuse to have any knowledge of God would be culpable for their ignorance.[14]

So we can see that Schellenberg does accept a version of the Easy Resistibility Principle. He admits that the evidence for God that God makes available is not so strong that it is impossible to resist. Those who wish not to know about God can achieve or maintain a state of ignorance. However, for Schellenberg, a loving God would make available evidence for his reality that is clear enough and strong enough that only culpable non-belief is possible. Schellenberg goes on to claim that not all unbelief is motivated by a desire to avoid God. There are sincere seekers for God who are unable to believe, and thus "honest inquirers have very good reason indeed to accept that not all failures to believe are due to the sin of the unbeliever, and in

---

[12] See J. L. Schellenberg, *Divine Hiddenness and Human Reason* (Ithaca, NY: Cornell University Press, 1993).
[13] Schellenberg, *Divine Hiddenness*, 27.
[14] Schellenberg, *Divine Hiddenness*, 27–8.

particular, that inculpable doubt occurs."[15] In effect Schellenberg is claiming that, if God truly exists, though the evidence for God should be resistible, it should also be powerful enough that it can be resisted only by those who do not wish to know God. Since there are cases of inculpable non-belief, it is clear that the evidence does not rise to this standard.

One could conclude from this that Schellenberg would say that one or both of the Pascalian constraints I have put forward must be in error. Either the Wide Accessibility Principle should be strengthened, so that it says that everyone who is willing to know God actually knows God, or the Easy Resistibility Principle should be modified, so that it says, not that the knowledge of God can be easily resisted, but that it can be resisted only at the cost of culpable irrationality. Schellenberg would affirm the latter because he thinks that, if the evidence for God is as strong as it should be, the only people who will fail to believe will be people who have culpably dealt with the evidence in irrational ways.[16] "A perfectly loving God—if those words mean anything—would ensure that some form of conscious and meaningful relationship with herself was always possible for capable and nonresistant finite persons."[17] So, if Schellenberg is right, then the fact that theistic natural signs satisfy the Wide Accessibility Principle and the Easy Resistibility Principle in the forms I have given them will not be significant. The knowledge of God should be far more available than it is; resistance to such knowledge should be harder than it is.

RESPONSES TO SCHELLENBERG

The first question to ask concerning Schellenberg's claims is whether the theistic natural signs in fact do meet the strengthened principles of availability and resistibility he would recommend. If Schellenberg is wrong in his contention that there are cases of inculpable non-belief,

---

[15] Schellenberg, *Divine Hiddenness*, 82.
[16] Schellenberg, *Divine Hiddenness*, 63.
[17] J. L. Schellenberg, *The Wisdom to Doubt: A Justification of Religious Skepticism* (Ithaca, NY: Cornell University Press, 2007), 202.

and all the cases in which the theistic natural signs fail to produce belief are ones in which the non-believer does not want to believe in God, then it is possible the theistic signs I have presented would in fact meet Schellenberg's requirement, if it should turn out to be the case that resistance to the signs is always motivated resistance.

Schellenberg himself thinks that an overwhelming case can be made that there are cases of inculpable non-belief. For such non-belief to be inculpable, Schellenberg thinks that the failure to believe must not be the result of inadequate or biased investigation or reflection, nor the result of self-deception that misreads the evidence.[18] It seems clear to him that there are individuals who meet such criteria. He cites cases in which individuals have devoted strenuous effort to investigation and reflection about God, and who appear to be honest and unbiased people. Some of them are people who claim to want very much to believe in God and yet find themselves unable to find enough evidence to produce belief.

Despite Schellenberg's argument here, it is far from obvious that there are cases of inculpable non-belief. Douglas Henry has argued very powerfully that it is reasonable to doubt that there are any such cases.[19] Schellenberg cites two different kinds of non-culpable non-belief: unreflective and reflective non-belief. In the first category Schellenberg includes "individuals—primarily from non-Western cultures—who have never so much as entertained the proposition 'God exists', let alone considered the question of its truth or falsity."[20] Henry questions the factual accuracy of this claim, citing anthropologists and ethnographers who regularly seem to find some conception of God in all tribal societies.[21] With respect to reflective non-belief, Henry rightly raises the daunting question as to how it is possible to have any assurance that any human is not self-deceived when claims are made that the person wants to believe in God. The

[18] Schellenberg, *Divine Hiddenness*, 65–9.
[19] See Douglas Henry, "Does Reasonable Nonbelief Exist?" *Faith and Philosophy*, 18 (2001), 75–92. Schellenberg responded in "On Reasonable Nonbelief and Perfect Love: Replies to Henry and Lehe," *Faith and Philosophy*, 22 (2005), 330–42. Henry carries the argument further in "Reasonable Doubts about Reasonable Nonbelief," *Faith and Philosophy*, 25 (2008), 276–89.
[20] Schellenberg, *Divine Hiddenness*, 58.
[21] Henry, "Reasonable Doubts," 278–9.

last question is given added pertinence by the Christian doctrine of original sin, which holds that the human race as a whole is fallen and in rebellion against God. Given the complexity of the human mind and the human heart, if humans are a sinful race, then all humans are, to some extent, in rebellion against God. If this were true, it would be exceedingly difficult to know whether any person, including oneself, is self-deceived.

However, despite the difficulty of knowing whether such non-culpable non-belief actually exists, I shall ignore this problem and proceed on the assumption that Schellenberg is right in claiming that some people do not know about God through no fault of their own. I make this assumption willingly, because it does seem to me that sometimes theistic natural signs are impaired in their operation by factors for which the individual is not to blame. If this is the case, then theistic natural signs will not meet Schellenberg's altered versions of the Wide Accessibility Principle and the Easy Resistibility Principle. Is this a significant problem for theistic natural signs? For a number of reasons I do not think that it is a problem. Let me begin with the general status of a priori claims about what God would or would not do.

Schellenberg says that his claim that God would not permit non-culpable non-belief, which is equivalent to the alternative modified versions of the Wide Accessibility Principle and the Easy Resistibility Principle I have discussed, is a conceptually necessary consequence of the claim that God is perfectly loving and loves human persons. However, our conceptual intuitions about such matters are surely defeasible, and, in some cases, highly uncertain. I would argue that, as our claims about what God would and would not do become more detailed, they necessarily become more uncertain. Perhaps we can be somewhat confident that, if God loves human persons, he will be devoted to their good. But can we be sure exactly what that good is? Even if we think that the ultimate good for a human can be known, and even if that good includes a loving and conscious relationship with God, do we know what path or paths might best lead to that good? It seems very dubious that we can infer anything concrete and specific about what God might will for me at 9:30 tomorrow morning from the claim that God loves me.

Schellenberg's intuitions about what a loving God would necessarily do are grounded in his intuitions about how loving human persons would treat each other. Humans who love each other desire those they love to share in a personal relationship of love, a relationship that requires some conscious awareness on the part of the lovers of each other. According to Schellenberg, since a loving relationship with God would be such an enormous good, a loving God would necessarily make such a relationship possible, and this, in turn, implies that God would make knowledge of himself possible for all who wished to have it.

However, even though I grant that there are analogies between divine and human love, there are also enormous disanalogies, and these disanalogies make detailed predictions about what a divine lover would do uncertain. In effect, Schellenberg is saying: "If I were God and loved human persons, this is how I would relate to them." The difficulty is that Schellenberg is not God; nor are any of the rest of us mere mortals. Since we are not God, we cannot be confident we know how we would relate to humans if we were. Consider the analogy of a small child, who believes that the essential expression of a parent's love is a gift of candy. The child might well think: "If I were a parent and really loved my children, I would give them all the candy they could possibly want." Of course a child who thought this would be expressing the limitations of his or her childish perspective; things look entirely different from the perspective of the parent, who has a different understanding of what is truly good for the child, and thus about what it means to express love for the child.

In many ways the difference between our human understanding of God and the good and God's understanding of himself and the good is vastly greater than the difference between the child's and the parent's perspective. The differences between parent and child are relative, but God is infinite and humans are finite. This does not mean we can have no idea of what God's love for us would be like; I agree with Schellenberg that God's love must resemble our human loves in some ways. However, it does mean that our intuitions about what God's love is like, and how that love will express itself, will be fallible, and highly fallible with respect to details.

If we reflect just a bit about how vastly God's situation is different from our own, these problems will become clear. One thing that seems evident is that, if there is a God, and if God desires a relationship with humans, it is very important to God *how* such a relationship is developed. He does not care only *that* humans enjoy such a relationship with him but also about how they acquire the relationship. This seems perfectly reasonable, since a relationship is partly constituted by its history. Presumably God could simply have created humans as "finished" beings with all the virtues and excellences he desires them to have. However, it is clear that God created humans as unfinished works-in-progress, and it seems plausible that he did so because he wanted them to play a role in their own development, and to play a role in the development of their relationship with himself. It seems at least possible that a final state that is attained through some kind of struggle is more valuable than one that is achieved without any effort.

If it is a necessary truth that there are no instances of non-culpable non-belief, then of course there must be no moment of time in which any person who would be willing to believe in God fails to know that God exists, and that in turn seems incompatible with admitting any process of struggle in which the knowledge of God might be lacking for a time. However, it seems quite possible that some persons might eventually enjoy a relation with God that is even more valuable because a conscious relation to God was something that took a long time to achieve. It seems possible that this is so, even if the person comes to enjoy a conscious relationship with God only after death. If God's purposes for humans do not end at the grave, and most religious perspectives do include beliefs about a continued life after death, then, if a person's relationship with God is enhanced by a process (in some cases a lengthy one) through which that relationship is created, these advantages over an eternity might swamp any privations that the person would endure in this life. So the claim that it is a necessary truth that God would not allow any person who wishes to know God to fail to believe in God at any moment seems dubious.

Schellenberg's complaint about the hiddenness of God is surely a special case of the general problem of evil. A failure to have a conscious relationship with God is clearly an evil, or at least a loss of a great good. Schellenberg in effect argues that a perfectly loving God who is also omniscient and all-powerful could prevent this evil and would do so, exactly as proposed by the traditional problem of evil for other evils. The problem of evil certainly presents a challenge for theistic belief, something recognized by both theists and atheists. However, it is by no means clear that the particular evil constituted by God's hiddenness makes the problem any more difficult. There are many goods that some people enjoy that are not enjoyed by others, and many others that are enjoyed by different people in different degrees. Some people enjoy a happy and secure family life; others are abused. Some are relatively healthy; others suffer painful and devastating illnesses. If there is no good answer to the problem of evil—no viable defense or theodicy, to use the language of contemporary philosophy of religion—then belief in God faces a daunting challenge. It is not clear to me that adding to the list of known evils the evil of failing to know God in this life changes the problem in any way. Someone who thinks that belief in God is still reasonable when children die of cancer is unlikely to think that belief in God is made unreasonable by the fact that some people who would like to know God in this life are unable to do so.

As I have already said, the problem of evil is generally answered through either a theodicy or a defense.[22] A theodicy attempts to explain why God allows evils, to give the reasons that justify God in doing so.[23] A defense argues that we have good reason to believe God has such reasons, even if we do not know what those reasons are. Part of a defense may consist of giving possible reasons why God might allow some evils, reasons that may figure in plausible accounts of why some evils may be justified. Such accounts might strengthen a defense in the following way: if we find that there are plausible reasons for God to allow evils in some cases, this gives some reason to think that God might have such reasons in other cases as well. Why believe this? One good reason might be this. If I have some knowledge of God and of God's character, this knowledge may properly be the ground of trust. If I know God is good, I may believe God has reasons for allowing evil, even if I do not know what those reasons are.[24]

[22] This distinction is made, for example, by Alvin Plantinga, *God, Freedom, and Evil* (New York: Harper & Row, 1974). See my earlier discussion of this point in Ch. 4, n. 29.

[23] For contemporary theodicies, see Richard Swinburne, *The Existence of God* (2nd edn.; Oxford: Oxford University Press, 2004), 236–72, and Peter van Inwagen (ed.), *Christian Faith and the Problem of Evil* (Grand Rapids, MI: Eerdmans, 2004).

[24] For a sketch of a defense along these lines, see my "Faith and the Problem of Evil," in *Faith beyond Reason: A Kierkegaardian Account* (Grand Rapids, MI: Eerdmans, 1998), 126–37.

A human analogy might help at this point. Suppose my wife has done something that appears to be unloving, such as failing to return home when she promised she would, and suppose I do not know why she has behaved in this manner. My failure to know what her reasons are does not mean I am unreasonable to believe she has good reasons for her actions. My faith in her and belief that she has good reasons for her behavior are justified by my knowledge of her character.

Some theodicy or defense along these lines will be important if belief in God is to be reasonable. Either a theodicy or a defense is possible or it is not. I strongly suspect that if a defense or a theodicy can be given for the problem of evil in general, then this same strategy will be adequate for dealing with the problem of the hiddenness of God. If no defense or theodicy can be given, then it will be difficult to mount a case for belief in God. Perhaps such a task is not impossible, since, even if there is serious evidence against the existence of God, that evidence might be overwhelmed by positive evidence. But, however difficult the task, I do not see how the problem of the hiddenness of God makes things any worse for the religious believer.

In dealing with the hiddenness problem, as with other forms of the problem of evil, I would not claim to have a theodicy. That is, I do not claim to know why God sometimes allows people who wish to know God to fail to do so. But I think we can imagine some possible reasons why God might do this, at least for some cases. One I have already noted: it may be that delaying the good of a conscious relationship to God makes that good even better once it is realized. But there are other possibilities as well.[25]

One is to recognize the social character of human beings. It is plausible to think that God's goal for humans is not simply for individual human persons to enjoy a relation with God, but for humans to be part of a community—the kingdom of God—composed of those who love God and the good. However, to be part of such a community, humans must be social beings, beings who are not self-sufficient as individuals but persons who necessarily live their lives by giving to others and receiving from others. In any case, it

---

[25] For a number of possibilities I do not discuss, see the articles in Daniel Howard-Snyder and Paul K. Moser (eds.), *Divine Hiddenness: New Essays* (Cambridge: Cambridge University Press, 2002).

seems clear that humans are social creatures of this sort, and that their character as social beings extends to their cognitive lives. Most of what all of us know and believe is due to those who have brought us up and the communities that continue to shape us. The power to be shaped by such communities is necessarily a power to be helped or hurt, depending on the nature of the community.

I believe that some of the most plausible possible cases of non-culpable non-belief are people who fail to know God because they have been taught by family and friends that God does not exist. It is hard to see how God could have created humans to be genuinely interdependent beings without allowing for the possibility that some people will, though no fault of their own, be prevented by their community from coming to know lots of things, including having knowledge about God. However, it seems very plausible that the goods made possible by our character as social beings outweigh the damage that is sometimes done, especially if God has ways of overcoming such damage, either in this life or in eternity.

However, it is evident that, besides making us social creatures, God has made us finite creatures. Indeed, what else could creatures be? God has made all kinds of finite creatures, with different kinds of powers and liabilities, and we humans have no justified grounds for complaining that we are the kind of finite creatures we are. As finite creatures, humans make mistakes. Sometimes the mistakes may be motivated ones for which we properly incur blame, but many of them simply seem to reflect our finitude. Such finitude would seem to imply that, no matter how strong and clear God made the evidence for himself, it would always be possible to make a mistake about that evidence.[26] There is no reason to think that all such mistakes would be blameworthy, and no reason to think that God could prevent them all, short of either vastly enhancing our cognitive powers or constantly intervening in our cognitive lives. So it is not clear that the stronger version of the Wide Accessibility Principle was within God's power to accomplish with respect to creatures such as ourselves.

Schellenberg seems to think that it would be easy for God to provide enough evidence to make non-culpable non-belief impossible, while

---

[26] Jonathan Kvanvig makes this point in "Divine Hiddenness: What is the Problem?" in Howard-Snyder and Moser (eds.), *Divine Hiddenness: New Essays*, 155.

still making it possible for those who do not wish to know God to avoid such knowledge. However, it is not clear that God could have accomplished this. Perhaps the epistemic environment that would be necessary to block all cases of non-culpable non-belief is one in which the evidence for God would be very clear and very powerful, so clear and powerful that not even a determined upbringing by atheist parents would suffice to block its effects. But evidence that is so clear and powerful would surely be very difficult for the willing non-believer to ignore, perhaps even impossible. But, even if it were not impossible, it seems plausible to think that God wishes those who do have a relation with him to enter such a relation willingly, with no hint of coercion or compulsion of belief. And, if that is so, perhaps God would not want to make it very difficult to evade knowledge of him; rather, he would want to allow people to escape from a knowledge of him without undue effort on their part.

Perhaps it is even better for those who do have religious faith that their belief stem from a situation that allows for some uncertainty, since such a situation allows one to demonstrate how much one cares about what one is committed to. A person who commits to a cause whose success is still uncertain shows that he or she loves that cause deeply. Such a commitment may also be a way of deepening one's love for that cause, since social psychologists tell us that our emotional attachments are to some degree influenced by our actions. If I have risked something for a cause, I will love that cause more, but if there is some uncertainty about God's reality, then a commitment to work toward the triumph of God's kingdom will also be uncertain, and therefore risky. Hence it is not implausible that allowing a degree of religious ambiguity that makes possible non-culpable non-belief also enhances and enriches possible forms of belief.

I conclude that my original versions of the Wide Accessibility Principle and the Easy Resistibility Principle are more reasonable than the enhanced versions someone impressed by Schellenberg's hiddenness argument might put forward. It seems plausible that God would make knowledge of his reality widely available, and the theistic natural signs, if genuine, do make this possible. It also seems plausible that the knowledge of God should be easily resistible, and so it is not surprising or particularly troublesome that the theistic natural signs do not compel belief in God, but rather allow for alternative interpretations and explanations.

BASIC BELIEFS AND THE PROBLEM OF JUSTIFICATION

A critic might respond at this point in the following way: "I suppose that the story you have told about theistic natural signs is a *possible* one. The things you have discussed, such as the experience of cosmic wonder and the apparent purposive order we observe in the natural world, as well as our sense of moral obligation and perception of humans as intrinsically valuable, do have some of the characteristics of natural signs. They have some degree of force that points toward belief in God, as evidenced by the fact that even non-believers appreciate their power. They are easily recognizable and in fact widely recognized, and very plausibly contribute to the formation of religious beliefs across many cultures. However, you have not shown that this possibility is an actuality. You need to show not merely that theistic natural signs are putative evidence for God, but that they provide genuine evidence."

One way of attempting to satisfy this challenge would be to try to convert the theistic natural signs into propositional evidence. Essentially, this is what happens when the signs are made the basis of the classical theistic arguments. As I have shown in Chapters 3–5, this can be done and has been done. Propositions such as "The universe exhibits beneficial order" and "There are objective moral obligations" become part of the evidence for the proposition that "God exists," through either deductive arguments or Swinburne-style inductive arguments. As we have seen in these discussions, there are many different arguments that can be developed from the natural signs, and some of the arguments have considerable force. Many people find them to be sound and convincing, and, to avoid their conclusions, critics are sometimes forced to make claims that are implausible (at least to some people), as when the "error theorist" about moral obligations denies we are ever truly morally obligated to perform an action. None of the arguments seems to be a proof, in the sense of "proof" that requires an argument that no reasonable person can reject. However, this failing is not really a failing. First of all, it seems unlikely that any philosophical arguments for any significant conclusion rise to this level of proof. And the Easy Resistibility Principle gives us a special reason to think that no such proof should be expected for God's reality.

So one way of answering the critic is to focus our attention on the sign, develop it into a proposition, and employ the proposition as a basis for an inference to some proposition about God's reality. However, if I am right about the character of theistic natural signs, this is not the only way the signs can function epistemically. If we focus solely on the propositional evidence they provide, we will fail to see a significant part of their value.

Theistic natural signs are modeled on Reidean natural signs. The most striking feature of Reidean natural signs is that they make possible basic knowledge, knowledge that is not the product of any inference or argument. I come to know such propositions as "There is a solid desk in front of me" or "My friend over there is sad and worried" by means of certain sensations (in the case of the desk) or perceptions (in the case of my friend). The natural signs are the means whereby I come to know these things, but they are not the basis of any inference or argument. Part of Reid's genius was to see, and to argue powerfully, that, unless we can come to know some things in this basic way, we could not know anything at all. After all, our ability to make inferences depends on knowing the premises of the arguments we are employing.

There still may be a sense in which Reidean natural signs can be seen as evidence. The signs are things that people are aware of, or can become aware of, and they do make certain truths evident to us. If we are open to the idea that there can be such a thing as non-propositional evidence, then Reidean natural signs may rightly be described as a type of evidence. The signs as evidence will consist of either sensations or observed features of the natural world that make certain truths evident to us. However, since neither sensations nor observed features of the natural world are propositions, we cannot say that they are evidence in the sense that they provide a basis for an inference to some other proposition that they make more probable, in the way that is commonly thought to be the case in probability theory, which allows us to estimate the probability of some proposition (the "hypothesis") relative to some other propositions (the "evidence" and the "background knowledge"). Alternatively, we could avoid the language of evidence altogether and simply ask whether the beliefs that are based on the theistic natural signs are justified.

Some philosophers, such as Paul Moser, claim that non-conceptual evidence can be a "probability-maker" for a proposition.[27] Moser argues for the view that "evidential probability derives ultimately from the subjective contents of one's non-propositional psychological states."[28] However, it is clear that the sense of probability employed here is non-epistemic. The psychological states make the propositions in question more probable in the sense that the truth of the propositions provides an explanation for the occurrence of those psychological states. However, this seems to presuppose that we know something about the causes of those psychological states. If we know it to be true that we are more likely to have a certain kind of experience when we are in the presence of a particular physical object, then one can say that the experience makes the presence of that object more probable or likely. Perhaps one could even speak of an "inference" from the perception to the object. However, this is not a normal inference. Or, if it is, it is because we have transformed the non-propositional experience into a proposition and reasoned as follows: "From the fact that I am being appeared to in a particular way, I infer that a particular kind of object is present to me." This kind of inference presupposes that I have knowledge of the connections between my experiences and the world; it is not the basis of such knowledge.

In a similar way, the proponent of theistic natural signs might say that the signs make the existence of God more probable. If we know that it is the case that God is the cause of the signs and that therefore the truth of the proposition "God exists" is part of the explanation for the occurrence of the signs, then we could certainly say the signs are probability-makers for propositions about God. However, the critic of theistic signs may well object that this presupposes the truth of the basic story about theistic natural signs and therefore cannot be used to justify that story.

---

[27] See Paul Moser, *Knowledge and Evidence* (Cambridge Studies in Philosophy; Cambridge: Cambridge University Press, 1989).
[28] Moser, *Knowledge and Evidence*, 7.

The problem stems from the fact that the whole purpose of natural signs, both Reidean and theistic, is to give us knowledge that is basic, non-inferential, and therefore not derived from anything else one knows. Let us suppose that at least some basic knowledge does depend on some kind of non-propositional evidence, something that makes the truth of the relevant propositions more evident. That still does not help us to determine, with regard to any specific instance of knowledge or even any type of knowledge, what is actual or genuine evidence.

How are we to decide when evidence is actual or genuine and when it is not? In posing this question, I am asking only whether theistic natural signs provide evidence in that weak sense of "evidence" in which evidence makes the truth of a belief more likely. I mean to ask whether they provide *some* reason for believing that there is a God. One may also say that the evidence would weakly justify the belief. The question as to whether a person is strongly justified in believing that there is a God will depend not solely on the theistic natural signs but on the total evidence that the person has. This will include questions about whether the person has defeaters for the belief in God, such as good reasons to believe there is no God. Even if theistic natural signs do provide evidence for belief in God, that evidence might be outweighed or undercut by such defeaters. I will discuss the idea of one's total evidence in the conclusion of this chapter, but the question of whether a person's overall evidence justifies belief in God must be distinguished from the question as to whether the theistic natural signs provide genuine evidence at all.

Most philosophers today adopt *fallibilist* answers to questions about what counts as good evidence. That is, they admit that, at least in the vast majority of cases, human beings might be mistaken in the judgments we make about what constitutes good evidence. Nor do we humans have any methods or procedures guaranteed to remedy this defect. However, even those contemporary philosophers who are fallibilists are deeply divided as to how we (fallibly) decide when our evidence is good evidence.

One of the fault lines on which the divide is most evident is the dispute between *internalists* and *externalists*.[29] There are many different versions of each type of epistemology, but, roughly, internalists claim that what justifies a person in a belief must be something internal to the person's consciousness. Justification must stem from something to which a person has mental access, something that the person is aware of or can easily become aware of on reflection. Externalists deny that justification must stem from some internally accessible mental state of the person. Instead, what justifies a belief (or gives it some other favorable epistemic status) for a person are facts about the relationship between that person and the external world. One common type of externalism is reliabilism, which says that beliefs are justified (or warranted, or have some other favorable epistemic status) when they are produced by reliable belief-forming practices.

The question as to how we determine that evidence for our basic beliefs is good evidence will be answered very differently by internalists and externalists, at least in most cases. For the internalist the natural focus of attention will be on some feature of the ground of the basic belief to which the subject has mental access. For the externalist the natural focus of attention will be on some facts about the way the belief was formed. In the next section I will try to look at the kinds of answer that can be offered by both internalists and externalists to the question as to how we decide that evidence for basic beliefs is good evidence. An alternative way of putting matters, if one wanted to avoid the language of evidence, would be to say that I shall examine the question as to how basic beliefs are justified from both internalist and externalist perspectives. The goal, of course, is to see what the implications of those answers might be for the question as to whether theistic natural signs count as good evidence in the sense that they might justify belief in God in a prima facie way. I shall argue that, whether one is an internalist or an externalist, if one

---

[29] For a classic discussion of these two types of epistemologies, see William Alston, "Internalism and Externalism in Epistemology," in *Epistemic Justification: Essays in the Theory of Knowledge* (Ithaca, NY: Cornell University Press, 1989), 185–226.

adopts an epistemological stance that is adequate for avoiding general skepticism, a strong case can be made for theistic natural signs as providing genuine evidence for God's reality.

EXTERNALIST AND INTERNALIST ACCOUNTS OF JUSTIFIED BASIC BELIEFS: IMPLICATIONS FOR THEISTIC NATURAL SIGNS

I shall look first at an externalist account of such matters, and then proceed to examine an internalist answer. As noted above, I shall assume that an epistemology that cannot provide a convincing account of how ordinary forms of basic knowledge, such as perceptual and memory beliefs, are justified, is a non-starter. It will not be especially surprising or worrisome to a religious believer if an epistemology that implies that we have no justified basic beliefs about the perceptual world also implies that we have no justified basic beliefs about God.

An Externalist Perspective

Both externalists and internalists agree that a belief that amounts to knowledge must be more than a lucky guess. What we know must be true, but, in a case where we have knowledge, the truth of our beliefs cannot be an accident. Hence, it is important that our beliefs have some such property as being justified or warranted, a property that should make a belief more likely to be true. William Alston expresses this idea by saying that justification requires that a belief be based on an adequate ground, and an adequate ground is one that is truth-conducive; a belief with an adequate ground is more likely to be true.[30] But how do we know, with respect to a basic belief, that it is based on an adequate ground? The most plausible answer from an externalist perspective is surely that the ground is one that we know usually produces true beliefs. Whether the ground be a particular

---

[30] See William Alston, "An Internalist Externalism," in *Epistemic Justification*, 227–45.

experience, a human faculty operating in particular circumstances, or something else, we must know that the ground is more likely to give us a true belief than not. An apparent problem with this kind of view is that it may be difficult or impossible to avoid circularity, in that we will have to rely on the grounds that are being questioned in order to determine whether those grounds have a good track record. But is circularity in this case something that must be avoided, or is it an unavoidable feature of the human situation?

An impressive case has been made by a variety of different philosophers that, with respect to our human faculties that produce basic knowledge, no non-circular or non-question-begging justification of those faculties can be given.[31] Human beings clearly have a variety of ways of forming basic beliefs, described in different language by different philosophers. These different "faculties," "belief-forming mechanisms," or "modules of our cognitive system" include such things as perception, memory, and rational intuition.[32] Thomas Reid argued persuasively that it is part of what he called "common sense" to trust our basic human faculties. Must we simply adopt a policy of trusting these faculties, or can this trust be rationally justified?

One might think that we can give a justification for the reliability of such faculties as perception or memory. Since these faculties give us mostly true beliefs, we are inductively justified in believing them to be reliable and therefore justified in relying on them. However, it is clear on reflection that any justification we offer of this type will be circular; we cannot know that perception is a reliable source of belief without relying on perception, and the same will be true of memory and other faculties. We can argue that these belief sources are justified by their track records, but we cannot know that they have good track records without relying on their trustworthiness.

---

[31] See, e.g., William Alston, "Epistemic Circularity," in *Epistemic Justification*, 319–49; Michael Bergmann, "Reidian Externalism," in Vincent F. Hendricks and Duncan Pritchard (eds.), *New Waves in Epistemology* (New Waves in Philosophy; New York: Palgrave Macmillan, 2008), ch. 3.

[32] Thomas Reid and many older philosophers prefer "faculties." Alvin Plantinga, in his *Warrant and Proper Function* (New York: Oxford University Press, 1993), uses the language of "faculties" as well as "belief-forming mechanisms." Jack C. Lyons describes these basic ways of knowing as "modules" in *Perception and Basic Beliefs: Zombies, Modules, and the Problem of the External World* (Oxford: Oxford University Press, 2009).

Michael Bergmann has recently argued that the reliability of our basic cognitive faculties is itself a deliverance of one of those faculties, the faculty that Reid called "common sense" and that has as part of its output the "first principles" that govern our epistemic lives.[33] If this is so, then belief in the reliability of perception and memory and other human faculties would be based on this first principle, and would not have to be based on circular "track-record" arguments. However, ultimately there is still circularity, since common sense is itself one of our faculties, and we cannot argue that it produces true beliefs without relying on it. So in the end even Bergmann concedes that "we simply can't check on the reliability of our belief sources without relying on our belief sources."[34] William Alston concurs, speaking about reliabilism in particular, but making a claim that applies to externalism in general:

Thus, for reliabilism there is no escape from epistemic circularity in the assessment of our fundamental sources of belief. Since the question of whether we have perceptual knowledge depends on whether perceptual, belief-forming mechanisms are reliable, as well as on whether perceptual beliefs are true, it is ineluctably an empirical question, one that we can tackle only by relying on perceptual beliefs to do so, thereby assuming, at least in practice, that those beliefs are reliably produced.[35]

Bergmann has argued that epistemic circularity of this sort can be benign. Roughly, he claims, circularity of this sort is a bad thing only when one has a "questioned source context," in which one has reason to doubt the output of a particular belief source.[36] Obviously, it will not

---

[33] See Michael Bergmann, "Epistemic Circularity: Malignant and Benign," *Philosophy and Phenomenological Research*, 69/3 (2004), 709–27. See particularly p. 723 for the discussion of common sense and first principles.

[34] Bergmann, "Epistemic Circularity," 725.

[35] William Alston, "Knowledge of God," in Marcus Hester (ed.), *Faith, Reason, and Skepticism: Essays* (Philadelphia: Temple University Press, 1992), 41.

[36] This is the main thrust of "Epistemic Circularity." It is worth noting that in *Justification without Awareness: A Defense of Epistemic Externalism* (Oxford: Oxford University Press, 2006), Bergmann slightly modifies this account of a "questioned source context." The revised version sees epistemic circularity as malignant, not just when a person has a reason to question a source, but also when the person should have a reason. See pp. 198–200 of *Justification without Awareness* and especially note 30 for a clear explanation of the changes. My thanks to Michael Bergmann for his help in clarifying these matters.

help much to appeal to a source when the credentials of the sources are doubtful. However, as Bergmann points out, in some cases a person has no reason to question a source and in such a case may naturally and properly rely on it to justify a meta-belief about the reliability of that source. However, whether benign or not, externalists argue that we have no choice but to trust the human faculties that generate our basic beliefs, even though we know that they are not infallible. We must either simply trust our faculties, or accept them because of reasons that are ultimately circular, since they also involve trusting our faculties. Any other policy would imply that we have no justified beliefs at all.

From an externalist point of view, the implications of this for theistic natural signs are clear. If theistic natural signs operate naturally to produce basic beliefs in God, then such beliefs should, like other basic beliefs that are produced by natural faculties, be trusted unless there are good reasons to think that these belief-forming processes are unreliable. If theistic natural signs generate mostly true beliefs, then they are a reliable source of true beliefs. If what they appear to make evident to us is usually true, then if we think of them as evidence they provide actual or genuine evidence.

Of course the non-believer is unlikely to accept any of this. The non-believer will probably argue, in an equally circular way, that the outputs of this process are not reliable, since there is no God and the beliefs generated by theistic natural signs are mostly false. In Bergmann's words, for the non-believer theistic natural signs operate in a "contested source context," and in such a context a circular argument is unlikely to change the non-believer's mind. In the next section, I shall say something about the value theistic natural signs may have to such a religious skeptic, but it is certainly unlikely that the skeptic will be moved by this kind of circular argument.

The non-believer will probably point to the chief disanalogy we noted between Reidean natural signs and theistic natural signs: theistic natural signs seem to be less universal and more easily resistible than most Reidean natural signs, and argue that this disanalogy means we are justified in being suspicious of theistic natural signs, even if we accept other basic sources of knowledge without any non-circular rational support. However, it is not clear that this disanalogy is so significant that it should override the default policy of trusting our human faculties. First, as we noted, even some Reidean natural signs can be modified, inhibited, and even blocked by other beliefs, so the disanalogy is not absolute. Second, if the Easy Resistibility Principle is plausible, as I have argued, then this disanalogy is precisely what one would expect of a genuine natural sign for God. So even if the non-believer rejects theistic natural signs as good evidence, it seems very reasonable for someone who sees these signs as natural signs with genuine force to rely on them in arriving at or confirming a belief in God's existence. If God is real, it seems very plausible such a person does have good evidence, or at least that the person is reasonable to think this is the case, even if the non-believer does not agree.

Some may find this result disappointing; they may have hoped for a more definitive judgment from a philosopher, some argument that would settle the issue one way or the other. However, it is not really surprising from an externalist point of view that this is the way things are, since externalists have a more modest perspective on the value and limits of epistemology than do some internalists.[37] Some philosophers have thought that the purpose of epistemology was to give us an account of knowledge that would allow us to tell when our knowledge was genuine and when it is not. The job of the epistemologist on this view would be, one might say, to give us something like a certificate of authenticity for knowledge claims, one that will guarantee that we have the real thing. The externalist rejects this picture. For the externalist, epistemology is theorizing about knowledge, but it must presuppose that the object of the theorizing exists, just as philosophy of art assumes that there is such a thing as art, and philosophy of science that there is such a thing as science. It is not the job of the philosopher to tell the scientist what counts as genuine science. In a similar way, it is not the job of the epistemologist to tell human beings which of their beliefs count as genuine knowledge.

Internalism

How do things look from the perspective of internalism? One might think that the internalist perspective is more promising to resolve

---

[37] See my discussion of "modest" and "ambitious" epistemology in *The Historical Christ and the Jesus of Faith: The Incarnational Narrative as History* (Oxford: Oxford University Press, 1996), 203–30.

such disputes as the argument about theistic natural signs. From the internalist perspective, it is not enough for justification for a belief to be formed in a reliable manner, or for a belief to be based on a ground that is in fact truth conducive and therefore adequate. Rather, the subject must be *aware* of such facts: know that the process that gave rise to the belief is reliable or that the ground of the belief is adequate. One might think that this awareness on the part of the subject gives justification that is not circular in the way that justifications of belief-forming processes are from an externalist perspective.

In reality it is not clear that an internalist perspective is as helpful as it might seem. Michael Bergmann has argued that internalism is subject to a dilemma.[38] The whole motivation for internalism lies in the intuition that, for a belief to be justified, the subject must be aware or potentially aware of "what the belief has going for it." The justification for a belief must therefore be something that lies within the mental purview of the subject. In laying out his dilemma, Bergmann begins by distinguishing strong awareness from weak awareness. He describes strong awareness of what justifies the belief as awareness that involves conceiving of the justifier as relevant in some way to the belief's justification or truth; all other awareness of what justifies the belief is weak awareness. Clearly, the awareness of what justifies the belief must be either strong or weak. The problem is that, if strong awareness is required, it looks like no belief is justified. This is because the awareness that justifies the belief will itself at least involve conceptualization, which will have to be justified, requiring a further conceptualization, on to infinity (with each additional conceptualization being more complex than the previous one).

If the internalist drops the idea of strong awareness as a requirement for justification, and opts only for weak awareness, in which the subject is aware of what justifies the belief but is not required to conceive of the justifier as relevant to the belief's justification, the other horn of

---

[38] Bergmann develops this dilemma in some detail in *Justification without Awareness*. See chapter 1, pp. 3–24, for an initial statement of the dilemma, which is then defended at length in the book as a whole. Bergmann gives a briefer version of the argument in "Reidian Externalism." I am grateful to Bergmann, both for correcting some earlier misunderstandings of his argument, and for helping me formulate the simplified summary of his argument that follows in the text.

the dilemma must be faced. For it is not clear how being aware of what, from some objective perspective, would justify a belief will satisfy the internalist intuition that a belief be justified from the perspective of the subject, if the subject does not and cannot recognize how the justifier is relevant to justification. Such a weak form of internalism seems to offer no real advantage over externalism.

There is another difficulty with internalist views of justification that is highly relevant to the problem of circularity we noted in connection with externalist views. Internalists want to say that it is not enough that a perceptual belief or memory belief is formed in a reliable way, or on the basis of a truth-conducive ground. They insist that it is important that we in some way know or are aware that the process is reliable or the ground is adequate. (This is, of course, what generates the awareness requirement that leads to regress problems in Bergmann's dilemma argument.) Internalists want to avoid circularity for perceptual and memory beliefs by appealing to what is variously called rational reflection or intuition. However, rational reflection is itself one of the basic sources of human beliefs, one of our human faculties. How do we know that reason itself is a reliable source of truth? There is little prospect of giving any justification here that is not circular. It looks as if the internalist, like the externalist, must simply posit a basic trust in at least one of our human faculties.[39]

Thomas Reid argued that there is an arbitrariness in demanding that our human faculties that give us basic beliefs other than reason be justified by reason, while accepting reason itself on trust: "Why, sir, should I believe the faculty of reason more than that of perception?—they came both out of the same shop, and were made by the same artist; and if he puts one piece of false ware into my hands, what should hinder him from putting another."[40] Reid expresses this thought within a theistic framework, but a naturalist who thinks our faculties are simply the product of natural evolution with no designer could make a similar point.

---

[39] William Alston argues very powerfully for this in "Knowledge of God," 22–4.

[40] Thomas Reid, *An Inquiry Into the Human Mind on the Principles of Common Sense: A Critical Edition*, ed. Derek R. Brookes (University Park, PA: Pennsylvania State University Press, 1997), 169.

The strength of the internalist perspective is also its weakness. The internalist insists that a belief be justified from the perspective of the believer. The internalist can argue that we have no alternative but to try to arrive at the truth, relying on how things *seem* to us, and that seems correct. If someone advises me to believe only what is true, I can follow that advice only by attempting to believe what seems true to me. The weakness is that we have no guarantee that how things seem to be to us is how they really are. Many skeptical scenarios describe situations in which a person is justified (internally) in believing what is false, as in familiar "brain-in-a-vat" or "evil-demon" stories. If diabolical scientists have put your brain in a vat and stimulated it so as to produce the experiences you are having, the beliefs you form as a result will be internally justified but false.

I think that to avoid a pervasive skepticism the internalist must at some point adopt something like what Michael Huemer has called the principle of phenomenal conservatism: "If it seems to S as if P, then S thereby has at least *prima facie* justification for believing that P."[41] If we are brains in a vat or live in an evil-demon world, and we follow this principle, we will be systematically wrong in the beliefs we hold. Nevertheless, Huemer argues, and I agree, that we have no choice but to follow some principle such as this. Of course, in the actual world, we quickly learn that things are not always as they seem; hence the justification provided by something's seeming to be the case to someone is only prima facie. However, if we did not generally rely on this principle, we could not discover the cases where things are not as they seem, nor anything else.

The principle of phenomenal conservatism defended by Huemer seems very similar to the "principle of credulity" Richard Swinburne defends in connection with his argument that religious experiences provide evidence for God's existence.[42] Swinburne states his principle in the following way: "It is a principle of rationality that (in the absence

---

[41] See Michael Huemer, *Skepticism and the Veil of Perception* (Studies in Epistemology and Cognitive Theory; Lanham, MD: Rowman & Littlefield, 2001), 98. I thank Trent Dougherty, who holds a similar position himself, for calling my attention to Huemer's exceptionally clear account of these matters. From my point of view, it is a plus that Huemer is himself a convinced atheist, and cannot therefore be accused of developing an epistemological view for the benefit of any religious belief.

[42] See Swinburne, *The Existence of God*, 303–15.

of special considerations) if it seems (epistemically) to a subject that *x* is present, then probably *x* is present; what one seems to perceive is probably so." Swinburne may mean for his principle of credulity to apply only to cases of perceptual appearing, but the intuition that underlies the principle seems identical to Huemer's principle. Swinburne argues convincingly that failure to adopt something like his principle of credulity results in a "skeptical bog," and he also argues that there is no good reason not to apply this principle to religious experience as well.[43]

When a person comes to believe in God by way of a theistic natural sign, should this be construed as a direct experience of God? The analogy with Reidean natural signs suggests that the answer is yes. For Reid we experience physical objects by means of sensations. In a similar manner, if God has created the signs in order to make humans aware of his reality, and if there is a natural tendency to form a basic belief in God when one encounters the sign, then theistic natural signs could be seen as one of the means whereby humans come to perceive God. However, since the terms "experience of God" and "religious experience" are often used to refer to particular episodes in which God appears to an individual, rather than a perception of God through some characteristic that is a structural, pervasive part of experienced reality, there might be reason to say that coming to believe in God through a theistic natural sign should not be called an instance of "experiencing God." However, regardless of whether we take the formation of belief in God through theistic natural signs as a religious experience or not, the principle of phenomenal conservatism would seem to support the claim that experiences involving the signs can provide support for belief in God. For clearly it is the case that—for many people—it seems to them that there is a God when they feel cosmic wonder, or experience beneficial order, or have a sense of being morally obligated. The principle of phenomenal conservatism says that we are prima facie justified in believing that things are as they seem to be. Those who "read" the signs as pointing to God's reality thus have prima facie justification for belief in God.

---

[43] Swinburne, *The Existence of God*, 303–6.

THEISTIC NATURAL SIGNS AS PROVIDING PRIMA FACIE EVIDENCE

I conclude that, whether one takes an externalist or internalist view of justification, a good case can be made that theistic natural signs do provide at least weak justification for belief in God. Externalists who are believers and find the signs convincing can say that the signs provide a truth-conducive ground for belief; we can conclude that their evidence is good evidence because it produces true beliefs. We find out what kind of evidence is good evidence by looking to see which kinds of evidence tend to lead us to the truth. To be sure, unbelievers will protest that this argument is circular; since they do not believe in God, they do not share the view that the theistic signs have a good track record in producing true beliefs. However, we have seen that circularity for basic beliefs may be benign, even inescapable.

Is this justification sufficient for knowledge? I believe that in some cases the answer is yes, but to make a case for this would require much more to be said about the concept of knowledge, and much would have to be specified about the particular cases to be discussed. However, many epistemologists certainly hold that one important condition for knowledge is that a belief be justified. At the very least, if belief in God is justified, it is a candidate for knowledge, assuming the belief is true.

A lot depends, at this point, on whether the non-believer claims to know that God does not exist, or at least claims to have good reason for believing that God does not exist, or whether the claim is simply that he or she does not know whether God exists. The former type of claim is a genuine challenge to the truth-conducive character of the theistic signs, and thus the person who makes such a challenge claims to have a defeater for the belief that the signs support. Such a person claims to have evidence *against* the reality of God's existence, a stronger claim than that one merely lacks evidence for God, and the person making such a challenge may be asked to show his cards, so to speak. It is no part of my argument to suggest that theistic natural signs are immune from such challenges. Theistic natural signs, even if they do provide prima facie evidence for God, are vulnerable to such challenges in principle, as is always the case for prima facie evidence.

Internalists who are believers may claim that grasping the signs "suggests" God's reality, to use Reid's own terminology. When they experience the signs, it seems to them to be the case that God stands behind the signs as the one to whom the signs point. Since it seems reasonable to say that we are at least prima facie justified in believing that things are as they appear to us to be, the signs seem to provide prima facie evidence for many people on an internalist account of things as well.

The non-believer will probably find this no more persuasive than the externalist claim that the signs have a good track record, since the signs can be interpreted or explained in alternative ways. Nevertheless, perhaps there is some value in the internalist account at this point, even for the non-believer. The believer may at least appeal to the non-believer to consider once again the force of the theistic natural signs. The non-believer may be urged to "come and stand over here and see how things look." The non-believer might be asked to consider whether it is possible that the operation of the signs has been inhibited or squelched by some cultural factor. (Just as the non-believer may ask the believer to consider whether the perceived force of the signs can be explained as a purely cultural construction.) If the signs constitute genuine non-propositional evidence, then there should be some genuine force to be perceived. In the end no philosophical account can replace the power of the sign itself.

CONCLUSIONS: THE THEISTIC SIGNS, SPECIAL REVELATION, AND THE OVERALL CASE FOR BELIEF IN GOD

I have argued that theistic natural signs can reasonably be viewed as providing prima facie evidence for belief in God. But is the evidence (and justification) provided only prima facie or could such theistic signs make belief in God reasonable in light of a person's overall epistemic situation? To tackle this question several other questions that relate to the issues must be answered. These include questions about the "information output" of the signs: what information do they give us about God? This obviously has great bearing on the question of what kinds of beliefs about God could be justified by the signs. These other questions also include queries about what other kinds of evidence, pro and con, propositional or non-propositional, we have access to about God. As we shall see, these questions are not distinct but interrelated.

Let me begin by considering the information output the signs provide. In Chapter 2 I claimed that we should consider the theistic signs as pointing us to God as a real being; their primary function is not furnishing propositional content but giving us an awareness of God as a reality. It is reasonable to think that they could not do this without also giving us some information about God, but I argued that the information content the signs provide is limited. This implies that those who make use of the signs may have widely varying beliefs about God, with many of those beliefs being erroneous. Some may be monotheists but some might be polytheists. The signs point toward some being or beings that lie behind the observed order of nature, but do not give us very detailed information about that reality.

To be sure, some information comes by way of the signs. Cosmic wonder suggests that whatever reality lies behind the natural universe exists in some deeper, more secure way than the contingent things that cry out for explanation. It has a firmer grip on reality than the transient realities we encounter in our world. Beneficial order suggests that what lies behind the universe is intelligent because purposive. Moral obligation suggests that whatever lies behind the universe is personal and cares about moral goodness; the reality must be a being capable of creating an obligation. A critic of religious belief may claim at this point that these natural signs by themselves could not give us any ultimate justification of belief in God as God is conceived of by Christians, Jews, and Muslims, because the signs leave so much undetermined.

I think the point that underlies this criticism is basically correct. The theistic signs may give us a *de re* awareness of God as a real being, but they underdetermine any beliefs about God we may form as a result. But, even if the critical point is sound, it does not mean that theistic natural signs are not valuable. Even if we cannot know very much about God from the signs—even whether God is one or many—that does not mean we do not learn anything. We might still come to know that naturalism—the doctrine that the natural, physical world is the whole of reality—is false. Even if we do not know much about what lies beyond and behind nature, it might be very valuable to know that there is something beyond and behind nature. I will say more later about why even this very limited knowledge might be valuable.

Meanwhile, it is worth pointing out that, in forming beliefs about God, one would not have to rely on theistic natural signs in isolation. It would be natural to *reflect* on the output of the signs, and very possible that reflection would give us reasons to think that some ways of thinking about the God the signs point to are more adequate than others. As Richard Swinburne has argued, for example, the view that one all-powerful and all-knowing God is responsible for the existence and order of the universe seems much more plausible than the view that the universe is the product of many gods, with varying finite degrees of power, because of the elegance and simplicity of the theistic view. Any view of God or gods as having some finite degree of power necessarily leads to the difficult question as to why that being should have just the amount of power it has. And polytheism by itself does not seem to account for the unity of the natural world, with its pervasive laws and structures. Hence, even if the signs by themselves do not lead to a determinate view of God, there may be good reasons on reflection to conceive of the reality the signs point to in fairly particular ways.

Of course the question of whether theistic natural signs could justify belief in God overall and not just in a prima facie way requires that we consider the overall epistemic situation. I think it is plausible to hold, with Alvin Plantinga, that some people are justified (perhaps also warranted) in having a belief in God that is properly basic.[44] Plantinga speaks of such beliefs as having a "ground," and I think it is plausible to see the theistic natural signs as providing at least some of the grounds for such beliefs. People who find the theistic natural

[44] See Alvin Plantinga, "Reason and Belief in God," in Alvin Plantinga and Nicholas Wolterstorff (eds.), *Faith and Rationality: Reason and Belief in God* (Notre Dame, IN: University of Notre Dame Press, 1983), 16–93, and also *Warranted Christian Belief* (New York: Oxford University Press, 2000).

signs to be powerful and are aware of no defeaters for belief in God are reasonable to believe in God just on their basis.

Philip Quinn and others have argued that, even if it is possible that some people have a proper basic belief in God in this way, many "sophisticated believers" are not in this position, because they are aware of "defeaters" for their belief, and even Plantinga admits that a properly basic belief is defeasible.[45] So, for those who see themselves in this kind of situation, perhaps the justification offered by theistic natural signs will be only prima facie, taken by itself, and will not be sufficient to justify belief without additional considerations. Such people will properly think about other reasons they might have for believing in God or for not believing.

Surely, for example, they will consider the problem of evil. As I have already noted, this is a long-standing problem for theistic belief. There are, I think, three types of responses available to the believer, though these are not all mutually exclusive and some of them might be combined. The first would be some kind of theodicy, explaining and justifying God's allowing evils of various kinds. The second type of response would be a defense, arguing that it is reasonable to believe God has good reasons for allowing evil, even if we do not know what those reasons are. (This defense strategy could also include giving possible reasons why God might allow some kinds of evils, without claiming that they are his actual reasons or that they explain all kinds of evil.[46]) The third type of response would be to argue that, even if evil does constitute evidence against God's reality, that evidence is outweighed by positive evidence, which might be found in religious experiences, in a special revelation from God, and even in the theistic natural signs. This book has focused on theistic natural signs, and not on the problem of evil. It would be foolish to tackle such a daunting problem in a few pages in the conclusion. But it is important to recognize that this is a problem that must be addressed in making any claim that theistic belief is justified overall. Like almost every problem in philosophy, there is no general agreement about whether any of

[45] See Philip L. Quinn, "In Search of the Foundations of Theism," *Faith and Philosophy*, 2/4 (1985), 481.
[46] As noted in Chapter 4, I am here using the term "defense" in a slightly stronger sense than was originally the case with Alvin Plantinga, who introduced it in this context.

the types of responses I have outlined can be successfully carried out. But it is worth noting that a variety of sophisticated responses to the problem have been developed.[47]

In addition to considering potential negative evidence, a sophisticated believer considering whether theistic belief is justified overall should also consider additional positive evidence. For example, the believer might find increased support from the inferential arguments that we have seen can be developed from the theistic natural signs. Some of these arguments may be convincing, in that the premises may be more plausible than their denials; in effect, the arguments may show that rejecting belief in God comes at a steep epistemic price. There may also be inferential arguments that are not rooted in natural signs *per se*, such as the "fine-tuning argument" from the nature of the constants discovered by contemporary physics that are required for the natural world to be as it is.[48]

Besides the evidence that can be developed into formal arguments, there is also the additional evidence provided by experiences of God. As I noted above, there is certainly a legitimate sense in which forming a belief in God through a theistic natural sign could be seen as a type of religious experience. However, I believe this kind of religious experience should be distinguished from a more direct kind of religious experience, in which people sense God as being present to them, or speaking to them, or comforting them, or calling them to some special task, and so on. Impressive arguments have been made by William Alston, Richard Swinburne, George Mavrodes, and

[47] For a forceful version of the problem of evil, see William L. Rowe, "The Problem of Evil and Some Varieties of Atheism," *American Philosophical Quarterly*, 16 (1979); repr. in Marilyn McCord Adams and Robert Merrihew Adams (eds.), *The Problem of Evil* (Oxford Readings in Philosophy; Oxford: Oxford University Press, 1990), 126–37. For responses to the problem, see Stephen J. Wykstra, "Rowe's Noseeum Arguments from Evil," in Daniel Howard-Snyder (ed.), *The Evidential Argument from Evil* (Indiana Series in the Philosophy of Religion; Bloomington, IN: Indiana University Press, 1996), 126–50; Plantinga, *God, Freedom, and Evil*; Swinburne, *The Existence of God*, 236–72; Richard Swinburne, "Some Major Strands of Theodicy," in Howard-Snyder (ed.), *The Evidential Argument from Evil*, 30–48; Marilyn McCord Adams, *Horrendous Evils and the Goodness of God* (Ithaca, NY: Cornell University Press, 1999); William P. Alston, "The Inductive Argument from Evil and the Human Cognitive Condition," Howard-Snyder (ed.), *The Evidential Argument from Evil*, 97–125.

[48] See my discussion in Chapter 3.

others that such experiences provide strong justification for belief in God.[49]

Finally, and I think most importantly, in considering the epistemological status of belief in God, the output of the theistic natural signs needs to be considered in relation to possible special revelations. The vast majority of those who believe in God are not "philosophical theists" but believers in God who are participants in a living religion. This means that their faith in God is not held as an isolated belief but is part of a much larger package of beliefs, and, in the case of Christianity, Judaism, and Islam, that larger package includes many beliefs held on the basis of something that is accepted as a special revelation from God.

In Chapter 1 I discussed the value of natural theology as providing the first element of a "two-stage apologetic."[50] There I argued that natural reasons to believe in God could make it much easier to defend the reasonableness of accepting a claim to special revelation. To put it simply, it makes much more sense to consider whether some alleged revelation from God is a genuine revelation if it is antecedently known that there is a God, or at least if belief in God seems a reasonable possibility. Special revelation claims, particularly in the case of Christianity, are often supported by claims that they are attested by miracles, as when Christians argue that Jesus's claim to be a prophet (or even to be something more than a prophet) are supported by the fact that Jesus was raised from the dead.[51] These miracle claims are also much easier to defend against Hume-style attacks if there is some reason to believe that there is a God; if naturalism is true, the probability of God's existence must be nil or very low, but if we have reason to believe that there is something beyond nature, miracles cannot be firmly ruled out.

One can therefore see that a case for belief in God on the basis of theistic natural signs may be very valuable for the religious believer

---

[49] Probably the strongest and most detailed case has been made by William Alston. See his *Perceiving God: The Epistemology of Religious Experience*. However, see also Swinburne, *The Existence of God*, and George I. Mavrodes, *Belief in God: A Study in the Epistemology of Religion* (Studies in Philosophy; New York: Random House, 1970).

[50] See "What is Natural Theology and Why Is It Valuable?" in Chapter 1.

[51] Richard Swinburne has used this line of argument extensively. See his *Revelation: From Metaphor to Analogy* (Oxford: Oxford University Press, 2007), and also *The Christian God* (Oxford: Oxford University Press, 1994).

who wishes to defend the reasonableness of a living faith. And here the modest result discussed earlier in this chapter, in which belief in some kind of God or gods is supported by theistic natural signs, may be valuable, even if the nature of God would be largely unknown if one had to rely solely on those signs. For the natural response to such a situation, in which one has some evidence of a reality beyond and behind the observed natural world but a large degree of ignorance about the nature of that reality, would be to desire and look for some further source of information about that reality. And that is precisely what special revelations claim to offer. From the point of view of a living religion, the meager output of theistic natural signs may not be a problem, but something to be welcomed. The limitations of natural theology may themselves be a sign that we should look for other sources of knowledge about God.

I have been examining the way in which theistic natural signs might offer some support for a living religion that is grounded in claims to have a special revelation. However, the epistemic support may go in the other direction as well. The idea that supportive epistemic relations may go in both directions is one that is familiar from scientific theories, which often gain some of their plausibility from the way that various parts of a theory dovetail and mutually support each other. The same may be true in the case of living religions. This means that, when considering whether theistic natural signs might make a significant contribution to belief in God that is justified overall, one must consider, not only additional arguments for God's existence and religious experiences, but the evidence that might support a more comprehensive body of beliefs that includes the claim that God exists.

The fact that there are natural signs that point to God makes it more reasonable to believe that a purported special revelation is genuine. However, evidence that a purported special revelation is genuine is also evidence that there is a God who might have given that special revelation. So not only is it the case that the theistic natural signs support the special revelation's claim to be genuine; the special revelation may also support the plausibility of the theistic natural signs. So long as the evidence components for various parts of a theory have some independence, the fact that the different parts of the theory support each other is not problematic. And there is some independence in this case, as the force of the natural signs can be grasped by those who are not committed to a special revelation claim, and the evidence for a special revelation being genuine (such as an observed miracle) might well be accessible to someone who fails to see the force of a theistic natural sign.

Perhaps this means that the language of "two-stage apologetics" is somewhat misleading. It suggests that natural theology is an independent project, something whose success or failure can be determined independently of special revelation. And I have argued that this is true to a degree: theistic natural signs can offer some degree of prima facie justification for belief in God that is independent of any special revelation claims. However, for most actual human beings, natural theology will not be truly independent of the comprehensive claims of a living religion, nor completely independent of the support that can be offered for those claims. In this context, theistic natural signs, as a part of natural theology, will be seen as providing part of that support, perhaps providing some modest degree of evidence for that comprehensive package by way of supporting some particular claims that are central to that package.

For the most part people do not invent or construct the concept of God. Rather, the concept is presented to them as part of the claims of a living faith. This means that many of the problems that are alleged to infect natural theology are not really problems. If we had to develop a comprehensive understanding of God on the basis of theistic natural signs, we would face daunting problems. However, if we are considering the claims of a living faith, things look different. We are presented with a comprehensive picture of God and God's nature that comes with an account of how that picture may be known to be true. One part of that picture may be something like this: "God wants to make it possible for humans to be aware of his reality, though he also wants them to be free not to believe. He therefore could be expected to provide signs of his reality that are easy to find, though also easy to explain away for those who do not wish to believe." The theistic natural signs I have considered seem to be exactly what this part of the theistic picture predicts, and therefore provide at least modest support for that picture.

Paul Moser has argued that there may be other reasons for the difficulties of natural theology, the output of which he terms "thin theism."[52] Moser argues that God is not interested in humans who merely know that God exists; rather, God desires humans to have a relationship with himself that is morally transformative. Such a relationship may require that the knowledge we have that God exists be embedded in a more extensive understanding of God, one that stems from a special revelation, and that challenges us and requires an existential response. I find this exceedingly plausible. However, even on this kind of view, natural theology may still be valuable. It provides some support for that "thick," more comprehensive package. And it may at least discomfort the dogmatic naturalist who refuses to consider the possibility of such a revelation. Natural signs for God may point to a mystery that prepares individuals for an encounter with a greater mystery, even if they do not by themselves justify belief in God.

[52] See Paul Moser, "Cognitive Idolatry and Divine Hiding," in Howard-Snyder and Moser (eds.), *Divine Hiddenness: New Essays*, 120–48.

Bibliography

Adams, Marilyn McCord, *Horrendous Evils and the Goodness of God* (Ithaca, NY: Cornell University Press, 1999).

—— and Adams, Robert Merrihew (eds.), *The Problem of Evil* (Oxford Readings in Philosophy; Oxford: Oxford University Press, 1990).

Adams, Robert Merrihew, *The Virtue of Faith and Other Essays in Philosophical Theology* (New York: Oxford University Press, 1987).

Allen, James, *Inference from Signs: Ancient Debates about the Nature of Evidence* (Oxford: Oxford University Press, 2001).

Alston, William P., *Epistemic Justification: Essays in the Theory of Knowledge* (Ithaca, NY: Cornell University Press, 1989).

—— "Epistemic Circularity," in *Epistemic Justification: Essays in the Theory of Knowledge* (Ithaca, NY: Cornell University Press, 1989), 319–49.

—— "Internalism and Externalism in Epistemology," in *Epistemic Justification: Essays in the Theory of Knowledge* (Ithaca, NY: Cornell University Press, 1989), 185–226.

—— "An Internalist Externalism," in *Epistemic Justification: Essays in the Theory of Knowledge* (Ithaca, NY: Cornell University Press, 1989), 227–45.

—— *Perceiving God: The Epistemology of Religious Experience* (Ithaca, NY: Cornell University Press, 1991).

—— "Knowledge of God," in Marcus Hester (ed.), *Faith, Reason, and Skepticism: Essays* (Philadelphia: Temple University Press, 1992), 6–49.

—— "The Inductive Argument from Evil and the Human Cognitive Condition," in Daniel Howard-Snyder (ed.), *The Evidential Argument from Evil* (Indiana Series in the Philosophy of Religion; Bloomington, IN: Indiana University Press, 1996), 97–125.

Anscombe, Elizabeth, "Modern Moral Philosophy," *Philosophy*, 33 (1958), 1–19.

Aquinas, Thomas, *Summa Theologica*, trans. Fathers of the English Dominican Province (New York: Benziger Bros., 1947–8; repr. Allen, TX: Thomas More, 1981).

—— *Summa contra Gentiles*, trans. Anton C. Pegis (Notre Dame, IN: University of Notre Dame Press, 1975).

Arnhart, Larry, *Darwinian Natural Right: The Biological Ethics of Human Nature* (SUNY Series in Philosophy and Biology; Albany, NY: State University of New York Press, 1998).

Atran, Scott, *In Gods We Trust: The Evolutionary Landscape of Religion* (Evolution and Cognition; Oxford: Oxford University Press, 2002).

Baier, Kurt, *The Moral Point of View: A Rational Basis of Ethics* (Contemporary Philosophy; Ithaca, NY: Cornell University Press, 1958).

Barrett, Justin L., *Why Would Anyone Believe in God?* (Cognitive Science of Religion Series; Walnut Creek, CA: AltaMira Press, 2004).

Barrow, John D., and Tipler, Frank J., *The Anthropic Cosmological Principle* (Oxford: Oxford University Press, 1988).

Barth, Karl, *The Epistle to the Romans*, trans. Edwyn C. Hoskyns (Oxford: Oxford University Press, 1933).

Bergmann, Michael, "Epistemic Circularity: Malignant and Benign," *Philosophy and Phenomenological Research*, 69/3 (2004), 709–27.

——*Justification without Awareness: A Defense of Epistemic Externalism* (Oxford: Oxford University Press, 2006).

——"Reidian Externalism," in Vincent F. Hendricks and Duncan Pritchard (eds.), *New Waves in Epistemology* (New Waves in Philosophy; New York: Palgrave Macmillan, 2008), ch. 3.

Berkeley, George, *A New Theory of Vision and Other Select Philosophical Writings* (Everyman Edition; New York: E. P. Dutton, 1910).

Boyd, Richard, "How to Be a Moral Realist," in Geoffrey Sayre-McCord (ed.), *Essays on Moral Realism* (Ithaca, NY: Cornell University Press, 1988), 181–228.

Boyer, Pascal, *The Naturalness of Religious Ideas: A Cognitive Theory of Religion* (Berkeley and Los Angeles: University of California Press, 1994).

Buras, Todd, "The Function of Sensations in Reid," *Journal of the History of Philosophy*, forthcoming.

Calvin, John, *Institutes of the Christian Religion*, ed. John T. McNeill, trans. Ford Lewis Battles, in collaboration with the editor, and a committee of advisers; 2 vols. (Library of Christian Classics 20–1; Philadelphia: Westminster, 1960).

Camus, Albert, *The Myth of Sisyphus, and Other Essays*, trans. Justin O'Brien (New York: Vintage, 1955).

Clark, Kelly, and Barrett, Justin, "Reidian Epistemology and the Cognitive Science of Religion," forthcoming.

Collins, Francis S., *The Language of God: A Scientist Presents Evidence for Belief* (New York: Free Press, 2006).

Collins, Robin, "God, Design, and Fine-Tuning," in Raymond Martin and Christopher Bernard (eds.), *God Matters: Readings in the Philosophy of Religion* (New York: Longman, 2003), 119–34.

Conee, Earl, and Feldman, Richard, *Evidentialism: Essays in Epistemology* (Oxford: Oxford University Press, 2004).

Craig, William Lane, *The Kalam Cosmological Argument* (London: Macmillan, 1979; repr. Eugene, OR: Wipf and Stock, 2000).
—— *The Cosmological Argument from Plato to Leibniz* (Library of Philosophy and Religion; London: Macmillan, 1980).
Cuneo, Terence, and van Woudenberg, René (eds.), *The Cambridge Companion to Thomas Reid* (Cambridge: Cambridge University Press, 2004).
Daniels, Norman, *Thomas Reid's "Inquiry": The Geometry of Visibles and the Case for Realism* (Stanford, CA: Stanford University Press, 1989), 84–7.
Dawkins, Richard, *The Blind Watchmaker: Why the Evidence of Evolution Reveals a Universe without Design* (New York: Norton, 1996).
—— *The God Delusion* (Boston: Houghton Mifflin, 2006).
Dennett, Daniel Clement, *Breaking the Spell: Religion as a Natural Phenomenon* (New York: Viking, 2006).
Descartes, René, *The Philosophical Works of Descartes*, trans. Elizabeth S. Haldane and G. R. T. Ross (2 vols.; Cambridge: Cambridge University Press, 1967).
Draper, Paul, "Natural Selection and the Problem of Evil," review in Paul Draper (ed.), *God or Blind Nature? Philosophers Debate the Evidence* (2007), www.infidels.org/library/modern/paul_draper/evil.html.
Duns Scotus, John, *Opera Omnia* (12 vols.; Hildesheim: Olms, 1968–9).
—— *Duns Scotus on the Will and Morality*, selected and translated with an introduction by Allan B. Wolter, OFM (Washington: Catholic University of American Press, 1986).
Dworkin, Ronald, *Taking Rights Seriously* (Cambridge, MA: Harvard University Press, 1977).
Evans, C. Stephen, *Subjectivity and Religious Belief: An Historical, Critical Study* (Grand Rapids, MI: Christian University Press, 1978).
—— *Philosophy of Religion: Thinking about Faith* (Contours of Christian Philosophy; Downers Grove, IL: InterVarsity Press, 1982).
—— *The Quest for Faith: Reason and Mystery as Pointers to God* (Downers Grove, IL: InterVarsity Press, 1986.
—— *The Historical Christ and the Jesus of Faith: The Incarnational Narrative as History* (Oxford: Oxford University Press, 1996).
—— *Why Believe? Reason and Mystery as Pointers to God* (Grand Rapids, MI: Eerdmans, 1996).
—— *Faith beyond Reason: A Kierkegaardian Account* (Reason and Religion Series; Grand Rapids, MI: Eerdmans, 1998).
—— "Faith and the Problem of Evil," in *Faith beyond Reason: A Kierkegaardian Account* (Grand Rapids, MI: Eerdmans, 1998),
—— and Manis, Zachary, *Philosophy of Religion: Thinking about Faith* (2nd edn.; Contours of Christian Philosophy; Downers Grove, IL: InterVarsity Press, 2009).

Flew, Antony, *The Presumption of Atheism and Other Philosophical Essays on God, Freedom, and Immortality* (London: Elek/Pemberton, 1976).

—— and Varghese, Roy Abraham, *There is a God: How the World's Most Notorious Atheist Changed his Mind* (New York: HarperOne, 2007).

Gauthier, David, *Morals by Agreement* (Oxford: Oxford University Press, 1986).

Gewirth, Alan, *Human Rights: Essays on Justification and Applications* (Chicago: University of Chicago Press, 1982).

Guthrie, Stewart Elliott, *Faces in the Clouds: A New Theory of Religion* (New York: Oxford University Press, 1993).

Hamer, Dean, *The God Gene: How Faith is Hardwired into our Genes* (New York: Doubleday, 2004).

Hardy, Lee, "Hume's Defense of True Religion," forthcoming.

—— "Kant's Reidianism: The Role of Common Sense in Kant's Epistemology of Religious Belief," forthcoming.

Harman, Gilbert, *Explaining Values and Other Essays in Moral Philosophy* (Oxford: Oxford University Press, 2000).

—— "Is There a Single True Morality," in *Explaining Value and Other Essays in Moral Philosophy* (Oxford: Oxford University Press, 2000).

—— "What is Moral Relativism," in *Explaining Value and Other Essays in Moral Philosophy* (Oxford: Oxford University Press, 2000).

—— and Thomson, Judith Jarvis, *Moral Relativism and Moral Objectivity* (Great Debates in Philosophy: Cambridge, MA: Blackwell, 1996).

Harris, Sam, *The End of Faith: Religion, Terror, and the Future of Reason* (New York: Norton, 2004).

Henry, Douglas, "Does Reasonable Nonbelief Exist?" *Faith and Philosophy*, 18 (2001), 75–92.

—— "Reasonable Doubts about Reasonable Nonbelief," *Faith and Philosophy*, 25 (2008), 276–89.

Hobbes, Thomas, *Leviathan*, ed. Richard Tuck (Cambridge Texts in the History of Political Thought; Cambridge: Cambridge University Press, 1996).

Howard-Snyder, Daniel, and Moser, Paul K. (eds.), *Divine Hiddenness: New Essays* (Cambridge: Cambridge University Press, 2002).

Huemer, Michael, *Skepticism and the Veil of Perception* (Studies in Epistemology and Cognitive Theory; Lanham, MD: Rowman & Littlefield, 2001).

The Humanist Manifesto II, www.americanhumanist.org/who_we_are/about_humanism/Humanist_Manifesto_II.

Hume, David, *A Treatise of Human Nature*, ed. L. A. Selby-Bigge (Oxford: Oxford University Press, 1888).

—— *An Enquiry Concerning Human Understanding*, ed. Eric Steinberg (Indianapolis: Hackett, 1977).

—— "Letter from a Gentleman to his Friend in Edinburgh," in *An Enquiry Concerning Human Understanding*, ed. Eric Steinberg (Indianapolis: Hackett, 1977),

—— "Of Miracles," in *An Enquiry Concerning Human Understanding*, ed. Eric Steinberg (Indianapolis: Hackett, 1977).

—— *Dialogues Concerning Natural Religion*, ed. Richard H. Popkin (Indianapolis: Hackett, 1980).

—— *Principal Writings on Religion: Including Dialogues Concerning Natural Religion and The Natural History of Religion*, ed. J. C. A. Gaskin (Oxford World's Classics; Oxford: Oxford University Press, 1998).

Inwagen, Peter van, "The Place of Chance in a World Sustained by God," in *God, Knowledge & Mystery: Essays in Philosophical Theology* (Ithaca, NY: Cornell University Press, 1995), 42–65.

—— "The Problem of Evil, the Problem of Air, and the Problem of Silence," in *God, Knowledge, Mystery* (Ithaca, NY: Cornell University Press, 1995), 66–95.

—— "The Argument from Evil," in Peter van Inwagen (ed.), *Christian Faith and the Problem of Evil* (Grand Rapids, MI: Eerdmans, 2004), 55–73.

—— *The Problem of Evil* (Oxford: Oxford University Press, 2006).

—— (ed.), *Christian Faith and the Problem of Evil* (Grand Rapids, MI: Eerdmans, 2004).

James, William, *Some Problems of Philosophy: A Beginning of an Introduction to Philosophy* (New York: Longmans, Green, and Co., 1916).

Kant, Immanuel, *Critique of Practical Reason*, trans. Lewis White Beck (Library of Liberal Arts 52; New York: Bobbs-Merrill, 1956).

—— *Groundwork of the Metaphysic of Morals*, trans. H. J. Paton (Harper Torchbooks, The Academy Library; New York: Harper & Row, 1964).

—— *Critique of Pure Reason*, trans. Norman Kemp Smith (New York: St Martin's, 1965).

—— *The One Possible Basis for a Demonstration of the Existence of God*, trans. Gordon Treash (New York: Abaris, 1979).

—— *Critique of Judgment*, trans. Werner S. Pluhar (Indianapolis: Hackett Publishing Company, 1987).

Kelemen, Deborah, "Are Children 'Intuitive Theists'? Reasoning about Purpose and Design in Nature," *Psychological Science*, 15 (2004), 295–6.

Kelly, Thomas, "Evidence," in *The Stanford Encyclopedia of Philosophy* (Stanford, CA: Stanford University, 2006), 1–2.

Kierkegaard, Søren, *Søren Kierkegaard's Journals and Papers*, ed. and trans. Howard V. Hong and Edna H. Hong (Bloomington, IN: Indiana University Press, 1967).

Kierkegaard, Søren, *The Sickness unto Death: A Christian Psychological Exposition for Upbuilding and Awakening*, ed. and trans. Howard V. Hong and Edna H. Hong (Kierkegaard's Writings 19; Princeton: Princeton University Press, 1980).

—— *Philosophical Fragments; Johannes Climacus*, ed. and trans. Howard V. Hong and Edna H. Hong (Kierkegaard's Writings 7; Princeton: Princeton University Press, 1985).

—— *Works of Love*, ed. and trans. Howard V. Hong and Edna H. Hong (Kierkegaard's Writings; Princeton: Princeton University Press, 1995).

Korsgaard, Christine M., with Cohen, G. A., et al. *The Sources of Normativity*, ed. Onora O'Neill (Cambridge and New York: Cambridge University Press, 1996).

Kvanvig, Jonathan, "Divine Hiddenness: What is the Problem?" in Daniel Howard-Snyder and Paul K. Moser (eds.), *Divine Hiddenness: New Essays* (Cambridge: Cambridge University Press, 2002), 149–63.

Leibniz, Gottfried Wilhelm, *The Philosophical Writings of Leibniz*, selected and trans. Mary Morris (Everyman's Library; Theology and Philosophy 905; London: Dent, 1934).

Leslie, John, *Universes* (London and New York: Routledge, 1989).

Lewis, C. S., *Mere Christianity* (London: Collins, 1952).

—— *Miracles* (San Francisco: HarperOne, 2001).

Livingstone, David N., *Darwin's Forgotten Defenders: The Encounter between Evangelical Theology and Evolutionary Thought* (Edinburgh: Scottish Academic Press, 1987; Grand Rapids, MI: Eerdmans, 1987).

Lyons, Jack C., *Perception and Basic Beliefs: Zombies, Modules, and the Problem of the External World* (Oxford: Oxford University Press, 2009).

MacIntyre, Alasdair, *After Virtue: A Study in Moral Theory* (London: Duckworth, 1981).

Mackie, J. L., *The Miracle of Theism: Arguments for and Against the Existence of God* (Oxford: Oxford University Press, 1982).

—— *Ethics: Inventing Right and Wrong* (London: Penguin, 1990).

Mavrodes, George I., *Belief in God: A Study in the Epistemology of Religion* (Studies in Philosophy; New York: Random House, 1970).

—— "Religion and the Queerness of Morality," in Robert Audi and William J. Wainwright (eds.), *Rationality, Religious Belief, and Moral Commitment: New Essays in the Philosophy of Religion* (Ithaca, NY: Cornell University Press, 1986), 213–26.

Moore, G. E., *Ethics* (Home University Library of Modern Knowledge 52; New York: Holt, 1912).

Moser, Paul K., *Knowledge and Evidence* (Cambridge Studies in Philosophy; Cambridge: Cambridge University Press, 1989).

—— "Cognitive Idolatry and Divine Hiding," in Daniel Howard-Snyder and Paul K. Moser (eds.), *Divine Hiddenness: New Essays* (Cambridge: Cambridge University Press, 2002), 120–48.

Murray, Michael, *Nature Red in Tooth and Claw: Theism and the Problem of Animal Suffering* (Oxford: Oxford University Press, 2008).

Nagel, Thomas, "What Is It Like to Be a Bat?" *Philosophical Review*, 83 (1974), 435–50.

Nietzsche, Friedrich, *The Gay Science: With a Prelude in German Rhymes and an Appendix of Songs*, ed. Bernard Williams, trans. Josefine Nauckhoff, poems translated by Adrian Del Caro (Cambridge Texts in the History of Philosophy; Cambridge: Cambridge University Press, 2001).

—— *On the Genealogy of Morals*, trans. Walter Kaufmann and R. J. Hollingdale (New York: Vintage, 1967).

—— *Twilight of the Idols* and *The Anti-Christ*, trans. R. J. Hollingdale, intro. Michael Tanner (Penguin Classics; London: Penguin Books, 1990).

Numbers, Ronald L., *The Creationists: From Scientific Creationism to Intelligent Design* (2nd edn.; Cambridge, MA: Harvard University Press, 2006).

Paley, William, *Natural Theology: Or Evidences of the Existence and Attributes of the Deity, Collected from the Appearances of Nature* (Boston: Gould & Lincoln, 1853).

Pascal, Blaise, *Pensées* (New York: E. P. Dutton, 1958).

—— *Pensées*, rev. edn., trans. A. J. Krailsheimer (London: Penguin, 1995).

Plantinga, Alvin, *God, Freedom, and Evil* (New York: Harper & Row, 1974).

—— "Reason and Belief in God," in Alvin Plantinga and Nicholas Wolterstorff (eds.), *Faith and Rationality: Reason and Belief in God* (Notre Dame, IN: University of Notre Dame Press, 1983), 16–93.

—— *Warrant and Proper Function* (New York: Oxford University Press, 1993).

—— *Warranted Christian Belief* (New York: Oxford University Press, 2000).

—— and Wolterstorff, Nicholas (eds.), *Faith and Rationality: Reason and Belief in God* (Notre Dame, IN: University of Notre Dame Press, 1983).

Pruss, Alexander R., *The Principle of Sufficient Reason: A Reassessment* (Cambridge Studies in Philosophy (New York: Cambridge University Press, 2006).

Quinn, Philip L., *Divine Commands and Moral Requirements* (Clarendon Library of Logic and Philosophy; Oxford: Oxford University Press, 1978).

—— "In Search of the Foundations of Theism," *Faith and Philosophy*, 2/4 (1985), 469–86.

Ratzsch, Del, *Nature, Design, and Science: The Status of Design in Natural Science* (SUNY Series in Philosophy and Biology; Albany, NY: State University of New York Press, 2001).

Ratzsch, Del, "Saturation, World Ensembles, and Design: Death by a Thousand Multiplications?" *Faith and Philosophy: Journal of the Society of Christian Philosophers*, 22/5 (2005), 667–86.

Rawls, John, *A Theory of Justice* Cambridge, MA: Belknap, 2005).

Reid, Thomas, *An Inquiry into the Human Mind on the Principles of Common Sense: A Critical Edition*, ed. Derek R. Brookes (University Park, PA: Pennsylvania State University Press, 1997).

—— *Essays on the Intellectual Powers of Man: A Critical Edition*, ed. Derek R. Brookes (University Park, PA: Pennsylvania State University Press, 2002).

Rowe, William L., *The Cosmological Argument* (Princeton: Princeton University Press, 1975).

—— "The Problem of Evil and Some Varieties of Atheism," *American Philosophical Quarterly*, 16 (1979); repr. in Marilyn McCord Adams and Robert Merrihew Adams (eds.), *The Problem of Evil* (Oxford Readings in Philosophy; Oxford: Oxford University Press, 1990), 126–37.

Rundle, Bede, *Why There is Something Rather than Nothing* (Oxford: Oxford University Press, 2004).

Russell, Bertrand, *Mysticism and Logic: And Other Essays* (New York: Barnes & Noble, 1917).

—— "A Free Man's Worship," in *Mysticism and Logic: And Other Essays* (New York: Barnes and Noble, 1917).

—— *Bertrand Russell on God and Religion*, ed. Al Seckel (Buffalo, NY: Prometheus Books, 1986).

Sartre, Jean-Paul, *Existentialism and Human Emotions* (New York: Philosophical Library, 1957).

Schellenberg, J. L., *Divine Hiddenness and Human Reason* (Ithaca, NY: Cornell University Press, 1993).

—— "On Reasonable Nonbelief and Perfect Love: Replies to Henry and Lehe," *Faith and Philosophy*, 22 (2005), 33–342.

—— *The Wisdom to Doubt: A Justification of Religious Skepticism* (Ithaca, NY: Cornell University Press, 2007).

Schleiermacher, Friedrich, *The Christian Faith*, trans. H. R. Mackintosh and J. S. Stewart (Edinburgh: T. & T. Clark, 1928).

Smart, J. J. C., *Our Place in the Universe: A Metaphysical Discussion* (Oxford: Blackwell, 1989).

Swinburne, Richard, *The Christian God* (Oxford: Oxford University Press, 1994).

—— "Some Major Strands of Theodicy," in Daniel Howard-Snyder (ed.), *The Evidential Argument from Evil* (Indiana Series in the Philosophy of Religion; Bloomington, IN: Indiana University Press, 1996), 30–48.

—— *The Existence of God* (2nd edn.; Oxford: Oxford University Press, 2004).

—— *Revelation: From Metaphor to Analogy* (Oxford: Oxford University Press, 2007).

Thomas, Lewis, "On the Uncertainty of Science," *Key Reporter*, 46 (Autumn 1980).

Tuggy, Dale, "Reid's Philosophy of Religion," in Terence Cuneo and René van Woudenberg (eds.), *The Cambridge Companion to Thomas Reid* (Cambridge: Cambridge University Press, 2004), 289–312.

van Cleve, James, "Reid's Theory of Perception," in Terence Cuneo and René van Woudenberg (eds.), *The Cambridge Companion to Thomas Reid* (Cambridge: Cambridge University Press, 2004), 101–33.

Waal, Frans de, *Good Natured: The Origins of Right and Wrong in Humans and Other Animals* (Cambridge, MA: Harvard University Press, 1996).

Wielenberg, Erik, "In Defense of Non-Natural, Non-Theistic Moral Realism," *Faith and Philosophy*, 26/1 (2009), 23–41.

Williams, Paul, *The Unexpected Way: On Converting from Buddhism to Catholicism* (Edinburgh: T. & T. Clark, 2002).

Williamson, Timothy, *Knowledge and its Limits* (Oxford: Oxford University Press, 2000).

Wilson, Edward O., *On Human Nature* (Bantam New Age Books; New York: Bantam Books, 1976).

Wisdom, John, *Philosophy and Psycho-Analysis* (New York: Philosophical Library, 1953).

Wolterstorff, Nicholas, *Thomas Reid and the Story of Epistemology* (Cambridge: Cambridge University Press, 2001).

—— *Justice: Rights and Wrongs* (Princeton: Princeton University Press, 2008).

Wykstra, Stephen J., "The Humean Obstacle to Evidential Arguments from Suffering: On Avoiding the Evils of Appearance," *International Journal for Philosophy of Religion*, 16 (1984), 73–93.

—— "Rowe's Noseeum Arguments from Evil," in Daniel Howard-Snyder (ed.), *The Evidential Argument from Evil* (Indiana Series in the Philosophy of Religion; Bloomington, IN: Indiana University Press, 1996), 126–50.

Yaffe, Gideon, "Reid on the Perception of Visible Figure," *Journal of Scottish Philosophy*, 1 (2003), 103–15.

Index

Made in the USA
Columbia, SC
22 May 2021